Hollywood in Monterey

1986

Hollywood in Monterey

Chronicles of a Cop

by

Sgt. Bill Cassara

BearManor Media

2020

Hollywood in Monterey: Chronicles of a Cop

© 2020 by Bill Cassara

Cassaracarmel@aol.com

Published in the United States of America by:

BearManor Media

4700 Millenia Blvd.
Suite 175 PMB 90497
Orlando, FL 32839

bearmanormedia.com

Printed in the United States.

Typesetting and layout by John Teehan

Cover photo of Sgt. Bill Cassara by Kit Parker (2000)

Cover design by Jack Taylor w/ inserts of Doris Day, Joan Fontaine, Phyllis Coates, and Clint Eastwood

Back cover image of Bill Cassara and Willie Mays (1984)

ISBN—978-1-62933-643-5

Dedicated to my wife and muse, Michelle

Table of Contents

Acknowledgments

Dave Allard, Mike and Nancy Bainter, Cliff Balcony, Lisa Ballantyne, Lloyd, Bill and Dotty Beardsley, Kimm Benton, John Burke, John Calzada, John Cassara, Gary Cohen, Bud Cook, Cassidy Cook, Tom Crompton, Lon Davis, John DiCarlo, John and Janet Duff, Bob Duncan, Pat Duval, Ron Fields, Bill Freeman, Paul Gardner, Jackie Gash, Rick Greene, Ron Guth, Tom Hagan, Larry Hannerfeld, Colin Hilton, Mike Kanalakis, Becky Kane, Del Kemptser, Glenn and Mark Kennedy, Mike Klein, Tim Krebs, Ted Meece, Shelly Milliman, Karen Nordstrand, Kit Parker, Chris Pascone, Ray Patterson, Terry Pfau, Jack Roth, Nick Santa Maria, Bob Satterfield, Randy Smith, John Soister, Stan Taffel, Jack Taylor, Tyler St. Mark, John Ullah, Irene Velasquez, Ed Watz, Jeffrey Weismann, the Wiley family, Nolan Zane, and Bob & Duon Zeroun. My Children, Diana (Dohnert) and Douglas Cassara, the gang at Niles, California, the Sons of the Desert, and all the men and women in law enforcement I had the pleasure of working with.

I am honored that Kit Parker of Kit Parker Films wrote the foreword to this book. He is an authority on films and is known worldwide, what a pal! To Pat Duval, a fellow deputy that inspired me with his people skills and his autobiography. Also to John Hansen, who is another colleague who wrote a book on his "career case." To Leonard Maltin who encouraged me in all my book projects. For Ben Ohmart, the owner of BearManor Media publishing who always gives me the green light. I would especially like to acknowledge Jack Taylor, an old friend and artist who designed the front and back cover. And to my late father, Sam Cassara, who taught me the old comedians.

Foreword

A life well lived in service to others…

I met Bill Cassara in 1986 when he was a Monterey County Deputy Sheriff. Bill discovered I was a lifelong Laurel and Hardy fan (as was he), and invited me to a Sons of the Desert (the Laurel & Hardy appreciation society) banquet where he introduced me to Stan Laurel's daughter, Lois Laurel Hawes. That alone was a big deal to any L&H fan, but the best part was it marked the beginning of a friendship between us. We were kindred spirits.

Next, he invited me to a "ride-a-long." This is where a citizen can spend a shift learning what peace officers contend with on a daily basis. In our case, it was an excuse to spend a whole day talking about old movies, which we definitely did, but a bonus was watching Bill interacting with the public. He was no "just the facts ma'am" cop, but a dedicated public servant with an uncanny talent for dealing with ordinary police issues, to those in distress. Crime victims knew he was their advocate just by his presence. Scofflaws, the opposite.

One ride-a-long led to another, and over time, our friendship grew.

At my prompting, Bill began shared his engaging life starting as a boy loving baseball, history and movies, which continues to this day. Both of us grew up watching Laurel & Hardy, but also The Three Stooges, Our Gang/The Little Rascals and The Adventures of Superman.

His policing "beat" was the beautiful Monterey Peninsula, which includes Carmel, Monterey, and Pebble Beach, has always been a magnet for stars, entertainers, sports figures and other VIP's. He interacted with many of them through the years.

Two examples were Doris Day and Joan Fontaine, classic movie stars known for protecting their privacy. They found Bill's self-effacing, non-star struck nature, as an endearing quality. They trusted him implicitly both as deputy sheriff and friend, as did many others.

I'll never forget our ride-a-longs listening to a master raconteur tell the story of his event filled-life. I even learned why cops like donuts.

Turn the pages, and don't forget to fasten your seatbelt…it's time for your ride-a-long with Bill.

– Kit Parker [*Kit Parker Films*]
Phoenix, Arizona

Prologue

WHAT IS A COP?

It's awkward having a policeman around the house. Friends drop in, a man with a badge opens the door, the temperature drops twenty degrees. You throw a party and that badge gets in the way. All of a sudden there isn't a straight man in the crowd. Everyone's a comedian.

– Dragnet's Sgt. Joe Friday (1967)

IN MOVIES AND TELEVISION, cops are usually portrayed as rubes, over-officious or bumbling comic characters. For some, the Keystone Cops come to mind, but in reality, the profession of law enforcement is a collection of problem solvers with abstract thinking capabilities. It may surprise most that cops are not "hatched" for the job. One has to be a human being first, with skills to socialize and empathize with people from of all walks of life. A police officer has to *communicate* effectively with the uneducated, the inebriated, the mentally ill, CEO's, doctors, and people from all walks of life. There is no one prototype; we all come from different backgrounds and experiences. The commonality is that we have a desire to help people and keep the peace. We consider ourselves victim advocates. Law enforcement is a team effort, starting with the dispatch operator. There are no "stars" in the profession and if one tries to step into the spotlight, their peers will put them back in place.

Many in law enforcement come from broken homes, were victims of crimes, or suffered family loss in traffic accidents; others simply answered the call of duty. One officer I know was kidnapped as a child and was rescued by a lawman, providing him with a desire to give back. Most of us had a different perspective growing up and we were ready for life's experiences.

For the record, I was never inspired to take up a career in the profession because of any television show, with the possible exception of *Car 54.*[1] I cared for my community while growing up in San Jose, California, by working with people and volunteering my time for non-profits. Law enforcement seemed like a natural progression to me. I set a goal to complete my education, considering myself a historian first. Everything just fell into place after that.

To live in an organized society there must be laws to protect people and property, with an order to it all. If there is no one to enforce those laws, then society crumbles into anarchy. Authority figures such as parents, teachers, bosses, government leaders, umpires, referees, and cops are frequently challenged. Human nature is such that no one likes being told what to do unless it is on their terms, and this creates friction. If a law is not to one's liking, change it through legal channels. When someone hurts another, that's when I step in.

Now that I'm retired from my profession, I spend my time researching, categorizing, collecting photo stills, and writing, all of which resulted in four published books on old Hollywood actors/comedians. There are many parallels to researching and investigating. While on the job, I had to write under pressure to articulate the facts of a crime scene and obtain witness/victim statements in order to disseminate suspect specifics. The detailed reports had to meet the approval of my supervisors, the filing district attorney, and were scrutinized during the court process. I was, in fact, already a professional writer.

At one time I was the official historian for the Monterey County Sheriff's Office, and I still describe myself as an archivist and a proud member of the community. I was a board member for the Monterey County Film Commission, the Arts Habitat, Crime Stoppers, and president of the Monterey County Peace Officers Association.

I was fortunate to have a thirty-year career in law enforcement, starting as a records clerk for San Jose PD in 1977, and working for the Santa Clara County Sheriff's Office. Most of my vocation came on the Monterey Peninsula in central California, starting with Seaside PD, then as a deputy for the Monterey County Sheriff's Office. In my long career, it was perhaps inevitable that I would meet some of the many celebrities who lived privately on the peninsula. Like all citizens, Doris Day, Clint Eastwood, Joan Fontaine, Phyllis Coates, Terry Melcher, and Ansel

---

1. *Car 54, Where Are You?* was a television comedy series (1961--1963) presenting New York City policemen in lighter moments of the job.

Adams depended on law enforcement to feel safe. Some were professional acquaintances but others developed into personal friendships. These stories will be recounted herein.

The history of the Monterey County Sheriff's Office is usually defined within the elected terms of each sheriff. Not as prominently recorded are the stories of the deputies themselves. This is an attempt at preserving some of those memories in book form, a non-fiction methodology in a chronological format. To write everything I experienced would be impossible to digest.

– Bill Cassara

Chapter One

The Magical Misty Tour

IT WAS A BEAUTIFUL DAY that Monday, September 10, 2001. All the hard work was done for the Monterey County Film Commission's tribute to Clint Eastwood's first directed film, *Play Misty for Me*. I was chairman of a committee to celebrate films that were shot on the Monterey Peninsula, and a big party was planned. There were over a hundred films to choose from, but *Misty* was decided upon as the definitive Carmel-Big Sur-Monterey film that showcased our corner of the world for unmatched locations.

We wanted to build up for our climactic Saturday on September 15, where the committee and staff were hosting a fund raiser for our non-profit. Not only was Clint Eastwood slated to attend the pre-screening party, we had bigwigs from Universal Studios attend to coincide with the 30th anniversary of the film's debut with the release of the DVD format of the film.

In preparation, a press release served as an invitation to all the locals who were seen in the film. It generated quite a response. Those who had been involved were invited, free of charge, to the screening at the Carmel Center Cinema.

With a pre-release copy of the DVD, one of our talented committee members edited together scenes of where to visit. Another committee member, Doug Lumsden, offered his luxury tour bus[2] to transport paid patrons around to the *Misty* spots. It was a modern, comfortable transporter with monitors in place, synchronized to show the movie scenes as we were to come up on it. I was set to use the microphone to describe the film and locations.

---

2. Monterey Scenic Tours was renamed Monterey Movie Tours after this event.

1

With Clint Eastwood at the Misty fundraiser

The Film Commission sent a press release out for the "Magical *Misty* Tour" along with details on how to attend the film showing. We got a big write-up from the local papers and the *San Jose Mercury News* picked up on it, recognizing the event as unique and newsworthy.

Columnist Glenn Lovell of the *Mercury* wrote the lead in: "A 'Play Misty for Me' Odyssey-Tour will take visitors to fatal attractions from 1971 thriller filmed around Monterey." Lovell also sought out co-star Jessica Walter, who had many fond memories of making the film. Although she gave an interview, she was unable to attend the actual event.

The event captivated the public's imagination and soon hit the wire services. Among the nationwide coverage, *Variety*, "the show business bible," mentioned the forthcoming event. Clint Eastwood himself cooperated by giving an interview to the *Monterey County Post*.

For only $25. the two-hour tour would start at KRML, the radio station where Eastwood's character,[3] was a disc jockey. An essential stop was the Monterey Sardine Factory Restaurant; the tour group would descend from the bus to take in the red-lined bar area where Jessica Walter's psychotic character first emerged. The bus was also to take the passengers to a cottage house at Bay View Avenue and Martin Street in

---

3. Clint Eastwood's fictional Dave Garver was a disc jockey who would spin cool jazz in the a.m. hours.

Carmel, where Dave Garver's, girlfriend lived. There were to be ten sites visited in all, culminating with a trip down Spindrift Road in the Carmel Highlands. It was a house on that road that served as the exteriors for the climactic scenes.

The commission was promptly inundated with requests to go on the tour bus; we sold out in the first few minutes it was offered to the public. The film was one thing, but a locations tour tickled the fancy of film buffs. We had only prepared for a single bus tour, logistics being the main consideration. However, this did not stop callers to absolutely beg to "Follow the bus around" or to have a fleet of buses available. That was not going to happen in the quaint towns on the peninsula.

As a non-profit organization, this event had everything going for it: star power, a scenic locations tour, an iconic film, and commitments from people traveling from across the country. There were only five days before the Saturday festivities---and then IT happened: The 9/11 assault on the twin towers in New York, the Pentagon in DC, and the plane crash in Pennsylvania. The impact of the atrocity was felt worldwide; a national emergency was declared, grounding all air traffic.

In preparation for our event in Carmel, Universal Studios had graciously provided the only 35mm print of *Play Misty for Me* known to exist. They shipped it by airplane on September 10th and it was set to arrive in Monterey the next day.

The committee members were the only ones who knew of the circumstances of the shipped film and we were all very nervous that the worst might go wrong. As the nation grew anxious over a possible imminent war on our soil, and watching the horrors slowly unveiling itself in New York City, the phones stopped ringing at the administration office of the film commission. We held steadfast hope that the plane and film were at the Monterey airport, but nothing was moving there. It took an extra effort to find and confirm that the plane had landed, but there was no one to confirm the status of the freight.

There was talk of postponing the event, but a local newspaperman encouraged us to continue, pointing out that, "*They* would win" if the show didn't go on. It was a bold move on the part of the commission. There was no guarantee of success of a turnout now even though many people had already committed their money.

The hours were melting away; we were hopeful in the two days remaining that the film would show up. Then the clock ticked down, with only a single day left. Word came from a freight distribution center that *one* of the reels was found. We had reason to believe the other reel had to be close by.

It was now the day of the event, Saturday September 15, 2001. The bus tour was greeted with rare enthusiasm and it went off without a hitch. By prior arrangement, we had actress Britt Lind[4] from the film aboard the bus. I had a rare thrill to introduce her to the tour group just as we came upon Ocean Avenue in Carmel. This is the scene where Clint's character bolts out to Anjelica because he mistakenly thinks it is his girlfriend (Donna Mills) from behind.

As the bus made its way, there was a separate frantic search for the other reel by the administrators of the commission; it was nowhere to be found. We did have the pre-release DVD of the movie, so a contingency plan emerged; find a local service that could electronically project the DVD version onto the screen. We found one, but it cost $500. for them to set it up. This was brand-new technology at the time.

Time was now out; the commission members had to be at the Crossroads private area for the gala party with the Universal people in attendance. I let the representative know what we were dealing with and our attention shifted to, "What is Clint Eastwood going to say?" This whole event was set up to honor the man and no one wanted to displease him.

Clint came dressed in a suit and tie with his wife, Dina. He was in a good mood and gave us some behind-the-scenes stories on the making of the film. On display was one of the flared, striped shirts Clint wore in the role. "We don't wear shirts like that anymore," he said, smiling. Photos were taken, wine was poured, and people were starting to fill up the cinema located across the parking lot. I was tapped on the shoulder by the president of the Film Commission, and told, "*You're* the chairperson for this event, and *you* are the person who has to tell Clint."

To say Clint Eastwood was fond of *Play Misty for Me* is quite an understatement; it had been his first directorial duty and his reputation was at stake upon its release. The story of the DJ who is stalked by a crazed fan was ground breaking and the backdrop of noticeable locations helped to tell the story. On its release, this film became a landmark success critically and commercially, and after thirty years, it had aged like fine wine.

I had met Clint a few times before but wasn't sure if he remembered me. When I introduced myself to him again he smiled and said, "So you're the big cheese for all this, huh?" I motioned for him to follow me to a

---

4. Britt Lind played the character of Anjelica, as she walks on Ocean Avenue in Carmel.

private area and told him all the details about only one reel showing up. He turned his face downward and away, reflecting his frustration. He really cared; this was his baby! I told him about our contingency plan and he was not excited about it.

The rest of the crowd started to walk to the theater as I stayed with Clint. Assured the film had started and the people were seated, we walked into the vacant lobby. There was a portal in the doors leading into the seating and we could see the projection fill the screen. Clint brightened up: "Hey, that DVD projects a pretty good image."

We tiptoed into the darkened cinema, where Clint took a prearranged vacant seat next to Dina and stayed for the duration of the picture. I sat directly behind them. Then there was that scene where his character and his leading lady are void of clothes under a natural waterfall to the tune of "The First Time Ever I Saw Your Face."[5] It was tastefully edited and made for a dreamy musical interlude. At that point, Dina looked at Clint and whispered in his ear, "Did you sleep with her?" Clint just looked straight ahead and shook his head; Dina gave him a soft jab on the shoulder.

---

5. "The First Time Ever I Saw Your Face" was a megahit sung by Roberta Flack and won a Grammy award for "Best Song of the Year" (1972).

Chapter Two

I Came My Way From San Jose

I **TOOK MY FIRST BREATH** on August 18, 1951, and was six weeks premature. Special handling was necessary at the hospital before they sent me home with my parents. We lived in San Jose, California, a vibrant city with a rich history and only 100,000 people. Now she is known as the capitol of "Silicon Valley"[6] with a population of over a million.

My dad, Sam Cassara, was a skilled carpenter, actually, a casket maker. To be polite in mixed company, he would describe himself as a "cabinet maker." He labored in this profession until he started his own business. His social life revolved around the San Jose Elks Club. He eventually became Exalted Ruler of this chapter. My mother was a night-nurse, taking care of mostly elderly, invalid patients.

I was raised Roman Catholic and my Sicilian-born grandparents were paramount in my life. My grandfather (Papa) was a barber and owned a shop in downtown San Jose, beginning in 1915. He was a man of few words but had a love for music and played a mean mandolin. In fact, he was a professional musician and often played for weddings in San Jose and Oakland. I often wished I could have been a silent observer during the years of my grandfather's barbershop heyday. All the breaking news and politics were discussed at these "men only" institutions, where the *Police Gazette* magazine was a favorite periodical. The Chicago Shaving Shop was on West San Fernando Street, walking distance from city hall and the professional offices of First and Market Streets. All the

---

6. A region of technology giants of the industry in Santa Clara County, stretching up the peninsula to San Francisco, 50 miles north.

With Clyde Manley of Manley's Donuts

important men came in for a shave before starting work and, according to my grandfather; he had the "best-a-barbershop" in San Jose. (In 1964, The Beatles burst onto the front pages of every American newspaper and magazine. My grandfather was distraught: he thought those four mop tops would put barbershops out of business.) Papa's claim to fame was witnessing the fall of the mighty Light Tower of San Jose on December 3, 1915. He retired in the early 1950s, after which he and my grandmother made their "trip of a lifetime" to Rome and the Vatican.

There are a couple of family legends that delighted me when I was growing up. My grandparents' first language was Sicilian and it was spoken at home until their children went to school. One afternoon as my grandmother was on an errand downtown, she noticed a movie theater marquee advertising *The Bride of Frankenstein*. She entered the cinema to enjoy a love story, but instead was scared out of her wits!

In later years, my grandfather told of the day that Herb Cain (a prominent columnist for the *San Francisco Chronicle*) was in town to promote a new book he had written, *Bagdad by the Bay*. It was chock full of old San Francisco and the news and characters of its time. My grandfather was well aware that Mr. Cain was in town and, from inside his barbershop, he noticed Cain parked out front. He put the requisite change in the parking meter and hurried off to his speaking engagement. Eventually, the meter expired with a red indicator. At that point my grandfather went to that meter and fed it coins. When Cain did return, my grandfather stepped outside to explain in his Italian accent, "I save you from getting a ticket-a." For this act of kindness, Cain gave my grandfather a copy of his book and inscribed it: "To John Cassara—thank you for saving me from having a fine time in San Jose! Thanks a lot." (1948). That book has been passed down to me.

I was enthralled by my grandparents' stories and my father's recollections of growing up in this city, especially how they lived in the Italian section, on North 13th Street. Their neighbors were the Fumagalli's (how I loved that name) and during Prohibition all the families made their own wine. It was part of their culture and no law was going to take that tradition away. The kids would yell at each other, "Your father's a bootlegger." My father laughingly told me in later years, "All our dads were bootleggers." I was entranced by history. I was especially attuned to the date of my father's birth year of 1919; it stirred in me a thirst for knowledge of what had transpired in both local and national times during that era.

The first movie I can remember seeing was the newly released cinema epic, *Around the World in 80 Days* (1956). This landmark movie was shown at the Coronet Theater in San Francisco, the only place in the Bay Area equipped to project a 70mm film. The atmosphere, the music, and the crowd made the experience thrilling, especially to this five-year-old. The prelude to the main feature was the French short film, *The Red Balloon*, which captured my imagination. I fell asleep halfway through the feature.

Movies were prominent in my boyhood: *Tom Thumb, The 7th Voyage of Sindbad,* and *Journey to the Center of the Earth* were standouts of visual and musical experience. However, it was *The Time Machine* that had an especially compelling effect on me. There was a scene in which a great war is beginning; chaos and panic are preceded by the terrifying sound of air raid sirens, a piercing pitch I experienced from school air-raid practice drills. In this futuristic movie (released 1960), the D-Day calamity registered on the time machine as August 18, 1966, the exact date of my fifteenth birthday. We were all living through a cold war at the time and there was a perceived nuclear threat in those days.

I recognized films as an art form, and truth be told, they also served as a "babysitter." My dad would typically drop me off and pick me up after the show. Being in a darkened cinema with the smell of popcorn was something transcending, almost transporting.

Speaking of babysitting, I had an adverse experience when I was a small child. I don't know how often this happened, but on this particular occasion my parents decided to have a night on the town. After my young brother, sister, and I were in bed asleep, my mother took the phone off the hook (in case anyone tried to call), then she and my father left the house. That very night my uncle passed away at a young age of a heart attack, and word reached my grandparents. They desperately tried to phone our house, but of course the line was busy . . . seemingly forever. My aunt and uncle took matters into their own hands; they came to the house, knocking on the door and windows in order to wake someone up. There was much concern. Just then, my parents arrived home. I never heard such yelling and crying at the same time. It was disturbing. Things were always frosty between my aunt and mother after that.

My escapism at home was television entertainment. I was, after all, a baby-boomer, part of the first generation brought up by this fascinating medium. I loved *The Adventures of Superman*; here was action, fantasy, and thrills, all wrapped up in a half-hour time slot. Criminal justice at that time was just as black and white as the monitor. It seemed it was the reporters who solved all the crimes and dutifully delivered the suspects to Inspector Henderson, that is if Superman didn't clunk the bad guys' heads together first. No depositions, no court trials, no civil penalties.

My preferred shows were the ones that made me laugh: the cartoons, The Three Stooges, and my pals Laurel & Hardy. I had a special connection to the comedy duo. My father would sit with me to watch Stan and Ollie and tell me stories of how he used to take his grandmother to watch them at the cinemas in downtown San Jose during the 1930s.

Everything in I Needed to Know I learned by Watching *The Little Rascals*

The Our Gang film series,[7] released for television as The Little Rascals, was shown daily on local television. I related to the kids in the series even though they were not contemporaries, the films having been made during the 1930s. There were life lessons to be gleaned by watching these short comedies: socialization, integration, schools, teachers, cops, truant officers, dog catchers, midgets, giants, bullies, sweethearts,

---

7. Produced by Hal Roach from 1922–1938.

freckles, cowlicks, hicks, hunger, free eats, Pete the Pup, honkey-donkey, monkeys, mules, medicine, running away, holidays, and social mores.

If television and movies were my entertainment, it didn't stop me from being active outdoors. In the late 1950s, my dad bought a house in the middle-class San Jose neighborhood of Willow Glen. It had been its own municipality back in the 1930s until annexed by the city. The "Willows," as it had once been known, was mostly orchard land until aggressive subdivisions were built. Our house had an original chicken coop attached to the back of the garage. All the shelves were knocked down and we neighborhood kids used it as a clubhouse.

When I wasn't on my bike, I was exploring the banks of the Guadalupe River, which ultimately winds up at the Lewis Canal.[8] This drainage channel was built of concrete, connecting to the closest point of the Guadalupe and Coyote River. It made for marvelous "cave" adventures. Household flashlights were not bright enough, so we experimented by making torches to see our way. They were a miserable failure and quite unlike the versions we saw in the movies. We even used a road flare—with mixed results.

Willow Glen had its own "downtown" on Lincoln Avenue. My favorite merchants were The Pronto Pup (where I got all my comic books and fountain treats), Ed's Hobby Shop, La Ville Delicatessen, and Willow Glen Pizza. The anchor for the community was the magnificent Garden Theater, where I saw every movie released between 1959 and 1969. On Saturdays there were special "kiddie matinees." For the special admission price of only a quarter, we saw movies specially geared for us. The program consisted of a cartoon, an old serial episode, and a feature. Westerns, comedies, and adventures were all bull's-eyes with us; so were science fiction movies. But if we determined that the special effects looked fake, we would boo loudly.

Most significant to me was [Clyde] Manley's Do-Nut Shop, because he became a friend and mentor to me over the years. I would often drop in during the slow-paced, warm afternoons where he invited me back to listen to the San Francisco Giants radio broadcasts. My hero back then was Willie Mays. Actually, he still is.

The San Francisco Giants first entered my awareness in 1962 when they went to the World Series and played the New York Yankees Mickey Mantle, Roger Maris, and Yogi Berra. We lost in the seventh game, bottom of the ninth with two outs and runners on second and third. Giant's first baseman

---

8. The Lewis Canal was built of concrete 1878 to drain the marshes of Willow Glen.

Willie McCovey's line-drive out to end it in the bottom of the ninth inning impacted us all. We were *that* close to winning the World Series until Bobby Richardson of the Yankees made the grab at second base.

After school let out for the day, my friends and I headed to Lincoln Avenue in Willow Glen, where we would often see a uniformed San Jose police officer assigned to this beat. He was a motorcycle cop and he was everywhere, or so it seemed. Every now and then he would get off his bike and drop in at the A&W drive-in and watch us play the baseball pinball machines. For a twenty-five-cent investment, we played three games and invariably won up to forty-five free games. The trouble was, we would cheer when the manually manipulated bat struck the metal ball over the ramp for a homer. The machine made electronic noises when one of us hit a grand slam, which was often. One day, the proprietor offered us a deal. If we didn't make noise, she would give us a free root beer at the end. We were able to contain ourselves from then on and the root beer never tasted better. I don't think they made a dime off of us.

My friend Larry and I used to play chess together and he introduced me to coin collecting as a hobby. We became experts when it came to knowing the value of each coin. On Saturdays we would bring our duplicates to the coin shops downtown to trade up. It was pure joy to snap a newly acquired coin into my book.

I spent a lot of time over at Larry's house. I loved his family, and they were generous to me. Larry had an uncle who was really intriguing. His name was Stanley Myron Handelman.[9] He was a professional stand-up comedian from New York City, and was occasionally seen on TV variety shows. He was a semi-regular on the Dean Martin Show. A couple of times a year he played the "Hungry Eye" in San Francisco and would stay over at Larry's folks' house. Much to our dismay, he never performed any of his routines for us. He preferred watching television with his parents. Stanley was very unassuming and wore his newspaper boy cap pulled tight over his head. His face was framed by large oval glasses, which became his signature look. Larry and I took him to the Santa Clara County fair one year and I was amazed at the number of people who recognized him.

Larry's mother was a school teacher, and a charming one at that. We were only kids but she enjoyed our company. One day I made a quip and she laughed out loud. She said, "You should be a comedian." Was the comment just an expression or was she being encouraging? After all, she grew up with Stanley Myron Handelman!

---

9. Stanley Myron Handelman was a semi-regular on the *Dean Martin Show* for television.

For income between the years 1963 and '66, I had a neighborhood paper route. I still remember the headlines of the day: The John F. Kennedy assassination, The Beatles' arrival in America, the death of Winston Churchill and yes, even the death of Stan Laurel. On Sundays I had to get up at 3 a.m. to get to my newspaper drop-off point and fold those papers. Sometimes the rubber bands snapped across my frozen fingers while I tried to roll them onto the thick *San Jose Mercury News*. My dog would run alongside me while I delivered that day's issue onto each customer's porch. Before delivery, I would warm up my hands by putting them in the middle of the freshly printed newspaper stack and read the headlines of the day. By the time dawn broke, I was finished. So I peddled my trusty Schwinn straight to the beacon of light emanating from Manley's Do-Nuts and thawed out in his shop. A freshly made cake donut awaited me to warm my insides and, of course, one for my dog (Fritz), who waited patiently outside.

A Fork in the Road

Being a newspaper boy provided me with good introduction for life; it was an enterprise with risks. We were billed at the end of the month for all the newspapers and it was up to us to make our collections from our customers. We did this during the evening and I don't know how many times we were told to "come back tomorrow." If all went well during the month, I would end up with twenty-five dollars net. With this, I paid for clothes, food, entertainment, and bus fair to downtown on Saturdays. We went to the movies and brought our duplication of coins (that we obtained from circulation) to the coin shops to trade for ones we didn't have. On Friday afternoon after deliveries, my fellow paperboys and I would meet at the local pizzeria for a one-dollar individual pizza.

On one particular afternoon, the burlap bags that draped over the rear fender of my bike got tangled up in the spokes of the rear tire. It acted as a sudden brake and physics took over. I rocketed over the handlebars and fractured my right wrist on impact, the right side of my face skidded on the pavement. I lost consciousness for a few moments but shock took over and I went back to finish my route. I had to stop my bike and throw with my left hand (terribly) to each remaining home.

The next day my dad took me to the hospital to mend my broken wrist; no one thought I had a concussion (though they didn't X-ray me). With a fresh cast and black eye, I went to school but could not participate in the physical education classes, so I was assigned to go to the library for an hour each day. Until then I had never gone there unless it was with the class. Little did I realize that a new chapter in my life was beginning. I learned how to find a specific book by searching through the cards in small pull-out wooden drawers. These rows of neatly typed 3 x 5 index cards were filed in alphabetical order, not by title, but by the author's last name first. I was impressed that adjacent to the author's name was his or her birthdate with an open right bracket if they were still living, or a death date. Somehow this really personalized the contents to me. I remember having a distinct thought: that authors never really die as long as their books are on the shelves.

I became a certified "library rat" and read anything I could find on the history of San Jose. I was first inspired by a book I bought, *Almost Forgotten* by Ralph Rambo. Here was a wonderfully illustrated text by the author with riveting stories about Santa Clara County history, starting in 1895. Mr. Rambo was sixty-eight years old when he published his book in 1963.

In the mid-1960s, my friend Maury and I took the Greyhound bus to Candlestick Park and watch the Giants. The tickets cost between fifty cents and $4.50 to see major league entertainment. In May of 1966, my friend Larry and I sat in the left field stands and saw Willie Mays hit his 512th homerun to pass Mel Ott; he hit it off the Dodger's Claude Osteen to right field, disappointing us (we wanted to catch the ball). That same year Maury and I invested $3.00 for special season tickets (The Knot Hole Gang), for the local minor league baseball team, the San Jose Bees.

By the time I was sixteen, I was working at a local restaurant, Uncle John's Pancake House. It was south of downtown and on the Monterey Highway; at the time it was U.S. 101, before the freeway was built. Restaurant work appealed to me; being able to eat for free was a plus. I was an energetic busboy and I learned early how to scan the room and anticipate customers' needs. My perspective changed when I worked the swing shift during the weekends: drunken adults would come in to try and sober up. San Jose Police officers would commonly come in to drink coffee during their break and the waitresses took special care of them. If there were jolly inebriants still in the party mood and they spotted a cop, the temperature dropped twenty degrees.

One day, Lee Marvin[10] came in for breakfast on his way north; a waitress had to serve him, but she was slightly intimidated. "What if I

---

10. Lee Marvin was best known for his no-nonsense role in TV's *M Squad* (1957–1960) as a detective with the Chicago Police Department.

spilled coffee on him?" she asked fearfully. In his legendary deep growl of a voice, he ordered rare steak and eggs and he wanted it "NOW." Yes, sir!

Cultural change was occurring right before my eyes in 1967; in San Francisco, the flower children coined it "The Summer of Love." In June of that year, the Monterey Pop Festival was all over the news. Performing artists from all over the world came to Monterey, the agreed-upon middle ground between San Francisco and Los Angeles. There was a rumor circulating that The Beatles were planning to perform as well. Young people amassed to the area for this odyssey. In the vernacular of the day, it was "a happening."

Many of the kids took up hitchhiking to take the road south; Monterey was only seventy-five miles away. Swarms of them came into the restaurant to grab a bite or "coffee up." The media labeled them as hippies, generalizing their look as "Arabs and beatniks."[11]

On my sixteenth birthday in August, I got my first car. It was a 1957 Dodge Coronet with giant "shark fins" adorning the backend. Not exactly a "Chick-magnet" back then, but it got my friends and me around. It drove like a tank at seventeen miles per gallon. Fortunately, gas was as cheap as twenty-five to thirty-five cents a gallon back then.

At the first opportunity we had, two of my friends and I drove to San Francisco to venture out and maybe go to a Giants game. We walked around the Haight-Ashbury district, trying to get an eyeful. It was not glamourous at all: there were old storefronts with hippie merchants selling their wares, the odor of incense was overwhelming. The merchants were all very paranoid, not that we were going to buy anything. We were mostly looking at the various posters they had for sale. I remember a dire warning; "if offered, don't take any sugar cubes," (they were allegedly laced with bad LSD).

It was in 1967 that my mother, who had been ill for quite some time, died of natural causes. My favorite memory of her was from the early 1960s, when I would accompany her to downtown antique stores. I was interested in the 1950s *Batman* and *Superman* comics, when the characters were still chasing bank robbers.

My mother had an artistic flair and was keen on the old 78-R.P.M. records (considered to be "junk" by most people). Each record cost a dime and she bought a stack. Once home, she warped the records (with a curling iron) to almost a clam shape and would create an artificial flower arrangement. Almost always, I looked at each record before they were

11. *Monterey Herald*, June 16, 1967.

worked on to read the title of the song, and while most were unfamiliar to me, they made an impression.

With the newfound freedom of my first car, it was my baseball-playing buddies with whom I spent most of my time. We ventured out on weekend nights to see movies at the drive-in theaters, ending the evening with a late-night snack at a coffee or pie place.

There was one film in particular that stayed with me: *In Cold Blood* (1967), Richard Brooks' stark adaptation of Truman Capote's bestselling non-fiction novel. The systematic killing of a rural family was unsettling and it stirred something inside of me. I was wholly empathetic and my blood boiled in outrage at the ultra-realism of the scenes depicting the victims' fate. The experience probably stoked my first thoughts of going into law enforcement as a career. Indeed, my school counselor set me up for a ride-a-long with a San Jose police officer in a special program to introduce students to the profession. I got an eyeful and was impressed by how the officer handled himself.

San Jose was growing up and quickly approaching 400,000 in population. The major sports teams concentrated their marketing on Santa Clara County. The San Francisco 49ers did their spring practice at San Jose State's Spartan Stadium; the San Francisco Warriors would train their pre-season team at San Jose's City College; and the Giants came to town to play the Santa Clara University's Bronco's at Buck Shaw Stadium for one celebrated game. Willie Mays usually led off in those games. The price was nominal to get a walk-up ticket.

In high school, my friends and I would go to all the varsity football and basketball games. Willow Glen High had the best athletes in the entire county, it seemed. The football team always finished first and the basketball team went undefeated during my senior year, and was officially ranked number two in the state of California.

My friends Charlie, Ice, Maury, Jinksy, and Burden all had something in common: we loved baseball. We would meet up at the school baseball diamond and play almost every day during the summer. Burden would keep the stats of each game, reproduced it in a typed box score format. Special games were written up with delicious old baseball vernacular. We informally named our unsupervised games The Random League. And that is exactly what it was—whoever showed up got to play. It was hardball versus wooden bats. What made our peer group unique was our imagination and organizational skills; we decided to shoot a movie, starring *us*! We put our funds together to buy army surplus items and, more importantly, film. We had no idea what we were doing, and even wrote up sheets of "stock" to sell for the project. One of our teachers contributed a couple of bucks.

Fortunately, one of our buddies was a photographer and he offered to shoot the action with a rented 16mm camera. The film was very expensive. We weren't satisfied to simply record ourselves playing baseball, or even make a story-driven short. The decision was made to shoot an epic called "Commando Raid." Without a script, we drove out to Pescadero Beach in San Mateo County and tried to emulate D-Day, with only a few of us to act it out. One special effect we were excited to set up was a close-up of a long-barreled play rifle. "*Cut!*" our director yelled when the shot was completed. Then we inserted a firecracker, lit it, and filmed it. We got the effect of a bang with smoke and fire; we were lucky the aluminum barrel didn't explode out in shrapnel. Back in San Jose, we shot a few scenes alongside the Los Gatos Creek. Resting up between takes, we had no idea that the nice patch we had discovered turned out to be poison oak. Production was at a standstill while those afflicted recovered.

We had an internal change in director, who preferred a comedy bent. Our "crew" went to the foothills adjacent to Monterey Highway onto unfenced private property. We had made a dummy for special effects and dressed it up in old clothes. The big scene was to take place on top of a cliff. It was of a fistfight between the enemy and the good guys. The cameraman took a good close-up of a "Hollywood" punch to the face, followed by "*Cut!*" The camera was then relocated down the cliff and took the position to shoot up at the site. On the word, "Action!" the dummy was thrown off the cliff as though it was the result of the fistfight. In mid-air, the dummy separated and the camera recorded the leg portion landing, followed by the torso and head. We fell down laughing at this unintentional blooper.

When the film was developed we watched with great anticipation, only to find out it was terrible. It was unintentionally funny, but we recorded something that was unique to us. Unfortunately, *Commando Raid* is a lost film.

My introduction to "show business" was prompted by our senior class talent contest. My friend and I decided to enter, but first we needed a routine. There was a pizza parlor that offered a free pie on Tuesday evenings for anyone who would get up onstage and perform. In preparation, Burden and I wrote a ridiculous patter routine in which we were imitating Boris Karloff and Bela Lugosi. In our grand finale, we were to recite the words of "Monster Mash."[12]

Preceding us was an act where a young African American male took the microphone and acted out a Bill Cosby comedy album with accuracy, poise, and perfect delivery. It was going to be a tough act to follow, but we were determined to earn our free pizza. For the act, we called ourselves The Blitz Brothers, and were introduced as such. We took the stage confidently until, in mid-sentence, I forgot my next line. Burden improvised and took up the slack; he continued doing *both* voices while I stage-laughed into the microphone like a demented Ed McMahon.[13] There was an elderly woman in the audience, stoked with beer, who laughed louder at us than at the talented Bill Cosby impersonator.

We tasted the fruit of our success that night (actually, a pepperoni pizza) as we reflected on the polishing we needed to do for the seniors at our high school. We changed the whole act around to be a little more physical and performed it in front of our fellow classmates. There were some laughs and we (remarkably) received some applause when we exited the stage. From then on we were "The Blitz Brothers," and some references to that effect were written in our 1969 high school yearbooks.

On June 20, 1969 was an event of historical significance; "Men landed on the moon." It was the dream of mankind to accomplish this feat and I watched it as it happened via our television set. With me was my grandfather who watched very patiently. I asked him, "Papa, you were a young man of seventeen years old when the Wright Brothers manned their first air flight, [1903] and here you are watching the moon landing. His one-word response; "Yep."

---

12. A 1962 novelty record by Bobby "Boris" Pickett.

13. Ed McMahon is best remembered as Johnny Carson's sidekick from *The Tonight Show* (1962–1992).

Chapter Three

Culture Change

AFTER GRADUATION I got a temporary job during the Santa Clara County Fair, working at the corn-on-the-cob stand. We shared the facility with a ham sandwich-and-beer booth and we frequently swapped wares. Just a short walk down the pavilion led to the main stage where top talent performed every year.

The war in Vietnam was raging, but my immediate concern was getting into college. I made it a firm goal to earn a four-year degree. I enrolled at San Jose City College, became a full-time student, and worked part-time at a coffee shop in a bowling alley. I was a waiter; starving students must eat. And besides, I did earn a meager living wage with those tips.

One afternoon, four elderly ladies sat down, ordered, and had a pleasant chat. In those days it was customary to pay by cash or check. When it came time to pay the bill, I noticed the name Arbuckle and blithely blurted out, "Arbuckle as in *Fatty* Arbuckle?" What a mistake! The response was quick and assertive, "We *don't* discuss him in *public*," one of the women said haughtily. So it was true; they *were* blood relations to Roscoe Arbuckle.[14]

The name Arbuckle was well known in Santa Clara valley, and not just because of Roscoe. He had a half-brother named Clyde, who happened to be the official San Jose historian. I finally met him when I

---

14. Roscoe "Fatty" Arbuckle (1887–1933) grew up in Santa Clara and had his first show business beginnings at San Jose's Unique Theater. He became a film star working for Mack Sennett and became a legendary performer and director. He was falsely implicated in the death of silent film actress Virginia Rappé. Arbuckle was acquitted after a third trial.

19

Posing in front our 1955 Chevy

volunteered for the San Jose Historical Museum, where I was trained to be a docent. With my San Jose pride, I relished that position. I helped transfer artifacts from a prior location to the new facility and assisted in identifying and cataloging the photos. Some of these were snapshots, one of which particularly caught my eye. It was dated 1938 and the image was of an unidentified big band. Written on the bottom was a name I certainly recognized: Art Carney.[15] I wanted to know more, such as what was the band's name? Where was the performance venue? That answer would come to me later in life.

That first year of the San Jose Historical Museum, I served as a docent and received many locals and tourists. One group came through that was from Germany and they were very intrigued about the photo displays of the old orchards and the drying procedures for fruits. San Jose was best known in those days as "the prune capital of the world." The group was impressed and someone said enthusiastically, "We *have* to try prunes!" I suggested, "Well, just don't eat too many at once." I'm not sure the translation came through.

Being a docent was my way of contributing to the local history; being a waiter was my attempt at earning a living. Each work day I returned to the coffee shop at the Futurama Bowl. I recall one gentleman seated at the counter enjoying a cup of coffee. He was apparently scouting me out. Before he left he told me, "You're too good for this place. Come in

15. Art Carney is best known as Ed Norton, Ralph Kramden's pal, on television's *The Honeymooners*.

and see me." He left his card identifying him as the manager of a very high-end restaurant in San Jose. I made it a point to show that business card to my boss. He valued me highly and was always generous with compliments. He often remarked how good I was with people. I usually devoured the newspaper every day and looked through the classified ads. On one particular day, something caught my eye. It was for a job at Intel Corporation in Santa Clara. This was the mid-seventies before the term "Silicon Valley" was an identifier, the computer industry was starting to boom. I went to the human resources department to fill out an application for the Intel job and couldn't believe how modern it was. Everyone looked very professional. While I was waiting in the lobby, I noticed on the employee board that the company had season tickets to all the Bay Area professional team games and sponsored company picnics. My imagination wondered.

Though the job was considered "low level," I have always been accustomed to starting at the bottom and working my way up. A thought occurred to me that perhaps I shouldn't pursue law enforcement but start a whole new career here. With steady pay increases and the opportunity for employee discounts on stock purchases, I gladly took the entrance examination. The results came back pretty fast, and the human resources employee told me they could not give the job to me. I was told that my aptitude test was too high for the low job they were trying to fill.

I told her, "I'm willing to work my way up..."

She said, "No, you wouldn't be happy here with that job. When we have some other positions available, come back and take the exams for those." I never did go back; instead, I concentrated on getting my four-year degree.

Wishy Washy Window Cleaners

One summer, my best friend and I started our own janitorial business. We called it "Wishy Washy Window Cleaners" and our slogan was "We'll Wash Your Panes Away." Our transportation was Charlie's 1955 Chevy station wagon. We packed up our tools and set off to knock on doors in the Willow Glen neighborhoods. To appear professional, we wore white lab coats and carried clipboards. We worked separately down both sides of the street, soliciting the housewives with our cleaning services.

At the end of one forgotten street, we rang the doorbell. Instead of a woman, a big, hulking man answered the door. We gave him our best pitch and he yelled over his shoulder, "Hey, Dorothy, you want your windows washed?" He explained it was his sister's house and then introduced himself. "I'm Dan Pastorini," he said, holding out his paw to shake. We gave him our business card. He convinced us to stay another half hour until his brother-in-law got home from work. We were offered beer, which we gratefully accepted.

I recognized Pastorini instantly; he was a local boy who went to Bellermine Prep School, where he was a standout athlete. He'd made a name for himself as quarterback for the Santa Clara Broncos, and made national headlines with his team. Even though Santa Clara was a small private college, Pastorini attracted scouts from professional football. He had just been drafted by the Houston Oilers as the number-three pick in the nation.

When the bemused brother-in-law returned home, we were introduced to him. His name was Dan House, and he was a prominent attorney downtown. Pastorini took him behind closed doors while Dorothy stayed with us. The attorney approached us and explained that he was Dan's agent and would represent him when the Oilers were ready to negotiate. Pastorini told us that they wanted to practice on us. The plan was for Charlie and me to prepare an estimate for washing all of Dorothy's windows and screens and come back with a price.

Charlie and I got the hint and went outside to discuss it. We had a regular price for each window washed, but they wanted to play this game. We went along with it, promptly doubling our normal price.

We had a formal appointment book and submitted our written quotation to them and waited for a response. They asked, "How long will the job require?" We told them, four hours. They took the book and told us they were going to make a counter offer; they then discussed it in their office for a while. When they returned, they submitted a strange counter offer. They explained that if we could do the job in half the time, they would double our price, but if it took longer than four hours we would be paid less. There was no hesitation; we agreed.

The next step was getting this all down in contract form. Lawyer House put it together and he, Dan Pastorini, Charlie, and I signed it. Dan asked, "Which one is Wishy and which one is Washy?" We debated between ourselves and pointed to each other. "He's Wishy, and I'm Washy," we both said, much to their amusement. After this, we all celebrated with a beer. Since we didn't have any more appointments that day, we were invited to hang around. The attorney explained that they were expecting a phone call any day for the Oilers to invite Dan and him to Houston to negotiate the contract.

Charlie and I started work on the house the next day and we did a damn good job in half the usual time. That set us up for our bonus. Just as the attorney arrived home, the phone rang. It was the Oilers summoning Dan and his brother-in-law to Houston. They decided to fly out the very next day.

By now, Dan considered us his good luck charms. He asked if we could come by every afternoon to check in on his sister while they were gone. There was a pool and plenty of beer if we agreed, and we did. Dorothy kept us busy, cleaning her bathrooms, and we even shampooed her carpets with the professional machines we rented. We were well paid for our services.

The phone call finally came; they had a deal with the Oilers and would be home the next day. There was a big party at the house when they returned. Many friends and associates dropped by to offer congratulations. Most of the neighbors—the same ones who had slammed their doors in our faces—were there as well. Dan became our best agent; he told those neighbors to hire us to wash their windows, and they did.

For the rest of that summer, Charlie and I would usually stop by in the late afternoon. As we walked up the driveway, we always heard a joyful greeting: "Hey, it's Wishy and Washy! Come in and have a beer."

The Real World

It was now 1971 and the Vietnam War was still raging, and with it, the draft lottery. I had a low draft number (109) and there was no guarantee I was going to be able to find enough units at San Jose State to be considered a full-time student. I was ordered by Uncle Sam to report to the local Greyhound bus station at 4:00 a.m. to be transported to downtown Oakland and the processing center. We did a lot of paperwork, testing, and medical examinations. They put us up for the night in shared rooms at an old dump of a hotel. This was the first step to being drafted. When I got back home, I went to see a recruitment officer and explained that I didn't want to be drafted, that I wanted to enlist—*if* I couldn't get my classes at San Jose State. He checked my aptitude scores and considered me "a man with an education" (I had sixty units at that time). I was eligible for quite a few interesting options.

My major was in the administration of justice, with a minor in sociology. The first day of registration at San Jose State was chaotic; people had been camping out for days to get a first shot at the various choices. Charlie and my buddy Lloyd accompanied me and spent the night on the lawn of the campus with sleeping bags. The following morning, classes began to fill up quickly. I was able to get only nine units confirmed, so I signed up on endlessly long waiting lists for other courses.

A full-time student had to carry twelve units, so I was desperate to find one more class. I went to all the ones for which I was on the waiting list, but the teachers announced they had a cutoff number and could not accommodate any more pupils. I had one last chance: I went to the home economics class and sat in. I was the only male, and still not high enough on the waiting list to be considered. After the class, I went to the female teacher's office and introduced myself. I explained that there should be a male point of view in this class. That did it! She boldly said, "I think so too; you're in."

With those twelve units, I was able to maintain my student deferment and stick with college for at least this one semester. My recruiting officer called and I told him the situation; he said he would hold onto my papers if things changed. As the semester wound down, I had a great experience being a student; and in home economics, being the lone male representative wasn't so bad either.

In the new year, my chances of getting drafted were becoming less likely: the war in Vietnam was winding down. It was time to get a full-time job and move out of the house. Lloyd and I went in together to share an apartment.

Just before my final exit from home, I was shocked to discover that someone had stolen my coin collection. The culprit left behind the now-empty metal box with the key emphatically placed on top. This was an "inside job." I was devastated. I had accumulated American coins since my youth and acquired them mostly from change and trading with coin collectors. Just at face value I had quite an investment. My expertise on the dates and condition was attained naturally through a trained eye and luck. I could even quote the value of each by the red or blue book that I had absorbed into my memory banks. I had accumulated rolls of steel-head pennies, wheat pennies, nickels, mercury dimes, Standing Liberty quarters, buffalo nickels, and even some Morgan silver dollars. It was a unique collection and one I would never be able to accrue again. Being the victim of burglary was an outrage, and I never forgot what it felt like. As a result, I could no longer even look at my change. I vowed to myself to continue my pursuit of a career in law enforcement.

I took a job working in a brand-new shopping center (Eastridge) in east San Jose. I worked for Gallenkamp's shoe store (a national chain) and learned the nuances of the job. Being a salesperson came naturally for me, and I learned the art of the power of suggestion and "closing the sale," a skill I used later in my law-enforcement career. I worked for a few years there while still going part-time to school.

Between the years 1973–1976, I also became a security guard at a metal salvage yard and was in charge of the junkyard dogs. I fed and secured them in the early morning hours so the workers could come in. One dog, Rocky, went absolutely crazy when he saw people at the gate and would whirl around and bark. In another yard, there was a dog named Wolf. He was sneaky and would lie in wait. I think I found a few back pockets on the inside of the gate from those who dared to enter.

My boss was a retired guard from San Quentin. I recall that he talked out of the side of his mouth when discussing things of importance. A few times he would drop by during my evening shift and would tip me off that he heard, "a local yard was going to be *hit*, so keep your eyes open." I tried to interpret that comment as an organized group was going to break in and steal scrap metal. It made no sense to me, but I did show heightened awareness.

For a brief time I also worked as a security guard at Meridian Corners, a new adult townhouse complex. I learned how to deal with drunks who wanted to ramble on to me about their domestic problems. Every Friday night, the complex hosted a gratuity bar so the renters could relax and drink where they lived. With invited guests, this became a big draw.

I was often summoned to help with unruly patrons who wanted to show the bartender how to make a "real drink." Once I had a customer dump his drink on me because the bartender wanted him out. Most things I learned in my law-enforcement classes were of little use in trying to reason with drunks. One technique was to appeal to a friend to help with the situation. I was surprised when the guy said, "It'll take more than you; he'll take on the whole lot of you." San Jose PD always assisted in those kinds of matters, and I became friendly with them. I was even invited for some ride-a-longs.

Riding with seasoned San Jose police officers was always a thrill, and I always dressed in a coat and tie. I especially liked when we scooted along on the closed-to-the-public Highway 280 that cut through the middle of the city. They had quite a reputation for being a progressive department with advanced teachings, including a field training program. I was impressed with the department; they were like the New York Yankees of law enforcement to me.

Roll call consisted of about a hundred officers being briefed on the events of the day and what to look out for. Each officer was responsible for looking at copies of felony crime reports from their previous shift and hit the streets in a marked patrol car, responding to calls for service in their assigned beats.

I still have vivid memories of my first contact with a heroin addict. The officer made a simple field contact on a person walking by. In a panic, the guy dropped his pack of cigarettes and started to walk away. The officer said, "Hey, you dropped this." He reached to pick up the Marlboro hard pack and it contained not cigarettes, but heroin paraphernalia. The guy denied it was his but we both saw him drop it when we drove up to him. It was later explained to me that this common packaging was called an "outfit."[16] He was arrested, and started to feel the effects of the drug in our backseat.

One time we responded to a burglary in progress and interrupted a heist of about a hundred guns still in their shipping boxes. They were piled next to the doorway so they could be loaded into the getaway vehicle. The suspects split when they sensed us coming. Detectives came out, and even the lab boys came to process the scene for evidence.

San Jose PD had so many specialized support units for patrol that the beat officers were free to respond call to call, take the original report and be ready for the next incident. Follow-ups were done by detectives.

College Experiences

While working full time, I continued to take classes at San Jose State. I look back at my college experience fondly and wouldn't trade it for anything. We had many celebrities drop in as arranged by the student union. One day, Muhammad Ali showed up, drawing a big crowd. Another big

---

16. "Outfit" is common street jargon for a carrying case of heroin, a cooking spoon and injection needles.

attraction was when Jane Fonda came to the campus to make a speech: she did *not* come as her Barbarella[17] persona (we never thought she would), but instead we saw her in activist mode. She scolded the crowd as "Apathetic San Jose State." Most of us cheered at that. While everyone was responding to her, I could see a squad of San Jose PD officers in riot gear standing in a nearby stairwell. I was not going to get in the middle of something like that. Fortunately, the rally was pretty quiet.

The same could not be said for the time President Richard Nixon visited San Jose on October 28, 1971. He was there to make a speech for GOP partisan followers at the city's civic auditorium. He also wanted to give a boost for his pal, Senator George Murphy (the former actor), who was running as the incumbent.

It was reported that nine hundred protestors surrounded the area where Nixon was set to depart and, apparently, the San Jose PD and the Secret Service were overwhelmed. President Nixon, Governor Reagan, and Senator Murphy all shared the same presidential limousine and had to wait in the convoy to get out. The crowd yelled obscenities at the president, who responded by climbing out of his limousine onto the top of the car. With lights shining on him, Nixon beamed and raised his arms to show the "V" for victory sign. It was an iconic moment captured in photographs. If the crowd was incensed before, they absolutely ignited with rage after the mocking gesture. Rocks and bottles were thrown at the caravan and there was a great deal of damage done to many of the cars. It was bad planning all around. The next day, this incident was covered by every newspaper in the world.

Since I considered myself a film buff, I took the opportunity to take film appreciation courses. It was thrilling to see early silent film in class when it wasn't available to see elsewhere. The courses were taught by Dr. Flick, the most appropriate name for a film professor that ever was.

A special memory I have was when Arthur C. Clarke was a featured speaker at the Daily Auditorium. Clarke was a renowned science fiction writer who wrote the novel and screenplay for the film *2001; A Space Odyssey* (1968). It was pretty damned impressive to watch the film and hear the author's comments at the conclusion.

I was also taken by another Stanley Kubrick–directed futuristic film: *A Clockwork Orange* (1971), a true cinematic achievement. I was so appalled by the rehabilitation/torture scenes that it became the scope of a

---

17. Jane Fonda starred in a futuristic film *Barbarella* (1968) in which she appeared in very provocative attire.

term paper I prepared for my sociology class. I not only got a good grade out of it, my teacher wrote on the returned copy, "You have the potential to write for publication." That comment has always been a source of inspiration to me.

The biggest film to hit where I lived was *Dirty Harry* (1971), starring Clint Eastwood. It was pure fantasy, but wildly entertaining. Harry's character is a grizzled detective who tackles everything with a vengeance. Like a comic book superhero, he rights all the criminal atrocities in San Francisco—if only the administration would just leave him alone.

There is a scene where Harry is assigned a new partner. At one point he asks him suspiciously, "Where did you go to school?" The reply, "I've got a degree from San Jose State," had the local cinema audience roaring its approval. Dirty Harry just squinted in disgust at his formally educated partner.

Lake Tahoe

The friendships I made in high school were still very close to me and we all stayed in contact during college. My high school friend, "Ice" was working as a cashier at Safeway to help pay his tuition at Stanford. At one point he organized our baseball buddies to go to Lake Tahoe for a weekend. Four of us went and spent most of our time at a friend's cabin.

It was very late at night and Ice and I walked to one of the casinos to get a late-night snack. By coincidence, we ran into a fellow Safeway employee who decided to join us. We were walking in the back parking lot towards the public entrance when a casino security guard drove adjacent to us, said something, and started to drive off. Just then, the stupid friend mouthed off by yelling, "Hey, don't smile, your face might crack!" Things went downhill fast from there. The security guard called in for backup and, before we got to the entrance, we were met by two guards with nightsticks. They asked what we were doing and we told them we were coming in for a bite to eat. We were tersely informed that the entrance was for guests only. We explained that we had previously used this entrance and that it leads to the casino. And furthermore, the door was unlocked and served as a public entry.

With sticks in hand, they marched us to their head of security in his office. I thought we'd be dealing with someone a little more intelligent.

I was wrong. The head guy asked for our identification, which we all provided.

"So, you're from California, huh? Well, this ain't California; we can do what we want." We had to repeat our reasons for coming into the casino, and they told us that there had been a lot of burglaries. We kept our mouths shut and let them go through the process of checking us out for any kind of warrants. We were squeaky clean.

A half hour passed and no progress had been made. I finally said, "Are we under arrest? If not, we can just walk out of here."

The boss stood up, grabbed his night stick from his desk, pounded it into his left palm and said, "You just *try* and leave here and see what happens. We take Californians into the desert and they're never found again."

With that, we just waited until they were done. After they filled out field interrogation cards on each of us, we were allowed to leave. Ice and I ditched the "friend" and went back to the cabin, fuming.

Back at the cabin, we told the story to our friends, one of whom was a pre-law student. Ice decided to call the casino and asked for highest manager they had on duty to lodge a complaint. Keep in mind that the casinos were still run by the Mafia back then, so it was a bit risky for us to challenge their medieval protection racket. The manager promised to call back after talking to the head security guy. The phone call came and the manager put the casino attorney on and we were asked to give our story again. I used the term "false imprisonment," and Ice made the point that his dad was a high roller at the casino.

The attorney apologized to us and smoothed it over by inviting us to dinner the next day, "on the house." Being young guys, (only 20 years old) we thought a compromise was in order. Ice and I arrived on schedule and were met by the manager and attorney. We were escorted to a very upscale restaurant and, in a very classy way, were encouraged to order anything we wanted. It was a splendid meal, and it was topped off by a complimentary bottle of wine. We were quite satisfied.

The manager and attorney came to check on us to ask how we were enjoying the meal. The mood suddenly changed; the manager (who talked and had the demeanor of actor Marc Lawrence[18]) said, "You guys are drinking wine and you're not twenty-one yet." We pointed out that it was they who gave it to us. At that point, we wisely shut up. We didn't want to wind up wearing cement shoes.

18. Marc Lawrence (1910–2005) specialized in playing gangster parts in films.

We did not overstay our welcome and left without drawing any attention, chalking it up to "life experiences." It did make an impression on me how unprofessional and uneducated the stooge security guards were.

San Jose Missions Baseball club

One of my passions during the 1970s was playing adult league softball with a team comprised of mostly old high school baseball friends. We called ourselves The Bad Sticks and had some notoriety throughout the league because we won more championships than not. One of the teams we faced each season was made up of off-duty police officers from San Jose PD. They were actually from a specialized unit from the Police Athletic League (P.A.L.).[19] We had a nice little rivalry.

In 1976, I had a unique job in professional baseball, working for the San Jose Missions, a brand-new franchise in the decades-old Pacific Coast League. For many years prior, the San Jose team was known as the Bees in the single-A, California League. It was a lower minor league about two steps away from the majors. The Missions played in the highest minor league (AAA) in baseball, an Oakland A's affiliate. When the Missions came to town, I sent my congratulations to the owner for landing the team in San Jose. He promptly hired me to sell season tickets, group sales, and work the box office at the municipal stadium in town. This was the same venue where I used to see ballgames with my buddy Maury back in 1966.

I was considered front-office personnel and hung around during the day, performing a variety of duties. The staff was relatively small; besides the owner, there was a general manager, an operations manager, and one support secretary. My favorite co-employee was a big-name, retired National League umpire, Chris Pelekoudas.[20] This respected career baseball man was bigger than life. He was a tough old bird of fifty-eight when the owner hired him as a front man for selling season tickets. The freshly retired umpire had name recognition in those days and was a

---

19. P.A.L. is a national youth crime-prevention program that emphasizes an athletic outlet and encourages education and bonding with local police departments.

20. Chris Pelekoudas (1918–1984) was a World War II veteran who became a major league umpire for the National League from 1960–1975. He had many encounters with the greats of the game, including Willie Mays, Hank Aaron, Sandy Koufax, and Gaylord Perry.

much sought-after speaker for various dinners and non-profit functions. Representing the Missions, he delighted the crowds with his fantastic stories of throwing baseball's best out of the game and giving a sales pitch. He always ended his talk, to great applause, with the words, "And remember, the umpire is *always right.*"

During the game, Pelekoudas could be found in a box seat directly behind home plate, overlooking the proceedings. My duties at the box office were completed after the fifth inning. One day I approached him between innings and asked, "Mr. Pelekoudas, may I sit with you?" He recognized me and barked, "Sit down." He was not in a relaxed mode. He was intensely watching the game, but not like a fan. His eyes were fixed on the home-plate umpire. It was the first time I ever viewed the game from the perspective of an impartial observer and it made an impression on me. Pelekoudas sometimes voiced his displeasure at calls the umpire missed. He would say, "Look at that rookie, why I'll . . ." I'm very sure the home base umpire knew of his presence and could hear the comments.

One day, there was an odd phone call that came into the general manager's office; it was a request for Mr. Pelekoudas to officiate a community college baseball game. In their words, "It's an emergency." The San Jose City College team was host to an important game against the Santa Cruz team, and one of the umpires couldn't be found. In that league, the norm is for two umpires to work the game. If there is only one umpire, the game is postponed, and no one wanted that.

There was no way Pelekoudas would be able to umpire; it was apparently against union rules. Nor would he want to put himself in that position. It looked like the game would be canceled, but I took a chance and volunteered. My boss squared it away, and I arrived at the campus ball field only a few minutes later. The two managers looked me up and down. Finally, the Santa Cruz manager asked about my umpire experience and when I replied, "slow-pitch softball," I could see his shoulders slump. Then, one said to each other, "Well, if it's okay with you, it's okay with me."

I really did feel I was a student of the game and could pull it off; the trick was to have a look of self-assurance. I would be working the bases, and my partner would be behind the plate. There was no time to lose, and my fellow umpire and I went over some signals that we would use to communicate with each other. We *anticipated* plays that might occur, even if the ballplayers were not cognizant of them. For instance, if there was a runner on first, we made sure the other knew of a possibility of the infield fly rule. We did this by hand signals to watch out for the possibility of a batter hitting a pop-up to the infielder and purposely dropping it to get a double play.

There were a couple of close plays on my end. Someone hit a high fly ball to deep centerfield and the outfielder went racing back. I ran out with the flight of the ball but stood stationary to see it clearly as it was coming down. It is important, for fear of distortion, not to have your head moving before the play is completed. The ball was blasted and bounced over the center fielder's head and onto the asphalt behind it. Unfortunately, the low cyclone fencing made it hard to distinguish if the ball bounced over the fence or was hit cleanly over for a home run. I relied on the centerfielder's body language; he looked straight down dejectedly, indicating to me that it was a homer. I gave the homerun sign to everyone else and there wasn't a peep. I had the call right.

Another play—an attempted steal at second base—challenged me. I anticipated this and was in position to make the call, and it was close. I called the runner safe and the Santa Cruz manager acted like he was losing his mind. I was very sure of myself and was not going to be intimidated. He was now coming out of the dugout towards me. It just so happened that I had recently read a book entitled, "Nice Guys Finish Last" by Leo Durocher. Leo "The lip" wrote that he always respected an umpire who met him halfway. So that's what I did.

As I approached the manager, he yelled at me, "What makes you think he was safe?"

I answered with conviction, "The runner beat the tag."

I had always wanted to know what managers say to the umpires with these kinds of calls; it seemed a frivolous argument. The purpose of this strategy is that the manager appears to be sticking up for his guy. The manager walked back to his dugout, knowing that he had gotten his two cents in and perhaps getting the benefit of the doubt for the next close call. In a team-unity gesture, the centerfielder jogged in after the third out and, in a show of contempt, spit his tobacco juice beside second base.

The rest of the ballgame went smoothly and I don't even remember who won, umpires don't care. The important thing was the contest had been played. I received 50 bucks and a sincere compliment, "Nice game," from both managers. I earned the respect of my fellow umpire, and the thought occurred to me that this wasn't a bad gig. I might have pursued that line of work if circumstances were different.

The experiences of objectively watching (and officiating) the game gave me a whole new appreciation for baseball. Most fans only watch "their team," and/or root for the stars on the field. This viewpoint allowed me to reflect how "the men in blue," were similar to men of the law. The umps are there to let the players play the game and are objective in their calls. Of course, if a play goes against a player/team, they sometimes convince themselves they are victims of some conspiracy. When situations get out of hand, the umpire has the authority to remove said player(s) from the game. Umpires are effectively the sergeant at arms, overseeing the proceedings. They hope for a quick non-confrontational game but are ready to enforce the rules under intense pressure.

Stress Oral Boards

Cop work was what I wanted to do, so I started taking civil service tests around the Bay Area. I was in good shape for the physical-agility tests, and I passed the written part alright. However, I didn't succeed well at the oral board interviews at first. I had to tell myself, "It is *supposed* to be hard." The questions presented were nothing like ones that job seekers would be subjected to in regular business. The board(s) would mostly be made up of a community representative, a person from human resources, a ranking officer, and usually, at least one sergeant. Sometimes, there were five on the board; other times, ten. There was no continuity from one board to the next except that they all had a designated antagonist.

Knowing in advance that there will be an adversary helps you learn not to take words personally. The theory behind all this is that police officers should be able to handle stress, be flexible, and maintain their dignity. They are screening potential officers to see if they have the basics to represent the department under intense scrutiny and to be an outstanding witness in court.

I participated in many oral board examinations and the more I did, the better I got. One typical question always seemed to surface: "If you witnessed a vehicle violation and the driver turned out to be your mother, would you give her a ticket?" There is no right or wrong answer to this; they want to know how you *think*. Whether you answer in the affirmative or negative, you'll get an argument from the antagonist to try and change your mind. And if you start contradicting yourself it will lead to a failing score.

I had an opportunity to give a different answer to one board, when asked if I would give my mother a ticket. I unwaveringly answered, "No."

The antagonist jumped up from her chair and confronted me, "Why not?"

My answer: "Because my mother died when I was sixteen." There was nothing else to say. Before the next question was asked, I made subtle eye contact with the uniformed sergeant who was observing. I was hoping that my answer let him know that I had experienced some of the realities of life. I'm not sure if my tactic was considered logical or one of arrogance. At the very least, I was sure to get noticed.

There were always "what-would-you-do-if" types of questions, and many of them were life and death related. It was always best to take a few seconds to think before responding, and not to get rattled when challenged. In one of those tense exchanges of questions and answers, one of the panel members leaned forward with his elbows on the table and instructed me, "Tell us a joke." It was a test to see if I could think on my feet.   I always passed the various tests, but I invariably wound up down in the eligibility list. In self-assessment, I must have been perceived as too green at that time in my life. They did me a favor by not hiring me then: I continued school and enjoyed my time experiencing what life had to offer. I was nurturing that all-encompassing "life experiences" attribute so important in law enforcement. Besides, obtaining my degree would also open up possible opportunities for careers in the field. Palo Alto PD *only* hired those applicants with four-year degrees; it was the same with the FBI. I could smell the end goal now.

Chapter Four

The Start of My Chosen Career

AFTER I GRADUATED WITH a bachelor of science degree from San Jose State University, I devoted myself to a full-time pursuit of my chosen profession. I had been a sheriff's reserve deputy for the Santa Clara County Sheriff's Office for one year, volunteering my time as needed. That same year I was hired by the San Jose Police Department as a records technician, working the midnight shift. A captain headed the division with a sergeant assigned on every watch but records personnel were made up of mostly non-sworn city employees. They were the ones who really ran the place.

Working in the records division was a unique opportunity to learn from a different support perspective. This was 1977, and San Jose PD had an annual lease with nearby IBM for their technical equipment. This was long before personal computers or word processing programs were available, although we had monitors for our in-house record keeping. One of my duties was entering data from the reports. I not only entered the pertinent information, I also had the opportunity to read the multitude of police reports that came in during my shift. Another task I had was typing up reports as dictated by the officers out on the beat. There were designated call boxes specifically for that purpose in different areas of the city.

I had ran DMV records, confirmed the warrants, worked the C.L.E.T.S. [21] machine and had instant access to all arrest records going back many years. In fact, one of our responsibilities was to enter data from the old index cards into the new computer system.

---

21. California Law Enforcement Technology Services gives state and local access to other agencies and federal crime data bases and the National Crime Information Center (NCIC).

Drawing of me by an inmate

Having full access to all information came with a big responsibility; these were confidential records and there were laws and penalties for abuse. There was one story I was told as an example of misuse. It pertained to the era (1974–1975) when Patty Hearst was kidnapped and held hostage. The whole nation was looking for her and it was the lead story for the media. One of our records personnel curiously queried the name, "Patty Hearst" into the C.L.E.T.S. database to see what would come up. What he didn't know is that the FBI had flagged the name, and it must have set off alarm bells. The FBI thought San Jose PD had found her and they scurried over to confirm what had happened. That records technician was held to answer for violation of specific laws and was no longer employed when I got there.

One of the legal tasks of the records division was purging reports that had long been adjudicated. Keeping the paper reports was a continuous space consideration. Of great interest to me was the destruction of an old homicide case that was still open[22] since 1933. It involved the infamous lynching case of two suspected kidnappers, Holmes and Thurmond. They were dragged from their jail cells by outraged citizens and hanged from trees in St. James Park, north of downtown San Jose. The suspects had admitted to kidnapping Brooke Hart, the son of an iconic department store owner, and caused a sensation by killing their victim. It was a national news story that hung over the citizens of San Jose for years. Many of the participants were photographed in the act of the lynching and they were susceptible to charges brought against them. Through the years, all details of the case were kept at the records division, and it was time to legally shred them. In practice, if all the likely suspects of any murder have died off, the department will quietly close out the case.

The department employed many interesting and dedicated employees. We all shared a common snack bar/eating room area and, often, the homicide detectives would come down to grab a cup of coffee and take a break during the process of writing their reports. Right outside our building was a civil defense structure that housed dispatchers. They took the incoming calls, determined its level of priority, and either sent a patrol car(s), referred them, or dropped them all together.

There was one old veteran dispatcher who was wheelchair bound. He loved baseball and would somehow obtain the resident addresses of old forgotten major league ballplayers. He would send them a personal check, "enough for a couple of beers." His thrill was getting the processed check returned with the original endorsement signature on the back. He kept the checks as a souvenir.

Our phones rang continuously, and back then, employees answered them directly. One late Friday evening a call came in from San Francisco PD. It was from the assistant chief, who was trying to reach our assistant chief regarding a mass arrest at Candlestick Park. Apparently, a group of off-duty SJPD officers went together to watch a Giants vs. Dodgers game, and a huge fight involving the Dodgers fans broke out. San Francisco PD rounded up the participants and sorted it out later, hence the phone call to our records division. That night gave the records sergeant and plenty to do.

---

22. An open case in law enforcement is one that the media's vernacular would call "unsolved."

A Sworn Officer of the Law

I might have remained a civilian at San Jose PD as it was a good job. My goal, though, was to become a peace officer as defined by 832 of the California Penal Code. I continued to take written, physical, and oral board examinations and was placed on three waiting lists. My chance came when I got a call from a sergeant from the administration division of the Santa Clara County Sheriff's Office in August of 1978 after all the qualifying tests. He asked if I was still interested in being a deputy sheriff? I spontaneously responded with "Wha-hoooo!" The old sergeant said, "I take that for being in the affirmative?"

I was assigned to the Sheriff's Academy for three months of hard study. The venue for the academy grounds was shared by San Jose PD and a unit of smaller police departments. We trained separately. Our class had about thirty recruits and we bonded very tightly, even though we lost a few along the way. We had physical training at the end of our classes and ran between three and five miles each weekday. The area where we jogged is now the site of the San Francisco 49ers' football stadium in Santa Clara.

There were two female deputy recruits in our class, and one of them was the granddaughter of a long-retired captain of the sheriff's office. She brought in a scrapbook that he had compiled over his career, with newspaper articles dating from the 1930s and '40s. The captain was the one the sheriff had sent, for extradition purposes, to pick up wanted criminals from other jurisdictions.

Our training officer was a member of the sheriff's office as well as a Vietnam veteran. He took on the training responsibilities for all the right reasons. It was a delicate balance to teach, grade our reports, and objectively giving us evaluations every month. He was also the one who gave recruits the final approval before graduation. During a Q&A session in class, he was asked, "Is your assignment to us considered punishment duty?" We all hooted at that one. Even *he* smiled at the notion.

Towards the end of our academy experience, it was mandatory for us to visit the county morgue as a class and observe an autopsy. Everyone was pretty loose about it until we were right outside, then there was a collective somber mood as we entered the room. There were three pathologists waiting for us. The first thing we were shown was a singular refrigerator drawer, [from a huge wall of them] which he pulled out. The corpse had been marked as a "John Doe." It was the body of a male in his mid-twenties who had died in a motorcycle accident.

It was on to the autopsy suite where there were three different gurneys. One was occupied by an old man, another held a middle-aged woman, and the third had a four-year-old child. We were told the child had gotten into the cabinet under the grandparent's sink; there she drank something that poisoned her system. I couldn't help but feel sorry for that unknown family and for what they must have been going through. As soon as the pathologist did the "Y-incision,"[23] our training officer fainted. There was a slight stirring in our group and I looked over to one of the doctors—he had a slight smile as though he was amused. I wondered if these doctors made a bet between themselves on how many in the group would pass out. Our training officer was dazed, but he got himself together. No one made a big deal out of it; we found out afterwards that our training officer had a four-year-old daughter at home. No one ever mentioned the incident again, not even in jest.

We had to stay for the other two autopsies and, fortunately, they weren't as traumatic. The middle aged woman, it was explained, was a tourist from Germany. During the postmortem examination, the doctor told us what she died of and added his thoughts about it, saying, "She probably didn't like doctors."

Working the Jail

Following the rigorous training at the academy and a public graduation ceremony, we freshly launched deputies received our new duties. Only a handful went to patrol; some went to the courts, and others to Elmwood,[24] but most of us were assigned to the main jail, where the facility housed those suspects awaiting trial. The inmates who were being held had to be classified as a danger to the public. The jail was maxed out in population every day. Most arrestees were released on their own recognizance after booking, while others were released on bail.

There were some dorm-like settings, some two-man cells, and—the most notorious of all—the "Murder Max" wing of single cells. Other dorms were named by the inmates: "Hollywood," "Siberia," "Snake Pit," and many other descriptive terms. The intake portion of the jail was painted in a very faint shade of green; the theory was that this color was

---

23. A precision cut from shoulder to shoulder and down the sternum to the navel.

24. Elmwood was considered "Rehab," the minimum security facility for already sentenced misdemeanors.

psychologically calming. Everyone, it seemed, smoked cigarettes, and a blue cloud hung over the area like a dense fog.

At first glance, the place looked like there was no organization to it. We newly minted graduates of the academy stuck out as "fresh fish." We had academy inspection haircuts, shined shoes, and uncertain dispositions. I quickly learned "officer presence," using body language to show confidence. As inmates walked by me by the dozens on their way to "chow," they would size me up. Some would try and engage me in a "mad dog" look.

During roll call, prior to our shift assignments, the rookies sat in the first row and the veterans chose to stay in back while the sergeants read details from the previous shift. Every three months saw a new graduating academy class, so the cycle repeated itself endlessly.

For our indoctrination, we were partnered with a field training officer who showed us the ropes. I was assigned an FTO who was so notorious, we had heard about him while still in the academy. His name was Deputy Fred Knox, but his reputation was such that we called him, "The School of Hard Knox." This silver-haired, twenty-five-year veteran deputy had seen it all. A former patrol officer, he once engaged in fisticuffs with a group of Hell's Angels who had him surrounded.

Knox wasn't afraid of anyone, but the thing that was most interesting to me was that every inmate in the jail knew who he was. Even the baddest of the bad would ask during the booking process, "Where's Knox?" They had a kind of professional respect for him.

That first week, I helped out in the booking area, where we had a whole "fish tank" full of fresh arrests waiting to get booked in for housing. My job was to ink the wheel, fingerprint and process the incoming inmates so we could classify and house them. Some of the inmates wanted to fight, bleed, or breathe on me. A few had fresh needle marks on their arms, with trickles of blood.

In the late 1970s, someone dubbed Santa Clara County as the P.C.P.[25] capital of the world. On the street it was sometimes called "angel dust." It is a powerful drug that was used at one time as an animal tranquilizer; in humans, the effects are unpredictable. Some suffer from hallucinations; most are paranoid but almost all are impervious to pain and are prone to violent behavior. There were many incidents of those who were so high, they had superhuman strength. One I remember had delusions that he was protecting the earth from invading Martians (in actuality, we deputies).

---

25. Phencyclidine.

It took five of us to grab each of his extremities to control him and make sure he didn't hurt himself or others. He was removed to a special safety cell for the night. When he came down from the drug the next day he had no recollection of the night before, and was probably a nice kid. The concept of "time out chairs," or stun guns were not invented yet.

After passing training, I was given my own working station on one of the many floors of the jail. It was quite the responsibility. We had no weapons, but we had instant communication at our desk and a portable radio. Trustees were the exception; they were allowed to come and go for work tasks during different shifts. They were screened and considered a lower risk for escape or violence, and they could be counted on to bring coffee to the deputies. As one of my sergeants said, "Just because they're trustees doesn't mean you can trust them." They were usually the runners, the ones to pass on information or contraband to the rest of the inmates.

The early-morning routine for deputies was to get inmates up for breakfast at 4:00 a.m., as some of them had court appearances to make and they had to make the jail-bus in time. There was a strict rule of not fraternizing with any of the incarcerated, which suited me fine. However, there was one inmate, a self-proclaimed sketch artist, who made a drawing of me from his viewpoint in his cell. Some of the inmates simply did not play well with others. There was one guy whose name I could never forget, try as I might: Charles Allen. He was a dangerous disrupter in the facility. I would meet up with him later in my career on the streets.

It was a pretty tight group of deputies. When we got off duty at 7:00 a.m., we would frequently meet at a local park and play softball. This was our "calm down time" before we went home and tried to sleep.

We housed some pretty notorious inmates in "Murder Max," but the one who freaked everyone out most was Richard Chase,[26] a serial killer who slayed six people in Sacramento in the span of a month. His crimes were so egregious that a change of venue was ordered and the high-profile trial took place in Santa Clara County. After all was said and done, the jury convicted him to death in May of 1979.

As soon as Chase was convicted, everyone—even the other inmates—wanted him out of our nice, clean jail. I was held over from my midnight shift and led to a small room where the shackled Chase was to wait for the transportation bus to take him to prison. I was assigned to "babysit" him to ensure that he didn't hurt himself. I was mere inches away from

---

26. Richard Chase was a cannibal who drank the blood of his victims and other unmentionable atrocities. He committed suicide in prison.

him, my chair facing his. Fixing my gaze, I saw that his white skin looked virtually transparent, with blue veins showing through. He looked anemic and I was afraid he had infectious hepatitis. Dubbed the "The Vampire of Sacramento" by the media, he was resigned to his fate and, fortunately, did not try to move or converse. Chase just stared down without blinking. I hated to breathe the same air as he. I wanted to burn my uniform when I got home.

Romance

Since high school I have enjoyed many love interests, some lighthearted, some serious. In 1977, I met a nice young lady from Monterey named Ruth. She and her girlfriend came up to take in a new nightclub in Campbell, called the Bodega. My friend Randy and I sought them out. It started with a dance and a cocktail, and I learned she was a grade school teacher in Monterey. We struck a commonality as we had both been docents in our community. We began to communicate via the telephone.

When Ruth's birthday rolled around, she invited to me to a party at her home on the Monterey peninsula. I was infatuated. We saw each other regularly on our days off and got pretty serious, to the point that we considered living together. I began to think how we could accomplish this feat. At first, I hoped that, after my jail duty assignment was completed, I would be able to rotate out to the south Santa Clara County Sheriff's Patrol Station in Gilroy. The idea seemed farfetched when I learned that, once assigned to the jail, it would take five years to rotate out, based on seniority.

I was really at a junction in my life. There were rumors circulating in the sheriff's office that the city of Cupertino was going to start up its own police force. In all the years prior, they had contracted out to the sheriff's office for all their patrol duties. If the city did have their own force, that would mean all the patrol officers would be bumped back down with the less senior people. There were also rumors that the board of supervisors wanted to hire non-sworn civilians to augment the jail staffing normally handled by deputy sheriffs.

In preparation for change, I participated in a physical agility test, a written civil-service test, and oral boards for both the San Jose and Seaside police departments. The latter would fit the best circumstances for my personal and professional needs. I was eager to be a "street cop" and to *help* people in their hour of need.

What sealed the deal for me was a serious incident that happened to a fellow academy mate. It was all over the news. Deputy Tony Cruz was escorting a suspect from the jail to a holding cell at court. Unbeknown to him, the inmate previously inflicted a scratch on his arm and convinced medical staff to bandage him up. It was all a ruse. The guy seized the opportunity to hide a prison-made knife (a shank), within the Ace bandage of his arm. At an opportune moment, the inmate requested to go to the bathroom, and Cruz escorted him. At a weak moment of attention, the inmate withdrew the shiv and stabbed Cruz in the neck. He crumpled down to the floor. The suspect then wrestled the deputy's .357 Magnum gun from his holster and shot him in the abdomen, then walked around behind Cruz's head. Tony told me later, "I thought he was going to blow my head off. I just lay there, pretending to be out."

With the commotion, court personnel approached the scene. The suspect decided to run, so with the gun in his hand he somehow managed to escape through a window on the second floor and fled on foot in his orange jail jumpsuit. The suspect ran up the street and hailed a city bus to stop and climbed aboard. Fortunately, an observant San Jose Police officer witnessed this and coordinated a stop of the bus. The suspect was arrested and, thankfully, no one on the bus was hurt.

As the suspect was being hustled back to the jail, medical personnel attended to Cruz. It did not look good. The media responded from all over the Bay Area: this was big news. By the time medical personnel were ready to put him in an ambulance, television cameras were broadcasting the aftermath. I saw it as it was broadcast live. "Not Tony!" I blurted out to the TV. Just then, a field reporter, Rico Chacon, from KTVU TV Channel 2 in San Francisco/San Jose, arrived on the scene. He was professional and sensitive in describing what had happened. He started off by saying, "Deputy Antonio Cruz was shot today . . ." There was a look of concern on his face that impressed me. I would come across Chacon later in my career.

Shortly after this incident, I received a call at home from Commander Gullet of Seaside PD. He asked if I was still interested in becoming an officer for their agency. This was the opportunity I had been looking for. I enthusiastically confirmed my intentions. He wanted to know how soon I could come down for a "chief's interview." I explained that I was working the night shift at the Santa Clara County Jail as a deputy, and asked if we could make the meeting on one of my days off. The commander said, "Wait, you mean you've already been through the academy?" This was gravy for any agency that did not have to run the expense and risk of putting a recruit through the academy. I made that appointment.

I called my girlfriend and we celebrated the good news: I would be moving to Monterey! Just before I was to leave for the interview, I received another phone call. This one was from a backgrounds officer from San Jose PD. He informed me that my name had come up on the waiting list. When the officer found out I was already a deputy, he said: "We love people who worked at the jail." He offered that they could do a quick update on my background and that he could slide me into their field training program. This was quite a moment. I didn't want to commit before my interview with the Seaside Police Chief. My chance at San Jose PD was temporarily put on hold.

As I drove down to the Monterey Peninsula, I had the feeling that I was a free agent who had already found a measure of success. As I approached the city limits, I had a flashback of the first time I had driven down for my oral board. I did not know Seaside as a native, but I studied it. I was proud when I caught the population posted on the city limits sign and memorized it in case I was asked. It was another one of those oral boards where an antagonist was planted to argue with whatever I was going to say. The question *did* come up, "What is the population of Seaside?" I immediately rattled off the number.

"Wrong!" said an outraged member of the board. "Do you realize that Seaside also takes in half the population of Fort Ord." [27]

"No sir, but I do now, thank you." I was not going to argue, but Fort Ord was its own federal entity in population, with strict military boundaries.

Seaside was a diversified city with a strong mix of all races—I knew that going in. Again, a tough question was asked of me: "Seaside has the highest crime rate on the peninsula. Why do you think that is so."

I answered, "Whenever there is a military base next to a city, it tends to attract vice and with it, crime." When I finally got the appointment for my chief's interview, the commander met me in the lobby and introduced me to Chief Ben Cooper. They had questions about my fiancée, such as "Who is she?" I told them of her profession and that she was raised in Seaside. There was another fact that stood out: she was of Filipino descent and her parents were heavily involved with the community. They were thrilled with that and, at the conclusion of the meeting, the chief offered

---

27. Fort Ord was an Army military installation off of Monterey Bay, between the cities of Marina and Seaside on the Monterey Peninsula, between the years 1918 and 1994.

me the job as police officer. I accepted and said I needed three weeks advance notice from my current position.

Back at work, the deputies at the jail congratulated me. I was sad to leave my peers, especially the ones with whom I had attended the academy with. I also met with the enthusiastic background officer at San Jose PD to give him my plans. He told me the eligibility list was "good for a year," so it was a positive parting. I have sometimes wondered if I made the right choice, but despite my love for the city and the history, it might have been best I did not have to see the *real* underbelly of San Jose. Whenever I came back, it was a joyful occasion. My fiancée and I settled into a Monterey residence and were married the following year.

The city of Monterey is a historical one. During the Spanish and Mexican regimes until 1850, it was the capital of California. There are more California Historical Landmarks in this city than any other in the State. I was drawn to the past and current cultures. There was so much to learn.

Chapter Five

Seaside By the Beautiful Sea

SEASIDE WAS A CITY of approximately 35,000 when I started working there in 1979. It was a blue-collar, hard-drinking, hard-fighting military town. Incorporated as a city in 1954, the area was at one time mostly sand dunes, the polar opposite of the green areas of Monterey, Carmel, Pacific Grove, Pebble Beach, and Big Sur. Many of the homes were built before the city had building codes, and numerous shanties were in pocket areas.

My first impressions of working in this town have remained vivid in my mind. The squad cars were bought as a fleet from the California Highway Patrol and had over 100,000 miles on them. There was no field training program or manual. I was assigned to drive around with the shift's sergeant for three days, trying to take it all in. At the end of that period, I was given a map of the city, and service calls of a simple nature were dispatched to me until I got my feet wet. After those three days I was assigned a beat; it was a "sink or swim" environment. I passed probation after six months.

There were about twenty-seven officers back then, working three different shifts. Besides the chief and commander, there were four lieutenants and four sergeants on the force. We began each shift exactly fifteen minutes before the patrol units could be relieved, making sure that the city wasn't without protection for even a few minutes. At the roll-call table, the sergeant would read pertinent information and assign us to our beats. The city was divided up into three beats and a traffic unit.

Seaside PD (1979)

Of the officers, only one had been there for eight years; the rest had fewer than three years of experience. There was quite a turnover in personnel and some perceived the department as a "training agency." The officers got their street experience and tended to move up to a better-paying position at the bigger agencies. My pay every two weeks was $484 net; we used to be amused about that figure because 484 of the California Penal Code was the legal definition of petty theft.

During my first weeks, there was a mass murder/suicide reported. A husband and father had shot his entire family before turning the gun on himself. The first responding officer was processing the scene along with the detective sergeant. As I drove up to assist, the sergeant was outside, waiting for the coroner. He lit up a cigar and said in contempt: "Ah, there's nothing like the smell of fresh blood in the morning." The cigar and smoke was to mask the stench entrenched in his nostrils. The first officer that arrived, a veteran of about two years, left the department soon afterwards to sell Amway products.

I had only been away from working at the jail for a month, and during an evening shift I pulled a car over due to some minor concern. Surprisingly, the driver was Charles Allen, the inmate I had dealt with at the Santa Clara County Jail. Apparently, he was released just about the time I left jail duties. "Cassara," he said as I leaned into the driver's side window, "what are you doing in my home town?" Before I could answer, he told me: "I'm going straight; you won't see me in jail anymore."

I offered encouragement, but his exact words were something I had heard from many inmates. Allen *may* have had good intentions, or perhaps he was simply trying to throw me off. Regardless, I think I might have spooked him with the coincidental meet-up. The reason I remember this so well is that, two weeks later, Charles Allen was found dead on a residential lawn in Seaside. He was a victim of a retaliation shooting.

On a quiet Sunday afternoon, I was dispatched to the high school, where there was a suspicious object at the end of the pool's diving board. They weren't kidding: it was a five-gallon bucket and flies were circling it. I had to climb that high dive ladder in my uniform, walk the plank, pick up the heavy bucket and its contents and somehow shuffle back and down the ladder to safety. The bucket was full of internal organs, but were they from an animal or a human? I called the sergeant to the scene because I could not figure out what we had, I suspected some kind of cult murder.

Sgt. Marv Dyke arrived with a cigarette dangling from his expressionless face. He surveyed the innards and, with his nicotine-stained right index finger, poked the heart. This old-school sergeant then told me, "These are pig guts; it's just the Happy[28] family." I had no idea what he meant or how he could have come up with his theory. I thought, How did he figure out who was responsible for this simply by poking an organ with his finger? Am I ever going to be able to do this? Dyke further explained, "The Happy family is mad because one of our officers gave one of them a ticket. They're poachers, and they like to take revenge." This was my introduction to the family that I—and every other police officer in Monterey County—would encounter time and again. Another weird call I remember was when I was detailed to the city cemetery for a theft of a grave liner—a term with which I was unfamiliar. I was led to an empty grave and the proprietor explained that the concrete insert had been stolen the night before. How did they accomplish this half-ton theft? There was a crane nearby that had been used for just such a purpose. Even more concerning: a locked shed had been broken into and great sacks of cement mix were stolen. I took the report and returned to the office, bewildered. The sergeant on duty looked over at the records supervisor and asked, "Did Barnaby H. get out of prison?" He had and was currently on parole. It was then explained to me just who this guy was: "A few years

---

28. A known criminal family that lived in the city.

back he stole an officer's patrol car and failed to yield. When he finally stopped, Sgt. Dyke snuck up behind him and used the butt of his shotgun to subdue him. "Oh," the sergeant added, "he used to work at the cemetery. I think he's your man."

I returned to the cemetery and asked an employee there, "Do you know a Barnaby H?"

"Yeah, he used to work here, operating the crane," I was told. "Yes, he would be able to do this, but he'd need a big truck to haul it."

I had no idea what to do next, but I wrote the report and submitted it at the end of my shift.

On a daily basis, someone from the *Monterey Herald* newspaper would come in and read a summary of our reports. This case was so unusual it became a news item, with my name listed as the contact person. Apparently, the phone in the office started ringing. Sgt. Kline advised, "This is how it works. When you get close, people start calling *you*."

I followed up by returning the call, and the guy was scared to death. He kept saying, "It was a joke. Some guy bet me I couldn't get it in my back yard."

I drove down and met the caller outside his residence. He led me to his backyard and—there it was! He explained that he had bought it from some guy for $50, so he could "put fish in it."

"What was the guy's name?" I asked.

"I don't know."

"Well, you're in possession of stolen property."

He began to panic. "No, no, I'll tell you who he is, but he might kill me. His name is Barnaby."

I found Barnaby at a local bar and arrested him for grand theft and burglary. Once in jail, he was put in a parole hold. The case eventually went to a preliminary hearing and he was bound over for trial. I testified there and, later, at a parole board hearing. As a result, ol' Barnaby was sent back to prison.

I really looked up to Officer Mike Bainter, a former English teacher at North Salinas High School, who had found his true calling in police work. Smart, with a couple of years on me, he took me under his wing and we (and our wives) soon became close friends. One day, he got into a shootout on his way to work while driving through the peaceful town of Pacific Grove. Bainter recognized a wanted felon, known on the streets as "Killer Joe," driving a car. Somehow, a shootout took place in broad daylight, and Killer Joe was ultimately taken into custody with the assistance of the local

PD. The felon was sent back to prison, but only after swearing vengeance on Bainter. The newspapers screamed, "Gun Fire Between Cars in Pacific Grove Captures Wanted Felon." Apparently, nothing like that had ever happened in this quiet, picturesque town.

Bainter and I had the opportunity to represent our department (actually, we were on our own time) for a local radio station (KOKQ) phone-in show. The host, a blind man in his thirties, loved his community. In the hour-long program, we answered questions pertaining to our professional background and, specifically, how we did the job. Callers participated in the show and it turned out to be a successful evening, although none of our other officers wanted any part of going on the air, live. Bainter and I just took it on. This would later have an influence on my career.

Our midnight shift started at 11 p.m. and usually we only had three officers and a supervisor on duty. That night it was Lt. Ralph Burdett, a tough-as-nails, eighteen-year veteran. His nickname was "Rotten Ralph."

This particular night we had to respond to a fight outside a bar between two motorcycle gangs. We strategically responded in full Code 3 (red lights and siren). As we approached, most of them ran away, although a few were still fighting. We were sorely outnumbered, so we sprayed the fighters with Chemical Mace. That weeded out some more but we wound up arresting about a half dozen and brought them to our station's holding cells. We began the booking process: photos, fingerprinting, paperwork, etc. One of them was so badly hurt, I was told to transport him to the hospital and "849ed[29] him.

As I was driving to the hospital, our two remaining officers were still at the station, processing the suspects. I heard the radio broadcast of a loud party at which there were dozens of drunken kids. The prior shift had already contacted the responsible party and it started to break up, but this was a "call-back"—and now there were more kids than ever. Lt. Burdett cut loose one of our officers to handle the call. Just as he was driving away from the scene, Officer Sysum blurted out on the radio, "I was just hit by a block of concrete; I think my arm's broken."

Lt. Burdett was angry that his officer had been hurt. He directed us back to the house to arrest anyone we saw outside for public intoxication. As we approached, the kids scattered. It was one busy night.

---

29. Cop jargon for section 849 of the California Penal Code that effectively gives the power to unarrest someone without charges if probable cause cannot be established.

Donuts

It might be true that cops eat donuts more than the average person—at least back then. The circumstances in Seaside were such that no restaurant stayed open during the midnight shift, but there was a Red's Donut Shop in a strip mall. When things started to calm down, usually after 3 a.m., Lt. Burdett would go into the shop and take a seat at the counter. We officers would then come in, one by one, to "coffee-up" and grab a bite.

Burdett held court at the counter, playing a dice game with us, and the loser had to pay for the donuts. This crafty, old hawk preyed on our rookie officers. It was mandatory to play dice with him, even if he cheated. To us, it was a source of amusement, a fun way to bond. He lost to me one day and he didn't like it. It was a bill for a dollar. Of course, he didn't pay me; instead, he wrote a note, which read: "I, Ralph Burdett, owe Bill Cassara one dollar, payable when he catches me," and then he signed it. That was worth more to me as a souvenir than the monetary amount. I held on to it until the day he died.

There was a notorious bar at the center of town that was an especially dangerous place for cops. I was in there one time on a case and noticed what looked like a big tip jar with cash inside—only this wasn't a "tip jar," it was pool money for whoever killed Lt. Burdett. I reported this to the lieutenant, who asked, "How much money is in there?" He then drove to the bar, went in, grabbed that jar, and counted its contents in front of the shocked patrons. He was insulted by the low total, so he threw in a couple of bucks himself. He had such a reputation that all the crooks in town were afraid of him. It was just how he liked it.

One of our officers, Mark Puskaric, grew up in this town and had a tremendous talent of finding stolen vehicles as he was driving around on his beat. He could remember stolen license plate numbers from the reports at briefings, retaining that information for weeks. He was a great investigator too, and he ultimately was hired by the district attorney's office. I remember a detail I was on with him when we received a burglary-in-progress call. Puskaric spotted the suspect going into a window. Puskaric went in after him and, when I reached the back porch, I heard a gun go off. My adrenalin was such that I put my shoulder to that locked back door and broke it down off its hinges. Lifting myself off the ground, I saw Puskaric in the other room, struggling with the suspect over a gun, the barrel of which was pointing all around. I tackled the guy and brought him into the station to book him. Sgt. Dike approached me and said, "Here's your gun." Apparently it flew out of my unfastened holster upon my impact with the door. There is no more of a sinking feeling than realizing your gun is missing.

During my tenure with the city, the force experienced substantial turnover within the ranks and in city personnel. A new city manager was brought in from Southern California. He downplayed the crime rate so as not to affect business and real estate values. He found a home in Seaside and, during the first night in residence, his wife told him that she heard a burglar downstairs. The city manager crept downstairs unclothed and got into a wrestling match with the intruder. Meanwhile, the wife had called the cops and we hauled the burglar away.

Dispatch Center

Everyone should know that, unlike fictional depictions on television and in movies, there are no stars in law enforcement. It is a team effort from the first call to the final justice in the courts. Dispatchers are the beginning of this chain; they take an incoming phone call and extract information to determine if it is an emergency, a nothing call, or a nut case. They take calls and disseminate information that sometimes is an officer threat and, just as easily, dispatch fire and medical while coordinating different agencies and units. It is a highly stressful job and they hardly ever get to know the outcome of an emergency because they're too busy taking other calls. 9-1-1 emergencies come in with such volume that the personnel receiving them occasionally become overwhelmed. I have strong respect for the men and women in that profession.

Dispatchers have heard it all, but some calls do get under their skin. One such call came in when I was working a beat in Seaside. My call number was "601," and I was told to phone dispatch for 10-36.[30] It seems one dispatcher had been receiving harassing phone calls all day, and she was tired of it. She had been able to hold the line open and identify the address from which the calls were emanating. The records division was able to confirm not only the caller's name, but that he had an outstanding warrant.

Surprisingly when I arrived at his residence, the guy opened the door and greeted me warmly. He had a police scanner going so he could hear all the radio traffic in Seaside. I invited him to come outside so we could

---

30. California 10-Code for "confidential Information."

discuss the situation. He then joyfully held out his arms, indicating that he wanted to be handcuffed. I arrested him on the warrant and placed him in the back seat of my patrol car. Then sensing his "thrill," I asked him if he'd like to talk on the radio. His face brightened up like a Christmas tree. "Now, when I say 'go,'" I said, "talk into the microphone and say "10-19,[31] one for booking." I then went on the air to my dispatcher and said, "Stand by." Then I put the microphone up to the cage separating me from the back seat and said, "Go." He proudly repeated his line. I got the microphone back and asked if she recognized the voice as the one she had been hearing all day. Her answer: "Affirmative, 601." Everyone was happy.

I admired Sgt. Mike Klein as a supervisor and as a person. He was born in Germany and retained genuine European manners. Hired by the force in 1969, he knew every bad guy in town. He had a way with people, showing sincerity and getting the job done with class. Klein used the words, "gentlemen," and "excellent," even in casual conversation. He was a true role model. Klein encouraged a team spirit and we responded in kind.

There was a crazy call to which Sgt. Klein and I responded one evening. A house had caught fire at the top of Hilby Avenue. We always respond to such an emergency to help if people are involved and/or traffic considerations. I was driving in a separate patrol car behind the sergeant. Suddenly, his car diverted immediately to the right, Seeing this, I innately made the same maneuver. It was lucky I did because I saw a bowling ball whizzing past me. The ball went shooting by me, in a sabotage attempt on our lives. The ball accelerated in speed as it rolled down the hill; it crossed Fremont Avenue and crashed through the glass front windows of the Sprouse-Ritz pharmacy store. After the call, Sgt. Klein and I surveyed the damage and waited for the owner to arrive. We had the chance to collect our thoughts about this freak occurrence. Klein remarked that if that ball had gone through our windshield it would have been like a cannonball hitting us. The Sprouse-Ritz building was eventually torn down. One Saturday afternoon, units received an alert from dispatch: it was a B.O.L. (Be on the Lookout) status update on an all-points bulletin that originated from San Jose. Bay Area banks were being hit by an armed robber with a distinct look and manner; the media had dubbed him "The Hollywood Bandit." On this day there was a break in the case. A witness observed him enter his car for a getaway. It was a yellow Volkswagen with personalized license plates. The letters were a name and easily remembered by the witness,

---

31. 10-19 is California 10-Code for return to the station.

who then passed the information on to dispatch. When communications center received the call, they quickly ran it for the registered owner. Most of the time cars are stolen for the job so it was lucky that, this time at least, the perpetrator used his own car as the getaway vehicle. San Jose PD tried without success to find this car, but it was being driven south and right to the registered address in Seaside.

We were set up for him and arrested the suspect just as he was pulling onto his street. His car was impounded and all the stolen money was in a bag on the passenger seat. He was brought to the station and booked; meanwhile, San Jose PD was notified. Sgt. Klein treated the suspect with respect and offered him a cigarette. As he lit up, the gentleman robber expressed an interest in talking to Sgt. Klein and, after waiving his rights, he admitted to this latest robbery. When the detectives from San Jose came, they escorted him back to their station, where the FBI met up with the team. A full confession on all the robberies was obtained.

There were some humorous incidents I remember in Seaside. One day, I was on patrol and drove through the parking lot of a K-Mart store. I saw a young dad drive his car into a "handicap only"– marked curbside. He and his young son exited and started walking when the dad saw me over his shoulder. He suddenly affected an unconvincing limp, which the youngster immediately began to mimic. Dad scolded him, saying, "Not *you!*"

On another occasion, I was taking a stolen vehicle report from a guy who lived in a very cramped apartment unit. As we sat down to discuss the dynamics of the case, his trained myna bird kept interrupting us by bombastically belting out, "*Ah, shaddup!*" The bird kept repeating this line—with a Brooklyn accent yet—much to my amusement and to the victim's chagrin.

John Lennon Gunned Down in New York

I was off duty on December 8, 1980 and watching *Sunset Boulevard* on television with my wife. Suddenly, there was an interruption for a special news bulletin: John Lennon had just been shot and killed in New York City. I was disgusted, outraged, and deeply saddened. Just then, I got a phone call from Mike Bainter, who was also off duty that night. He suggested we meet at a coffee shop and discuss this sudden impact on our lives. Mike's wife, Nancy (a high school French teacher), joined us and we talked about what we knew of the incident. Mostly, though, we reminisced about the music.

I first saw The Beatles on TV the night they debuted on *The Ed Sullivan Show*, February 9, 1964. Being a newspaper boy, I followed their career through all of their musical stages. The Beatles, both as a band and as individuals, had a big influence on me. When the Bainter's and I learned a New York City police officer decided not to wait for an ambulance and to transport John to the hospital himself, we felt a momentary sense of pride. Although it was not common knowledge in later years, I learned that John's widow, Yoko, annually contributed an undisclosed amount to the NYPD fallen officers' fund. Lennon was such a genius and he made so many people happy, it is a tragedy that one nut took him away from us.

This is one of my favorite John Lennon quotes, although it is quite chilling."Part of our policy is not to be taken seriously because I think our opposition, whoever they may be in all their manifest forms, don't know how to handle humour, you know. And we're humourists, we're Laurel & Hardy, that's John and Yoko. And we stand a better chance under that guise 'cuz all the serious people like Martin Luther King, Kennedy and Gandhi got shot."[32]

Street Hookers

Since Seaside was known as a vice town—with drugs, money, and military personnel—it tended to attract hookers and "Johns." Some had pimps they had to answer to, but all were severely addicted to drugs, mostly heroin. As officers of the law, we kept an eye on them because they were so vulnerable. They were often victims of abuse, and more than a few were killed or overdosed.

The "Ladies of the Night" were supposed to report to the local clinic on a monthly basis and, if we saw any new ones hitting the streets, we would cite them per city ordinance to report to the clinic to make sure they were clean. There was no way to stop the epidemic, but we tried to at least to ensure the girls' medical safety.

One incident I recall from a swing shift involved three drunken military men who stepped up to the front counter to report a "robbery." I listened to their story, as did Lt. Burdett. The men had approached a prostitute on the street to arrange for a hookup. Apparently, after being

---

32. Beatles Interviews www.Database: John Lennon & Yoko Ono Interview: Apple Offices, London 5/8/1969.

paid up front, the young lady jumped into her pimp's car and took off. Rip-offs like this were common and, on occasion, a John would report it. When Lt. Rotten Ralph heard this particular complaint, he grabbed the three by the scruff of their necks and took them to the drunk tank. He told them, "You just copped to a crime. A prostitution transaction is illegal, and this ain't the better business bureau." The following morning, the miscreants were released without charges after sobering up.

Some of the hookers lived close by in motels, but others were driven in from outside the county. We noticed that when a new girl showed up, a turf war would break out near the bars. One day, a beautiful, tall blonde made her presence known when she showed up to "hook." She was a creature of the mean streets, with a tough disposition and salty language to match. It was one of those evening shifts when I was dispatched to an overdose at a seedy motel room. The door was opened, so I walked in and announced myself. At first, it appeared that no one was there. I then noticed that the same prostitute was lying unconscious in the bathtub, submerged in buckets of ice. This is an oft-used "street" method to revive someone who has overdosed. Checking her pulse, I was able to determine that she was still alive. I immediately called for an ambulance. While awaiting its arrival, I looked around for the obvious source of her overdose, but found no drug paraphernalia. After the ambulance crew showed up and began working on her, a couple of pimps walked in, doing their best to look innocent.

The victim was ready to be rushed to the hospital, but medical staff needed to know what kind of drug she had used. I confronted the two, and neither one admitted to knowing her. I yelled at them, "All I want to know is what kind of drug she used! The hospital won't be able to help her without knowing if she took an upper or a downer." They calmly shrugged their collective shoulders. I blasted at them, "This woman needs help and, if she dies, I'm coming after *you* for a murder charge." That didn't work either. Fortunately, she was revived at the hospital, only to return to the street the next day. I talked to her about the incident and she expressed complete indifference. Before long, she left the area.

Sometimes, I thought about those unfortunate girls and wondered what their lives must be like. Once, many years later, I was in a very high-end store in Carmel and was approached by a female clerk; she asked, "Do you remember me?" I did not. "Let sleeping dogs lie," she said. That's when I recognized her: she had been one of the most drugged-out girls on the street back in the day. Whenever I had a rookie with me, I used to drive to her spot on the corner and ask to see her arm. She had a long track of needle marks[33] going up her limb. I was happy to learn that she had kicked the habit, raised a son, and had a nice job to support herself. It is important for cops to hear happy endings every now and then; it reassures us that, occasionally at least, we have a positive impact on people.

During one of my midnight shift calls, I was dispatched to an apartment complex where a complaint had been made about a continuously crying baby. I knocked politely, but there was no answer, I then gave it a solid "police knock," the type that everyone in the complex can hear. There still was no answer, but I heard the baby crying. Concerned for the infant's welfare and, given the exigent circumstances, I opened the *unlocked* door and looked around for the parents. They were nowhere to be found. The five-month-old child was in her crib, still crying. I felt so much empathy for that baby.

I called Child Protective Services, but it was going to take at least a couple of hours before they could respond. I didn't want to just wait for the parents to return, and besides, my fellow beat officers would soon have to take my other pending details. Sometimes, a cop has to take the initiative. I told C.P.S. to meet me at the station. I then wrote a somewhat nasty note for the parents, explaining that I took their baby and instructing them to come to the station the instant they read my message. I dutifully left my business card with the note.

There was no supervisor on duty, and what I did next was not taught in the academy. I lifted that child with plenty of blankets and placed her in the front seat of my patrol car. I turned on the red and yellow lights, but no siren. I drove extra slowly until I reached the station, and then explained to the female records supervisor that she would be in charge of the baby until C.P.S. came. I then went back out to my beat, took pending details and waited until the parents, C.P.S., or both, arrived. A good while later, the mother and her boyfriend sheepishly walked into the station. They explained that they had gone out for a night of dancing and drinking and couldn't find a babysitter, so they chanced it. When C.P.S. came, things started to be sorted out. I cited the mother for child abandonment and forwarded the report to C.P.S. for their follow-up. The baby was returned to the mother.

It all turned out well, but I had exposed myself (and the department) to severe risk if something had gone wrong. The result: the detail was handled, I solved the immediate problem, and no one brought up the subject with me afterwards. That's how things rolled in Seaside: decide, solve the issue, and get ready for the next call.

In my thirty-year experience in law enforcement, I was injured only twice. Both incidents involved women who lived in Seaside. The first time

---

33. Called a "snake" in street terms

was the result of a domestic call between two female roommates. One of the young ladies called in to report that her car had been stolen, although she provided no clue as to who might have stolen it. I took down the information and had Records enter the details into C.L.E.T.S., which is standard procedure.

A few hours later, the same party called 9-1-1 to report that the suspect had returned with the car and that she wished to press charges. Officer Sysum and I responded and once we were inside, the two really started mouthing off to each other. As is usual, we tried to separate the two combatants. I suggested to one of the woman that we step outside so she could tell me her version of the events. As I walked her through the living room, she suddenly bolted toward her roommate and gave her a roundhouse slug to the jaw. I grabbed her from behind and she bit my arm, causing me to fall backwards, with her on top, facing up. She also had the presence of mind to grab the handle of my gun and tried to yank it out of my holster. She was subdued, thanks to my partner. I needed medical attention and it was documented, but in the end, such injuries were always chocked up as an administration-defined "hazard of the job."

We had very good officers at Seaside, and it was the tightest unit with whom I have ever worked. One of our more senior officers was K. C. Smith. He had grown up in the area and knew the streets and their players. He talked to everyone and, after a handshake, he would offer them his own business card (the city did not provide them). He often passed on information that was highly beneficial to us, but it was the rapport he had with those in the underground that impressed me most. Every time he made an arrest and needed an interview, he asked the guy in the back seat, "Hey, are you hungry?" Then he pulled up to the drive-in window at a Burger King and order hamburgers. It must have been an interesting sight at the drive-up window.

There was a time when Lt. Burdett and I stopped a burglary in progress at the new car center. Most of the time these guys didn't carry identification, so when the suspect was asked for his I.D., he proudly presented J. C. Smith's business card. The good lieutenant tore it up and said, "A goddamned K.C. Smith get-out-of-jail-free -card." And that's what we called them from then on.

I have the highest respect for officers who work undercover; they have to isolate themselves from their families to generate a different identity. If cops are considered "good actors," then the ones going underground should be eligible to receive the Academy Award.

It was important to know that we had an undercover officer in the city—the dynamic "Z-man." If there was an urgent call, like a robbery alarm at a liquor store, he would pass the marked units to beat us there. Z-man introduced me to a partner of his from the Monterey County Sheriff's Office who also worked undercover. It was hard to comprehend that he was on our side. A Vietnam veteran, he presented himself as a heroin addict, with his small stature, long stringy hair, and Rasputin-like beard. It was necessary to know what he looked like because if we saw him working on the street, we were instructed to leave him alone. If we "burned him" by inadvertently treating him differently than other derelicts, his life would have been in jeopardy. This undercover detective impressed me greatly. I had no idea that our paths would cross many times throughout our careers. Ideally, a police force is made up of diverse and intelligent officers, Seaside PD being a shining example of this. We had two highly capable female patrol officers, which was much to our advantage. Sometimes suspects or victims, both male and female were more comfortable conversing with them than with male officers. Another of our female officers was Ira Lively, an African American who worked Juvenile crimes. She was the darling of the NAACP. We also had an esteemed African American lieutenant, Dave Butler, who had pushed a patrol car in the city since 1964. Lt. Butler was easily one of the nicest individuals in law enforcement. Unfortunately, he died only a month after retiring.

When I was first hired on the force, it was a common practice to distribute badge numbers on a seniority basis. I was given badge number 27. As the attrition of police officers mounted, we would move up in badge numbers as well. The turnover was such that by the end of my two years with Seaside, I had become number 9 in tenure. It was a goal of the officers to finally obtain status as a "single digit midget."

With the departure of our senior officers, we received many new rookies to take their place. These recruits learned quickly, but there is no substitute for experience. In just two years on the department, I had seen murders, body dumps, drug addicts, gun fire, and domestic disturbances. Whenever I pulled onto a side street, pedestrians would stop in their tracks until I passed by. We did traffic investigations, stolen vehicle reports and stakeouts. We wrote our reports in longhand in the field until the end of shift or a fresh arrest, after which we could use the typewriter. If one was in the station too long and the fellow beat officers had to take your calls, you might just find a piece of cheese in your mail box. And no one wanted to be called a "Station rat."

Chapter Six

It Happened In Monterey

MY WIFE AND I HAD NOW been living in Monterey for two years, and we loved it. I have always been drawn to this great meeting of land and sea. In some literary quarters, the peninsula and Salinas valley is known as "Steinbeck Country." The books of John Steinbeck often feature the backdrop of the exquisite beauty and eccentric characters the author had encountered during his time here growing up.

This area was famous for its resident artists, writers, and photographers, including Robert Louis Stevenson, Jack London, Robinson Jeffers, Henry Miller, Edward Weston, Salvador Dali, and Ansel Adams. The communities of Monterey, Carmel, Carmel Valley, Big Sur, Pacific Grove, and Pebble Beach have attracted many Hollywood celebrities through the years, such as Bing Crosby, Clint Eastwood, Doris Day, Joan Fontaine, Kim Novak, Jean Arthur, Betty White, Paul Anka, Merv Griffin, Reggie Jackson, Peter Tork, and Allen Funt, to name a few. I never went out of my way to meet these celebrities, but it was important to know where they lived and to look out for them.

The first time I met anyone of a celebrity background was in Monterey in the early 1980s. George Fenneman was in town to promote Home Savings of America. He was the company's spokesman and was doing a lot of commercials. What I most revered him for was former position as announcer and straight-man for Groucho Marx on the long-running quiz show *You Bet Your Life*. As a devoted Marx Brothers fan, I naturally

John DiCarlo and I (1981)

wanted to meet anyone who had worked with Groucho. There were only a few people on hand at the bank opening, and I'm not sure if they were there for the same reason as I. George received everyone cordially, shaking hands and handing out books on early TV. There was a photo of him and Groucho from the *You Bet Your Life* days, which he inscribed for me. After asking him a few questions, he asked that I "wait around." After completing his obligations to the company, he sat down with me. He still described himself as a "Groucho fan." He told of the period when he was growing up in San Francisco and the Marx Bros. came to work out some business for one of their films for MGM. Mr. Fenneman told me he went to the theater to watch them perform every matinee. There was so much adlibbing, he said, that each day, "it was like watching an entirely new show."

Seems Like Old Times, a 1980 comedy featuring Chevy Chase and Goldie Hawn, was shot in Carmel. It was exciting for locals to view this film as the first shots were from the air, sweeping over Highway 1 and the artichoke fields near Monastery Beach. The plot was similar to the "screwball" comedies of the 1930s and '40s, with lots of mix-ups and a zany courtroom scene. The plot has Chase's character

forced by his kidnappers to commit a bank robbery in Carmel. We see him at a rural gas station that was on Highway 68, going toward Salinas. Not surprisingly, the bank robbery triggers a manhunt. One laughable moment (to we locals, anyway) comes when a supervisor asks his detectives how they intend to go about the case. One of them answered: "Oh, you know, dogs, helicopters…" The cinema audience snickered at that because Carmel PD only had one detective, no dogs, and no chopper within its one square mile.

That same year (1980), Goldie Hawn was featured in *Private Benjamin*, which contained yet another local reference. Goldie's character was at an Army recruitment office and they were trying to entice her to join by offering exotic places where she might be stationed. They showed her a photo of the Monterey marina and told her it was Ft. Ord. The locals were very familiar with the dilapidated Army facility (some called it Ft. Pneumonia). It was a hilarious moment.

In August of 1981, I was one of eight thousand people to see Bob Hope perform at the Monterey County Fair. I loved his early films but it seemed to me that he had become far less humorous from the sixties on, especially on his TV specials. I staked out a seat fairly close to the stage to watch him in action, although my expectations were low. Just then, Bob strolled out onstage to the strains of his theme song, "Thanks for the Memories." In his customary fashion, he began with a topical monologue. He was slaying the politicians, fruit-flies, medflies, and air-traffic controllers in his patented machine-gun delivery. I had never laughed so hard in my life.

This was only four years after Bob's pal Bing Crosby died. Bing, of course, was heavily associated with the region. In the early years of the Crosby Pro-Am, Bob was always on hand to play as a celebrity amateur. Not surprisingly, he was much loved in this military town due to the many tours he had taken to entertain the troops, dating back to the Second World War.

Bob was supported by his longtime orchestra leader, Les Brown (and His Band of Renown). Bob sang a couple of songs from his movies—"Buttons and Bows" was one I remember. He had the audience in the palm of his hand for a full hour, making hilarious observations that all seemed spontaneous. At one point, a very good-looking woman got up from her chair and walked right up to the middle aisle to take a photo. Bob stopped in mid-sentence and gawked at her as she returned to her seat. The seventy-eight-year-old comedian made comic fodder out of the situation by just staring at her. At that moment, his pre-1960's persona was fully on display, and the crowd loved it.

Around this time I walked into the local book store and found *the* book for me: *The Great Movie Shorts*, by Leonard Maltin. I had been a fan of this author ever since he released his movie guide book back in 1969, but his new book featured elaborate write ups of comedy two-reelers. He not only wrote about Laurel & Hardy, Our Gang, Edgar Kennedy, Andy Clyde, Leon Errol, The Three Stooges, Charley Chase, Buster Keaton, Joe McDoakes (George O'Hanlon), and Robert Benchley, he also wrote about the studios and gave a short synopsis for each one of the shorts discussed. On top of it all, he included two hundred photos.

It was from Mr. Maltin's book that I learned Edgar Kennedy had been born in Monterey County. It may have seemed like a small detail, but it was a driving point to me. I wondered, "Just exactly *where* was he born?" No local seemed to know, so for a number of years this mystery became a minor fascination with me. It was a combination of Mr. Maltin's book and the popularity of the home video market that re-sparked my interest in films in general, and comedies in particular.

Monterey County Sheriff's Office

My fellow officers in Seaside were slowly moving on to other departments. This made me start to think about where I should spend the rest of my career. I was, by this time, an established officer of the law, but I wanted to stay in Monterey County. A flyer was circulated that garnered my attention: the Monterey County Sheriff's Office was hiring. Having worked for a sheriff's office before, I knew there were better career opportunities than one could find in a tiny city.

Monterey County was huge, encompassing over 3,281 square miles; in comparison, the State of Rhode Island is 1,214. The sheriff's jurisdiction for patrol responsibilities covered the unincorporated areas outside the chartered cities of Salinas, Gonzales, Soledad, Greenfield, King City, Marina, Seaside, Monterey, Del Rey Oaks, Sand City, Pacific Grove, and Carmel. Ft. Ord was its own entity, on federal land.[34] The county is bisected north and south by State highways 101 and Highway 1 going down the coast. Going east to west is the Carmel River to the Pacific Ocean.

The beats are incredibly large in Monterey County. There is a main office in Salinas, a substation in King City, and another in Monterey. The sheriff is also responsible for the courts, the jail, the civil, public administration, records/county warrants, and coroner duties.[35]

---

34. Ft. Ord as a military base has mostly been annexed by the cities of Seaside and Marina.

35. The Monterey County Board of Supervisors discontinued the Office of the Coroner as its own separate county department in 1984 and assigned the responsibilities under

I was hired by Sheriff Bud Cook in 1981 after undergoing the usual battery of background checks, medical, psychological, and a polygraph examinations. They even gave me a "hearing test" in the form of a tuning fork behind my head. I was to identify which direction I could hear the pitch and tone. It was not very sophisticated, but it was the norm.

Sheriff Bud Cook was to be admired; he was hired in 1957 after completing his military service. He served in every rank until he was elected sheriff in 1978. He was a tall man, and the Stetson hat he always wore in public gave him a commanding presence; he was also trustworthy, ethical, and uncommonly intelligent. In a sense, he *was* the Sheriff's Office, serving three consecutive four-year terms. There was no need for a public information office during the Bud Cook years. This sheriff knew his domain and after a quick briefing, could articulate all the facts and background with aplomb.

My first day on the job had me performing administrative duties at the main office on Alisal Street in downtown Salinas. This had been the sheriff's headquarters since the 1930s. The jail was adjacent to the administration building, garnering national attention when agricultural leader Cesar Chavez was incarcerated for twenty days in 1970 for his participation in a lettuce strike. Dignitaries such as Ethel Kennedy came to visit. It drew the news media to document the incident.

A new correctional facility was built in 1977 and relocated in the county area. When I was hired, the old jail fell into disuse, with the exception of an administrative sergeant and a civilian (in charge of training) who had offices there. The jail cells were empty and served as storage of county records. I recall seeing volumes of bound records rotting away with insect and rodent infestation; they were eventually removed and destroyed. There is no telling how much important information was lost.

I was considered a "lateral entry" deputy and didn't have to work the jail; I went straight to patrol duties at the Monterey station. We had four big beats to cover: Pebble Beach, the unincorporated areas of Monterey, Carmel, Carmel Valley, and Big Sur.

The "mouth of the valley" is the general area where Highway 1 meets Carmel Valley Road. Just a few miles south is Point Lobos, a state park. The distance between C.V.R. going south through Big Sur to the county line of San Luis Obispo County is seventy-five miles of a rugged coastline. East of this area are the Carmel Highlands, Palo Colorado, state parks,

the Sheriff's jurisdiction.

and the Los Padres National Forest. Response time could amount to hours, especially when there was a stranded or lost hiker in the forest or camp areas.

Built in 1969, the Monterey substation also held a communications center for the peninsula agencies (with the exception of Carmel). The district attorney's office was here, along with the civil and superior courts, juvenile courts, judges' chambers, probation, support personnel, and our downstairs office. We were in the bowels of the courthouse and was heavily fortified as a bomb shelter.

The deputies who worked there were all very senior, ten-, twenty-, and thirty-year veterans who had experienced countless emergencies and rescues. They were very comfortable with themselves as professionals and each had a unique style. The sergeants relied heavily on their judgment and expertise.

They had been on the job when "the mouth" was mainly peaceful farmland, punctuated by a landmark old barnyard off Carmel Valley Road and Highway 1. They saw firsthand the development of a predominantly rural area into a vibrant era of commercial establishments and new housing projects. They were on duty when the overflow of "hippies" from the Monterey Pop Festival continued their trek south on Highway 1 to Big Sur. According to Deputy Pat Duval, "The females beckoned the deputies to "take off your clothes and join us."

There was no welcoming committee waiting for me my first day at the Monterey roll-call room, where the unofficial code was: "Don't talk unless you've been here for five years." One of the first to acknowledge me was Deputy Hank Klamput; he was about fifty years old; wore glasses, and with white hair and a mustache, looked like the fictional Geppetto. He greeted me with: "You were sucking hind tit when I was taking paper, Cassara." Those older deputies either didn't see you at all or they gave you grief. The hazing was to be expected; it was all part of the pecking order until you proved yourself.

The deputies were assigned and scheduled by seniority, the day shift in Monterey was made up of the most senior officers who had worked with one another for several years. When I was going through the field training program, I was assigned the day shift and was very entertained by the stories that were told during roll call. Sometimes, they told the same story over and over if they had a new audience. They laughed freely, but the one distinctly robust laugh I liked most belonged to Deputy Jim "Trigger" Tregea.

This enabled me not only to work with the older guys but to see Sergeant John Crisan, the shift supervisor, in action. He was an absolute legend in Monterey County, both out in the field and in the department. Crisan was born in 1932 and raised in communist Romania, escaping that country when he was a boy. Crisan joined the department in 1961 and was in charge of the new search-and-recovery team back in the day. The tools were rudimentary compared to modern technology, but over the years this dedicated team was very successful when it came to finding lost hikers and recovering the bodies of those who had plunged to their deaths from the steep cliffs of the county. The Big Sur residents had affection for him and, as a sign of respect, called him Sheriff John. At the office, he was jovial and had a very easy style of management. Outside the office, he was known to introduce deputies to Slivovitz, a brandy associated with his native land. He had been a sergeant for eighteen years before he was promoted to lieutenant.

Once Crisan became a staff member, Sgt. John Calzada took his place as day shift supervisor. Calzada was a native New Yorker and came to Monterey County by way of his military services. A man with a great legal mind and a sense of humor, he once described the day crew as "Comedy Central" during roll call. There were cigarette trays on the roll-call room tables back then , and about half of the deputies smoked. Roll call was read by the sergeant and it always started glumly by reading printed synopses from the national California Law Enforcement System (C.L.E.T.S), listing whichever officer who had been killed in the line of duty the previous day. There seemed to be a few almost every day. The ones with the most impact were those who died in California and the ones who were killed "only a few weeks before retirement." If one of the officers was killed enacting traffic enforcement, Tregea might cut the tension by saying, "That's why I don't pull people over for traffic violations—it's too dangerous." The seemingly crude remark always set off a chain of laughter. To do this job, one has to find humor whenever possible.

One of the most notable deputies we ever had was Pat Duval, the "singing sheriff." An African American, he came from a small town in Florida, where his dad was also a policeman for 30 years. Pat was musically inclined at a young age; he went on to have voice lessons to train for a possible career in opera. Duval finished up his stint in the Army at Ft. Ord and, like many others before him, he fell in love with the Monterey Peninsula. He was hired by our office in 1967 and continued his singing on the side. He volunteered his time for many fundraisers, including the Bing Crosby National Pro-Am. Pebble Beach resident Clint Eastwood took notice of Pat and cast him in a couple of his films. He is a bailiff in *Sudden Impact* (1983), and a detective in *The Rookie* (1990). For a while, Pat was the resident singer at the Ragged Point Inn (on the way to Big Sur). When off duty, Pat drove around in a used Mercedes, bearing a personalized license plate: EN4CER.[36]

Deputy Duval was always in good humor; before roll call, he would sing just about any show tune that came into his head, including selections from *Oklahoma!* and *Show Boat.* He occasionally dabbled in country western, rock 'n' roll, and Motown, but when it came to my favorite group, The Beatles, he had no interest whatever. I remember him saying, "*What* is 'Yellow Submarine'?" Despite this, he was a one-man goodwill ambassador to the people of Monterey County; he participated in flag ceremonies, sang at funerals, and even performed the national anthem at Candlestick Park before a San Francisco Giants game. He was always showcased at the Salinas Rodeo, during which he would ride in on his horse and sing, "California, I Love You." Off duty, he regularly went horseback riding with Kim Novak. Doris Day loved him; she even had him sing on her *Doris Day Best Friends* show in the mid-1980s. A whole book could be written about Pat Duval, and one has: *From Colored Town to Pebble Beach: The Story of the Singing Sheriff.* It is his autobiography, published in 2014.

The most senior deputy was Bob "The Rock" Batson. He was a grumpy, huge bear of a man with occasional bursts of wit. Batson claimed a seat at the corner of the roll-call table, a spot nobody else sat, not even on his days off. The deputies used to like to tell the story of a day when one of our administrative lieutenants came over from the Salinas office. The lieutenant arrived early and decided to sit in the first chair he saw. When Batson came into the room, he politely advised the lieutenant that he was sitting in "his" chair and that he would have to move. The administrator tried to laugh it off by remarking, "So, is your name on the chair or something?" Batson said, "As a matter of fact, it is." He calmly picked up the chair, spilling the lieutenant onto the floor. Batson showed the underside of the chair for all to see and, sure enough, there was his name. That lieutenant was so embarrassed that he never came to the Monterey substation again. If anyone else had done such a stunt they might have been fired, it was explained "It's just Batson being Batson."

---

36. This is in reference to Clint Eastwood's *The Enforcer* film, a sequel to *Dirty Harry.*

Deputy Don "Root" Oliver, from Texas, had that rare combination of common sense and charm. In addition, he was a professional musician, playing guitar in a Country Western band that he had formed. Then there was Bob "Bud" Thompson, and a nicer, warmer human being I have never met. He could instantly bring a sense of calm to a situation with his demeanor and pet phrase: "Hey Bud, what's going on?"

On swing shift, Deputy John Burke was the most senior. He was also the team leader in the Sheriff's Search and Rescue Team. He was tall, willowy, and agile. He knew every rancher on the Carmel Valley and Big Sur areas, and his voice was a booming bass. The first time I rode with him, we were assigned to the Big Sur beat, which we covered in the department's four-wheel drive truck. While Burke drove with his left hand, his right hand held a Styrofoam cup where he spit out his tobacco juices. My job was to take reports, and hold the spit-cup when he made the turns.

All of our sheriff's personnel were colorful in their own way. Our lieutenant, for example, wore a mustache and was the very image of Richard Boone's Paladin character from *Have Gun Will Travel*. He even had a business card with a chess piece emblazoned on it. Deputy Jess Mason was another unique public servant. He had a relaxed manner and didn't speak much at roll call. He had a type of personality that when he *did* speak, everyone listened. Mason was a first-class scuba diver and was always in the water to photograph something or to recover drowning victims. So aquatic was he that we suspected he had gills.

Mason moved with the stealth of a Native American and was an important team member of the Sheriff's Search and Rescue Squad. Sometimes it seemed people would drive to Monterey just to lose their lives driving over the cliffs or drowning in the Pacific Ocean. One of the most notorious areas of drowning accidents is Monastery Beach, which we called "Mortuary Beach."

Mason was well known and respected in the Big Sur area. I remember a time in the 1990s when a huge landslide buried Highway 1. Cal-Trans sent out a bulldozer to clear the roadway just before another landslide hit. The bulldozer was leaning hazardly over the edge, with the operator inside his cage—one tiny movement could have sent the man plummeting to his death. The rescue was precarious as there was no safe ground to reach him. That didn't stop Mason, who coordinated a Cal-Trans "Cherry Picker" to the area. He got in the bucket and was lifted to the victim. Mason helped the traumatized man out of the cage to safety. Everyone called him a hero, but it was just another day on the job for Deputy Mason.

My two field training officers in each separate month were Deputy Greg Clark and Wayne Harvey. Clark was young, sharp, and destined for promotions. What I liked about him is that he liked to have fun on the job. Over the years we teamed up to perpetrate a few practical jokes on our fellow deputies and sergeants. Writing phony memos and circulating them was a specialty.

Deputy Harvey had me in stitches during my month with him; he was like a ventriloquist in that he could project an animated face and talk through the side of his mouth without moving his lips. Using this unique skill, he would make snide comments under his breath, much like W.C. Fields does in his films. Harvey was also great with the public. He would get out of his car and converse with tourists and pose for pictures. There were plenty of tourists all through the peninsula at any given time.

I remember an interval when Harvey and I grabbed some coffee at the Carmel Center (later called Crossroads). As I was getting up to leave, Harvey hit the bathroom. Outside, I met a nice English lady, who seemed unusually excited to see me. She had a napkin in her hand and explained that her son's favorite show on the "telly" was *CHIPs*, and asked if I would autograph the napkin. I felt obligated to tell her, "*CHIPs* is the California Highway Patrol; we're the county sheriff. I was going to sign, but I saw Harvey coming toward us from the bathroom. I pointed to him and explained that *he* was from *CHIPs* and to ask him. She bounced over to him and Deputy Harvey graciously signed his autograph.

I had previously worked with Deputy Harvey's brother, a sergeant, in Seaside. So, perhaps my reputation preceded me. The goal of my training was simply to get familiar with the area and the many distinct ways of the sheriff's office as it was incredibly different from Seaside. When we would drive by, people on the street actually waved at us.

The Monterey substation had a culture far separate from any other agency, including the other offices of the sheriff. There were slang words indigenous to these deputies. Here are just a handful of examples:

- **A Wet Owl** refers to anyone suckered into taking a detail that a senior deputy had slyly off-loaded.
- **Blue Room** is slang for the place (say a sergeant's office) for anyone about to be scolded, disciplined, or simply "called on the carpet." **Twinkie** is a yellow "Post-it" note on one's report (usually for corrections to be made).

- **O.T.R.** is the term used on the radio for a common meeting place at a church parking lot between beats 7 and 8. Instead of articulating the name of the church, O.T.R. meant "Old Time Religion." **Root** is welcoming in place of a deputies' name. Example: "Hey, root, how's it going?"
- **Abalone** is a name for those senior deputies who had settled into their careers and are clogging up all the good shifts and days off. The metaphor being, "They grab onto a rock and hang on."
- **Weaver** refers to the non-sworn who want to talk shop.
- **Cone of Silence** is any gossipy personal information (not to be confused with confidential and sensitive case-related discussions). The origin of the phrase came from the television show *Get Smart* (in a non-functioning sound-proof bubble).
- **Seaside Woods** is a radio term used primarily by midnight deputies who have gone out on a break at Red's donuts in Seaside. Dispatchers were clued into this location.
- **Woofing** is someone who talks too much.
- **Kifing** (or Kifer) is slang for someone cheating on one's spouse or girlfriend.

After my three-month training was completed, I took my rightful place in seniority on the midnight shift, where I settled in nicely. We had a new sergeant (Mike Kanalakis) on our watch who completed his stint as an officer in the Air Force before becoming a deputy. He was a big barrel chested man, slightly officious, and kept us in line (sort of). I worked with this professional for most of my career and he eventually was elected sheriff.

My first day off training meant I had my own beat and, unlike working conditions in the city, at night it was pitch dark. There were no street lights in the county, and addresses had to be illuminated by our spotlight. I went from call to call that evening. Back then, there was a big hall at the Mission Ranch where all the locals would drink, dance, and get into fights. After we cleared that up, I had to go Code-3 across the valley to aid in a similar incident.

I was hit with a bad case of laryngitis, but there was no way I was going to call in sick on my first day on the beat. At some point, I was doubled up with Deputy Dave Allard for the shift and I'll always be grateful to him for giving me some cough drops to help soothe my sore throat. As soon as I was off duty I went to the local hospital, where I was diagnosed as having strep throat. Fortunately, I had my scheduled days off to recover.

One of my favorite working partners on the midnight shift was Deputy John DiCarlo. Of Italian descent (he could even speak it), he had grown up in Rochester, New York. He was a baseball fan and a damned good player. John got things done in his own style—think Yogi Berra and you have Deputy DiCarlo. He was gentle, with an unassuming manner; he was also an iron man who never called in sick a day in his career, not unlike Lou Gehrig.

John went on to be a coroner investigator and I later worked with him as a sergeant. One of the qualities I liked about him was that he was a great singer and often sang in Italian for stage plays at the Wharf Theater in Monterey. His whole family was involved in those productions.

Murder

There was a homicide case I was involved with in 1982 that has stayed with me for some reason. On September 9 of that year, suspicious circumstances in my beat unfolded early that a.m. Nurse Sarah Dane, from Monterey's Eskaton Hospital, was overdue at work by two hours, prompting a phone call from the staff to her mother's house. Sarah lived in a small cottage adjacent to the main home at the end of Middle Canyon Road, so her mom walked over to check on her. She found blood at the scene. In a state of hysteria, she dialed 9-1-1.

I was first to arrive and got the basic information from Mrs. Dane; I then relayed it to my backup, Deputy Duval. We did not know if there was a suspect still inside so we entered with guns drawn. No one was in the house, but it was obvious from the amount of blood and debris that there had been a struggle. She was definitely kidnapped and it looked even worse. I put out a B.O.L. for the nurse's car, contained the scene, and notified our sergeant. The detectives arrived in short order.

We acquired more details about Sarah Dane from her mother and asked for a recent photo as we needed to get out an all-points bulletin. When I saw her picture I immediately recognized her—we had collaborated in a manner of speaking while we were both on duty at the hospital. It was only a few months before this incident, but I was assigned to guard a suspect who was undergoing an operation after being shot by a CHP officer during a standoff. Twenty-six-year-old Nurse Dane was in her official capacity and we had plenty of time to talk and compare notes. She had an easy smile and laughed effortlessly. I liked her. It made me angry that such a charming creature could be victimized in her own home. The case was almost personal for me, which is a bad thing for a cop.

After the A.P.B was issued, CHP notified us that the victim's car was towed at 4:30 a.m. after finding it grounded on a median center in Marina. Detectives went to the tow yard and—there it was: Sarah's body had been stuffed inside a sleeping bag on the floor of the back seat. The suspect drove but it was unclear if he intentionally dumped the car or lost control of it. Forensics processed the physical evidence and a coroner investigator took possession of the body. Now we needed a suspect.

Enter Detective Freeman, the lead investigator in this case. These were the days before DNA technology was available to law enforcement, but there was still fingerprints and physical evidence in the form of hair samples intertwined with the victim's bodily fluid.

In the meantime, a suspect was developed: it was the victim's brother-in-law, Thomas William Perkins, of San Jose. According to later testimony, Perkins' wife informed him that she had decided to seek a divorce. This occurred the previous night of Sarah's murder. Perkins warned his wife that he would retaliate in a way that would really hurt her. Then he took off, ostensibly on a drinking binge. The following day, he did not show up for his job as a roofer.

During the period Perkins was unaccounted for, Detective Freeman returned to the victim's house and stayed there overnight in complete darkness. He was hoping that Perkins would return to the house to retrieve evidence or further spook Sarah's mom. Freeman sat in that house with its blood-soaked carpets and bedroom; he looked at every item Sarah had. He even went through her photos, getting a real sense of who she was.

Finally, after a few days, Freeman was tipped off that the suspect had finally showed up for work. Freeman, who had already clued in San Jose PD on the case, now gave the green light for a special unit of SJPD to arrest Perkins on probable cause. They took him to the police station where he was processed for physical examination, which included his hair. Perkins was a cocky ex-con: "You won't find any evidence; I already washed my hair."

Thank you for your spontaneous statement, I thought to myself.

Detective Freeman was waiting to interview him at the PD and read him his rights.

Perkins not only waived them, he taunted Freeman, saying "You'll *never* get my cooperation."

It took too much time for the lab to compare Perkin's hair with that of victim's. After his seventy-two hours of incarceration, he had to be released for "lack of evidence." The Monterey County District Attorney wanted to wait until more conclusive evidence was brought forth.

We were all hoping for quick justice to prevail but, instead, the case stretched out into days, months, and years. Perkins initiated contact many times with Freeman, goading and mocking him. Finally, a deputy district attorney decided to take the case on and Perkins was arrested on murder charges. While cooling his heels in Monterey County Jail, a break developed.

Perkins bragged about the killing and abduction to an inmate who had been charged with homicide. The informant was willing to turn state's evidence against Perkins without the promise of any breaks for his own crime.

Three long years passed following the homicide and the trial was finally set to begin.

Local media covered every development of the case. It created a sensation when the informant had to testify against the defendant. The informant was called to the stand to recount in detail what the suspect had said to him, which he proceeded to do in an overly polite tone. It remained to be seen if his testimony carried any weight. The assigned public defender sought to attack the credibility and went right at it. "Aren't you concerned for your life for being known as a jailhouse snitch"? The informant maintained his poise and testified, "I wanted to do what was right. I wasn't promised any breaks, nor do I expect them."

This was not a jury trial; the defense chose to have the presiding judge rule on the case.

On February 16, 1985, the judge pronounced the defendant guilty of homicide and sentenced him to thirty-five years in state prison. The newspapers printed the verdict in bold lettering, using the same font they had used to inform their readers of Sarah Perkins' tragic death. The judge later remarked that there was more than enough evidence to convict Perkins based of physical evidence alone. The family finally got the closure they deserved and the now convicted murderer was put away. The outcome was bittersweet for me.

Cannery Row, the Movie (1983)

The *Monterey Herald* broke the news: John Steinbeck's novel *Cannery Row* was going to be filmed at the Monterey Wharf and Cannery Row. I followed the story with interest since I lived just up the street on Prescott Avenue, although I was disappointed when I learned that most of the filming was done on a soundstage in a Hollywood studio. There was some advanced filming scenes in Monterey, but the stars (Nick Nolte and Debra Winger) stayed in Los Angeles. The finished product could have been so much better, I hated the studio's "cotton candy skies" visual effect.

Divorce

For the next three years I lived my life upside down, working until dawn and sleeping during the day. My wife spent her days teaching; weekends were reserved for tennis. It was going to take years for me to rotate off the midnight shift. As so often happens in law enforcement, the crazy working hours contributed to our drifting apart. She decided that she did not want children because she thought it would make her "crazy." I couldn't believe that such a fine teacher and lover of children harbored such an anxiety. I took the first step in seeking divorce, bought her out and refinanced, and continued living in the home on Prescott Avenue. We both made the same salary, so there was no alimony; it was a pretty clean split. Looking back on it all, it was because of her that I pulled up stakes in San Jose and moved to Monterey. I will be eternally grateful to her for that.

My favorite working partner was Deputy Tom Crompton. Born and raised in the Los Angeles area, he kept me entertained with his boyhood stories of sneaking onto the movie studio lots. We had similar physical characteristics: same age, mustache, glasses, and slightly receding hairlines. When people told us that we looked alike, we reacted as though we it never occurred to us. At the coffee shop a couple of times we liked to fool with a waitress of foreign born, the only difference between us was that Crompton ordered his coffee black and I had cream with my coffee. If she moved out of sight, we switched places in opposite booths and, as a way of extending the joke, we swapped glasses.

Crompton and I had a great working relationship: he was a perfect "Bad Cop" to my "Good Cop." There was one night I remember especially well. We were playing a cassette of the soundtrack to *A Clockwork Orange*, the part where a speeded up version of *The William Tell Overture*[37] was played. But the fiercely dynamic orchestral version was better known to us as *The Lone Ranger* theme tune from radio and television. It must have been 2 a.m. when we got a call from the Pacific Valley in Big Sur. A honeymooning couple had been staying in a campground and got spooked; they didn't know where they had left the car and they were stranded somewhere on Highway 1.

We had a long, foggy drive ahead of us, about an hour and a half even going Code-3. At about ten minutes to go for our destination, one of us had the bright idea to play *The Lone Ranger* theme and hold the P.A.[38] system microphone to the cassette speaker. The result was a beautiful blaring of, not a siren, but musical accompaniment of our approach. With our white Sheriff's car, it was almost like the Lone Ranger arriving himself: "A fiery horse with the speed of light, a cloud of dust, and a hearty 'Hi-O, Silver!'"

When we arrived we found the young couple terribly cold and frightened, not to mention confused. Crompton and I played it deadpan as though it was how we *always* responded in emergencies. The couple from Kansas explained that their camping equipment, food, and clothing were back at the campsite and asked if we would hike-in to help them. Of course we did.

Afterward, we put the items in the trunk of the car and they got into the back seat. On cue, we cranked up the overhead revolving red and yellow lights and blasted the music over the P.A. system. I snuck a glance back from the rear view mirror and it looked like they were in shock. We found their car a couple of miles away and helped them get situated. Then, as before, we took off northbound just as we had come. Once we were out of sight and sound range, we had to pull over—we were laughing so hard. We imagined what they said to the folks back home; "In California the cops don't use sirens; they use the *Lone Ranger* theme song." Moments of levity in law enforcement are sometimes fleeting, but they are rich when they happen.

KWAV Radio Shooting

A contrasting experience occurred during the pre-dawn hours of October 1983. Deputy Crompton and I were doubled up again that night. We picked up scanner traffic dispatching a Monterey PD unit to suspicious

---

37. This overture was composed by Gioachino Rossini in 1828.

38. A public address system.

circumstances at radio station KWAV on Garden Road. The Monterey units were tied up on something else, so Crompton and I offered to go. We blacked out our lights and as we approached, we could hear gunshots coming from inside the radio station.

The front glass door was blasted out, with several spend shotgun rounds scattered everywhere. I got on the air to report, "Shooting in progress," and to roll back up. Numerous shots continued from inside; we did not know if there were multiple shooters or what the targets were. We took a position on the corner of the station to maintain visual with the entrance and to see the unlit outer wall. I had my shotgun trained for whatever was next. Just then, a side door burst open in the dark. I yelled, "FREEZE!" I could make out the outline of the person—it was a female, who screamed as soon as she saw me. The shots continued inside and the female ran past us, got into her car, and drove off.

We heard sirens in the distance when a suspect emerged from where he entered. Crompton ordered him to drop his shotgun and put his hands in the air. Crompton cuffed him and we dutifully handed him over to Monterey PD when they arrived and took over the investigation.

There were fifty shots fired methodically all through the transmitter and station. The suspect, later identified as Norbert Schenk of Santa Cruz, was shooting everything off the walls. The disc jockey (Sandy Shores) was on the air when she heard the shots getting closer. She called 9-1-1 and the dispatcher told her to hide, which she did, under the console. Schenk blasted the record off the turntable, putting the station off the air. The title of the record was "Never Say Die."

Ms. Shores later divulged that as the gunman stopped to reload, she stood up and pleaded for her life. She asked if she could leave. Schenk agreed, but advised her to "hurry up."

Schenk had been living in his van parked outside the station. He later told police, "The station was ruining my life, so I ruined the station." He believed that the radio station was bugging his van and poisoning his mind. He was charged with five felony counts, ranging from firing a gun into an occupied dwelling to vandalism. He was held in jail on $100,000 bail.

This incident became national news the next day; every media outlet covered the story and hit on the point of how vulnerable news agencies were, especially lone females broadcasting on all night radio. Everyone wanted to interview Sandy Shores and the station manager. Interestingly enough, they later married each other. It's funny how life works out.

A preliminary trial was held on November 22, 1983. I testified, as did investigators from Monterey PD. Judge Thomas deemed there was sufficient evidence to hold Schenk over for trial. Court reconvened in January of 1984 and the judge ruled that the defendant was deemed mentally unfit. He was sent to Atascadero State Hospital to receive treatment. That was the last I ever heard about him.

Chapter Seven

Settling In

AS 1983 ENDED AND 1984 BEGAN, I was assigned to the day shift. What a pleasure it was to actually have full visibility and see my beat during the daylight (after the inevitable fog dissipated, of course).

Big Sur

Big Sur beat is so incredibly vast that most people have a hard time describing it. For deputies' purposes it starts just south of the Carmel Highlands/Point Lobos area and continues for seventy-five miles to the San Luis Obispo county line. The Pacific Ocean is on the west and, going east, is the Los Padres National Forest.

A central nerve to Big Sur is the Esalen Institute, which was founded in the early 1960s by two Stanford graduates. It became a mecca for the "counter culture." The twenty-seven-acre-setting features natural springs overlooking jagged edges of cliffs. It appears to some as the "edge of the earth," or perhaps the edge of the universe.

In September 1969, a week after Woodstock, folk singer Joan Baez, a resident of Carmel Valley, hosted a music event at Esalen. This event seemingly drew every youngster who *couldn't* make Woodstock, some estimated that over ten thousand people tried to make it to the rather small venue. The crowd spilled over with music lovers, blocking Highway One with their vehicles, all of which were loaded with gear and hitchhikers. In

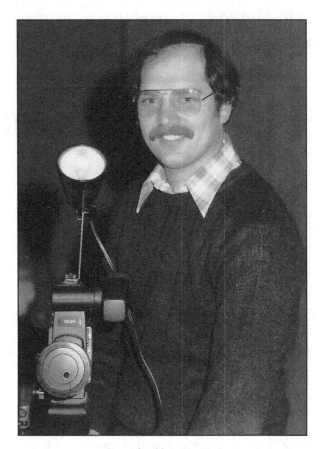

Cassara's Video Services

addition to Baez, the festival included Crosby, Stills, Nash and Young, Joni Mitchell, John Sebastian, and others.

The event was filmed and released as a movie in 1971. The documentary had footage of two Monterey County Deputies trying to deal with the crowds outside the facility. Deputy Roger Chatterton,[39] who was interviewed for the documentary, was most accommodating and served as a professional presence to ensure safety. It was a really low-key affair, which was fortunate. There was no other backup for miles, with the exception of one highway patrol unit. There were only a few times I had to go into the institute during my career, usually for a bench warrant or a domestic. As I recall, everyone panicked at the sight of my patrol car.

---

39. Roger Chatterton rose through the ranks of the department and was a captain when I was hired,

Big Sur was a mecca to some and represented many things to many people, but it did not have a "downtown" area. I was often amused by travelers who were smack dab in Big Sur and waived me down asking, "Just where *is* Big Sur?" I usually answered all questions, but if a tourist asked a local, they might have heard; "Big Sur is not as much a place as it is a state of mind."

A story that has been handed down since the early seventies concerns a deputy who had observed a big Winnebago heading south on Highway 1 and two guys on top hanging onto the rail. Going down that highway with all the turns and cliffs made such a stunt even more dangerous. The vehicle was pulled over and as he talked to the driver, the two guys on top sheepishly made their way down. They were Jack Nicholson and Art Garfunkel. The deputy said, "You can just *guess* what was in their vehicle." It was suggested that they get *inside* the Winnebago, which they did immediately with no trace of objection.

Cassara's Videotaping Services

I always thought I had a pretty good eye for the camera, but I was never going to be a cameraman in Hollywood. By 1984, the technology had improved in the home video market, I was encouraged to buy a portable video camera in San Jose for about $3,000. The lens was commercial grade and I had a custom-made tripod. I'd be willing to bet that no one else in the peninsula's private sector had a rig like mine.

I bought the camera gear originally as a hobby, augmenting it with two video cassette recorders. I was able to play a tape on one and do an edit on the other. It was very rudimentary, but tape-to-tape editing recording was an innovation back then.

I sought approval from the sheriff to start a part-time business: Cassara's Videotaping Services. I mainly videotaped weddings and special events. In March of 1984, I was contracted to videotape the wedding of David Hasselhoff and Catherine Hickman. Hasselhoff was internationally known at that time as the star of television's *Knight Rider*.

I met the young couple at Carmel's Highlands Inn, where we talked business. The wedding was very confidential because there was an incredible amount of interest as to where and when the wedding was to be. We were sitting down and overlooking the beautiful view over the Pacific Ocean when a woman boldly walked up to Hasselhoff and stared at the contours of his face. He did not look up, but that didn't discourage the woman. Without looking away, she blurted out to Catherine, "Got a pen, honey?" I was surprised that a cat fight didn't break out.

The wedding was set at the gazebo at the ocean side of the Inn, which was inaccessible to casual viewers. Since Hasselhoff was a big television star, it attracted the paparazzi. They were lined up on the entrance road and, with telescopic lenses, they tried desperately to seize the moment. "Dave," they kept yelling, "turn around!" Unfortunately, their yelling was recorded on the soundtrack and sometimes drowned out the ceremony.

There was another memorable gig I did during the spring of 1984. A Southern California woman found my business in the Yellow pages and called me. She was scheduled to run with the Olympic Torch through Carmel Valley and wanted it recorded. I was wondering how I could capture more than just a side view, as the crowds were thick on the street. I hitched a ride on top of the trunk of a slow-moving sheriff's unit that had been assigned to front the runner(s) through Monterey County. I got a great recording of her running the full length and was happy to be part of her history.

Playing Baseball with Willie Mays

Through the years I kept my allegiance to the San Francisco Giants with all their highs and lows. My dream of playing major league baseball dissipated in the reality of life. However, in January of 1984, I became aware of the very first "fantasy camp." It was a five-day event and featured now-retired members of the Giants. Those who had signed on to participate included Bobby Thompson, Monte Irvin, Sal "The Barber" Maglie, Juan Marichal, Tito Fuentes, Mike McCormick, Jimmy Ray Hart, Jose Pagan, Bobby Bonds, Stu Miller, Jim Davenport, Wes Westrum, Leon Wagner, and Willie Mays.

The concept was the old Giants were to participate as coaches for baseball fans who had dreamed of wearing the team's uniform and playing the game with the actual team members, The experience included airfare, a suite, breakfast buffet, and an open bar at night. I weighed the option; a lifetime of memories verses a great cost. Since I was in between wives at the moment, I decided to go.

I signed up to for the "Baseball Fantasies Fulfilled" program that was run by a fellow named Max Shapiro. As a result, I was placed on a roster along with doctors, lawyers, and stockbrokers. I was the only cop. The roster was given to members of the San Francisco media during a press conference. This was a brand new concept and a newsworthy one. I received a call at home from a reporter for KPIX television in San Francisco. He had noticed that I was in law enforcement and found that interesting. He explained that his station was paying for his participation in the camp and wanted to confirm if I would be available for an interview. The edited report was broadcast in the Bay Area television market.

It was a warm January at Diablo Stadium in Tempe, Arizona, the site of the training facilities. I was one of about forty would-be-ballplayers, also known as "campers." We did everything a big league ballplayer would experience; some even practiced chewing tobacco and spitting during an interview. We each had our own open locker with our official Giants uniform. A past Giant great, Mike McCormick, was one of our coaches. While we were suiting up, he yelled at us, "Okay, you rookies, be sure and wear your cup on the *inside*."

Each day after breakfast, we'd suit up in our Giants uniforms and were bused (along with the pros) to the ballpark. We "campers" were divided up into teams and practiced drills during the morning. At noon, we broke for lunch and ate what the veterans called "dugout food": sandwiches, beans, and a cup of soup. It was good nourishment for the rest of the afternoon, for that is when we would actually play a game against the other camper teams. Afterward, the veterans put on a batting practice for us.

During one of those days, Bobby Bonds' son strolled over from his nearby college. We all knew about Barry Bonds,[40] even back then. He took a seat in the dugout and casually answered our questions. "If they walk me," he said, "I just steal second; it's like a double." His physique was as slender as a greyhound's. I remember thinking, "He might be another Gary Maddox!"[41]

A couple of days into the week, a uniformed Willie Mays strode into camp. He was now fifty-three years old. Everyone brightened when Willie arrived; he started teasing his old teammates, and they loved it. Willie had an infectious laugh and high energy. He joined us in batting practice, peppering the balls over and against the fences.

---

40. Barry Bonds started his professional career two years later and went on to break Babe Ruth's record for homeruns.

41. Gary Maddox was a slender speedster and centerfielder for the Giants and Pittsburg Pirates.

After getting back to the hotel, we showered and got dressed for "Happy Hour" refreshments. We had our own private area and the old Giants started talking about baseball stories, ones we never heard before. They had us in stitches. The veterans always incorporated Willie into the stories. There was one about how Willie took a loss extra hard and was sitting around, moping about it. Leon Wagner told the story: "We lost a close game and I started to get ready for a date that night, but poor Willie couldn't shake the loss. He felt responsible for it."

In the following days, Willie continued as a roving coach. I was taking batting practice away from the others and I heard a voice from behind say, "Hmm, not bad." It was Willie Mays, talking to *me*! He came over and said, "Let me see your hands." I opened them and Willie said, "No callouses." Then he opened up his bear-sized paws to show me his built-up callouses across the base of his fingers. In those days, batters didn't use batting gloves to reduce friction. Willie told me, "That's what spring training's for, to build up your calluses." Willie treated everyone like they were *ballplayers*.

Then came the big day: we "campers" got to play a game against the Giants—before a crowd in the stands (including former Giants owner, Horace Stoneman). They killed us, of course. It was surreal to look on the field to see Bobby Thompson at first, Tito Fuentes at second, Jose Pagan at shortstop, Jimmy Ray Heart at third, Leon Wagner in Left field, the incomparable Willie Mays in center and Juan Marichal on the hill. In my only time at bat, I managed to fly out to Bobby Bonds in right field, but I got to see Marichal's signature high leg-kick and Willie Mays glide around centerfield making his distinctive "basket catches."

That night there was a big banquet with all the players. I was heading toward the bus when two of the Giants spotted me. Jose Pagan and Tito Fuentes were in a car with their wives and they invited me to get in. I gladly accepted; they didn't have to do that. It made me think how generous those guys, the heroes of my youth, actually were. It reinforced in me that the culture of baseball was unique, something I had now experienced firsthand.

Chapter Eight

Head 'em Off At the Pass

F.T.O.

In 1984, I became a field training officer after only three years on the force. I would have this assignment for over four years and broke in many new deputies, some of whom went on to surpass me in rank. It was a privilege to break in rookies and to work one-on-one with them. There is so much to absorb: the office had a training manual and we covered all the steps before proceeding. The main issue for most of the recruits was learning the geography. Rookies are discouraged from talking during roll-call, so they remained silent until they were in the car.

Most had worked our jail before their transfer and knew the basics concerning uniform and rank. Those with jail experience were accustomed to emergency backup response within minutes. This was not the case out in the field. We always told them to watch the street signs so they knew where they were, but some of the outer regions were so isolated that backup might take hours to get there. It was therefore important to be self-sufficient and use common sense. The people referred to us as "The Sheriff," or "The Man," so we had to be diplomatic problem solvers.

Sometimes, on a slow Sunday morning, I would go out early with the trainee to get donuts to bring back for roll-call. I would drop him off in front of Reds' Donut Shop and have him buy a dozen donuts, which would always turn heads and evoked comments: "I guess cops really

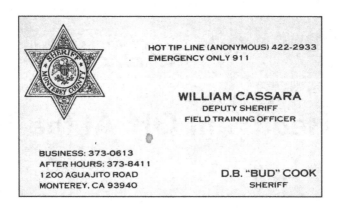

do like donuts!" It was a mild form of initiation and it was all in fun. Deputies were often asked to take pictures with tourists, and we always accommodated them—after all, we were the goodwill ambassadors for Monterey County. Very often, the European visitors would look at our patrol car and remark, "We thought sheriffs rode *horses*." What I could never figure out was why they asked to be photographed with us putting handcuffs on them. And if that wasn't enough, they wanted to pose in the back seat of the patrol car!

There were many emergency calls I responded to over the years, but I remember the non-routine ones best. I was on patrol during the day shift on the Holman Highway, just passing the Community Hospital of the Monterey Peninsula, when I saw a traffic jam. An elderly man in an electrically powered wheelchair was riding on the highway. I positioned myself behind him and had to pull him over with a quick toot from my siren.

My first words were, "What do you think you're doing?"

He replied, "I'm going home." Apparently he got into an argument with his wife upon being released from the hospital, so he took off. That'll teach her.

I gathered him up, put the wheelchair in the trunk, and took him home. I couldn't resist telling him that he didn't have a license to drive that thing on the road. He was just a few feet away from the Highway 1 onramp to the freeway—that section of the highway was called Carmel Hill for a reason. If he had gotten onto the ramp, gravity would have taken over and he would have been flying down the hill without any breaks. If I hadn't been there at that particular moment, it would have been a bad day for everyone. I probably saved his skin, but I was even more concerned for his welfare once he was reunited with his wife.

While patrolling the long road up of Robinson Canyon Road, there was a car parked overlooking the crest and the motor was running. A garden hose was attached to the exhaust pipe and into the vehicle. Inside was an elderly man, a woman, and a dog. They were all unconscious ... or dead. The door and windows were locked, so I used my fire extinguisher to break the window and unlocked the door. I had fire and medical rolling, and fortunately, the fresh air revived the man and the dog. The woman could not be revived at the scene and was taken by ambulance to the hospital. The male explained that his wife had Alzheimer's disease, so he had decided their whole little family should go out together. I had to tell his grown children about the predicament, and the news was not well received.

Because the woman was not a willing victim, I had no choice but to write a report, charging the man with attempted homicide. It became big news the following day. The district attorney was duty bound to take the case, the result was the man was placed on probation and issued a restraining order so he couldn't come near his wife. It was a sad state of affairs.

In the days before our department had a bomb squad, I was dispatched to investigate a "suspicious package" at a Pebble Beach residence. The reporting party was a retired federal judge who received a strange piece of mail enclosed in a large manila envelope. It was bulging from the inside and reinforced by heavy tape. The judge was certain that it came from someone he had once sentenced, but there was no return address on the envelope.

What was there to do? While the judge hid outside with his fingers in his ears, I used a pair of scissors and opened the package, inside of which was a scribbled note wrapped around a pint of some sort of liquid. The note identified the sender, who was appreciative of the judge for a kindness he had shown. The bottled contents were homemade moonshine.

"I thought it was a bomb!" the judge said with much relief. "You are a very brave man!" "Either that or a very stupid one," I said.

"I thought you would transport it to the airport to test it in the city's X-Ray machine."

"That's exactly what I would *not* do," I said. "I'd be endangering everyone's lives during the transport and at the airport." I just did what needed to be done, nowadays procedures would be different.

Most bomb scares are filled with tension, especially when they involve public places. I once responded to a residential call concerning a "bomb on the front porch." When I arrived at the scene, I learned it wasn't a bomb at all; it was a "bum."

Among other distinctions, Pebble Beach was the "alarm capital of the world." Seemingly every residence had one, which was encouraged, but the constant false alarms made us unavailable for other emergencies. With every alarm, we had to respond as though a burglary was in progress, which required us to check every possible point of entry. Some of those old mansions were right over the Pacific Ocean, making it life-endangering to get around. When electricity went out in the region, it triggered many alarms, and we had to clear each one. Windswept nights caused trees to fall and alarms to be activated. I had just negotiated one of those windy little roads in Pebble Beach to check on an alarm activation, and when I tried to return, a huge tree was now blocking the road. I had to call emergency services to send out a crew to chainsaw the tree so I could pass. It occurred to me that the tree blocking the road had fallen just after I passed through, it missed me by a few minutes.

Pebble (as we called it) was pitch dark once nightfall descended. Del Monte Forest had its own security force that covered the area 24/7 and helped out when they could. I'll never forget the time when someone was throwing dummies in front of moving cars, it scared the wits out of drivers. This heightened the security force's awareness. One foggy night, the same thing happened to one of them. I was summoned to the scene, took the dummy as evidence, and documented it in a report. The bogus body was homemade and was dressed in men's clothing; it was stuffed with what felt like wadded-up paper. Not expecting much, I took it to the office and performed a pseudo autopsy on the figure. It was filled with copies of *The Wall Street Journal*; each issue had a mailing label on it identifying the subscriber. There was no guarantee the papers were from the owner; they could have been recovered from someone else's trash. I checked with security, who had a roster of all the residents, and got a match with the name and address.

The next afternoon I took the dummy along and knocked on the suspect's door. A lady answered and was a little surprised at my presence. There was no guarantee that anyone associated with this house had been involved in the prank. Nevertheless, I showed her the clothes and she confirmed that they belonged to her son. Just then, her darling boy walked in and was confronted by his mom. There was some 'splainin' to do. The teenager had been sneaking out at night with his buddies. They wore dark clothing and were equipped with walkie-talkies to communicate with each other. After the confrontation, we weren't bothered with flung dummies anymore.

Animals on the roadway in the rural area were not uncommon. Once I came upon traffic backed up on Highway 1 because there was a rider-less horse clip-clopping along. He obviously got loose from one of the ranches, but he posed a big safety risk on the highway, this was tourist season. I turned on my red lights to warn oncoming traffic to heed to the side of the road. To some motorists, it must have looked like I was trying to make a traffic stop on the horse. I positioned myself to get adjacent to him and went at his pace so as not to spook him. I radioed for a backup unit to *"head him off at the pass,"* and they did. I was able to run my car just ahead of the animal and veered it onto a less busy road behind Carmel High School. My beat partner, Deputy English, came in from the other direction and boxed him into a residential backyard. We were able to contain the horse until the S.P.C.A. came to take him. The owner of the house was not home at the time of this incident, but he must have been surprised when he found some "road apples" in his yard.

During the evening hours, it was even more dangerous when animals were on the road; there were times when darkness and fog combined to hamper visibility, resulting in injuries or death. One such incident still gives me the chills. It was in the early morning hours and all was quiet on Highway 1, south of the Carmel River. As usual, there was fog in the air and the roadways were slick. There was no traffic until a motorcyclist hit a herd of boars heading to the slough on the opposite side of the road. He slid off his bike, breaking his leg. This riled up the boars, and they might have eaten the downed motorcyclist alive had it not been for the deputy who had witness the accident from a distance away. I responded, too, and helped the guy into the patrol car while until the fire and ambulance crew arrived. We also pushed the bike to the side of the road.

I was waiting in my patrol car for a tow truck when more wild boars came out of the slue and wallowed in the blood—it was like a scene from a Stephen King novel. As a result of this incident, Cal-trans made a special sign reading "Wild Pigs Crossing," to alert drivers. The yellow sign was even illustrated. I was often asked if the sign was "a joke," or perhaps "a cute little Carmel touch to delight the tourists?" In response, I told them the story. It remains the only sign of its kind on a California state highway.

One of my most unusual calls started off as a routine house burglary. There was a break-in at a doctor's house outside of Carmel and, as I took note of the items taken, I recognized it as a "kids-type burglary:

stolen items included small things like change, stereo equipment, and a television set.

Kiddie burglars sometimes break into homes during the day when the owners are at work. Instead of carrying the items through the neighborhood, they stash them, only to recover them later under the cloak of darkness. Keeping this in mind, I walked around the woodsy property to look for stolen property. The doctor had a greenhouse that was unlocked, so I opened the door to take a look. There was a long, wooden, oblong box inside that was not secure; this, I felt, would be a perfect place to hide a stash of goods. What I found when I looked inside shocked me. There were about a dozen human legs, severed at the ankle and thigh and chemically preserved. They were heavily bound in thick, clear commercial plastic wrap. This was like a short story by Edgar Allan Poe. Was the doctor, in fact, a mad scientist? I had communications center dispatch the on-duty coroner investigator to the location, Just then, the doctor saw me and walked toward my direction, looking perturbed. I pointed to the find and asked him, "What are these?"

He replied sternly, "What are you looking in *there* for?"

Boy, was *that* a wrong answer. I could have been addressing "Doctor Serial Killer," with victims in the basement. He went back into the house when the coroner investigator McCabe arrived. I figured these guys had seen just about everything, but McCabe took one look and was as astonished as I was. He took over the scene and we waited until the head coroner communicated with us.

It turned out that the good doctor was a licensed obstetrician. I imagined him keeping his patients' amputated limbs as some sort of souvenir, perhaps for some kind of experimentation. The coroner, although not affiliated with the sheriff's department during this time, had a good rapport with those in the medical profession. He had us back off the case and informed us that the doctor was authorized to have these limbs in his possession. And I thought it was against the law to have human body parts in a residential neighborhood! I wondered what would have happened if the kids found this. Come to think of it, maybe they had and ran off, forever cured of their thieving impulses.

Chapter Nine

Celebrities

ANSEL ADAMS, ONE OF THE MOST widely acclaimed photographers in history, lived out his last years in the Carmel Highlands, on Spindrift Road in the county jurisdiction. The house was as impressive as his black-and-white portraits and nestled at the natural end of the road; it was a geological marvel in that, from the inside, one could observe 180 degrees from any point. Uncluttered views allowed for picturesque images of the Pacific Ocean and the rugged shoreline. He was one of those important people living in the Monterey Peninsula of whom we had to be aware.

When Ansel Adams died on April 22, 1984, he had lived a long life and his inevitable passing had been fully expected by members of his family. There was to be a private memorial at an undisclosed location and, as part of the preparation, a family member wanted to hire a deputy to stay in the house while the service was being held. It was a smart move because thieves often target such occurrences. There was a mechanism in place for a private hiring, indicated by a sign-up sheet for "outside employment." I grabbed it out of a sense of duty.

I arrived in my uniform and parked the patrol car in front as a deterrent to trespassers. I was not sure what to expect inside when I rang the doorbell. A kindly, gray-haired lady introduced herself; she was Virginia Rose, Mr. Adams' widow She showed me around the house and made me feel comfortable. At one point, she motioned for me to follow her downstairs to a room that had been a particular favorite of her husband's.

Escorting Doris Day

The gracious Mrs. Adams interacted with me in a manner that made feel as though I were a personal guest.

I don't recall how the subject came up, but she told me that she and her husband planned a public exhibition of their work in Carmel for 1981. There was to be a private viewing the night before and, among their special invited guests, were John Lennon and his wife, Yoko Ono. They confirmed that they would be coming and then the unthinkable happened, as we all know, John Lennon was gunned down in front of his home in December

1980. The exhibition went on, but Mr. and Mrs. Adams regretted never having met John and Yoko, whom they respected as artists. Following this, she left with the other family members for the memorial. I was now alone in Ansel Adams' house. The tastefully decorated rooms featured stunning, oversized portraits and row upon row of leather-bound books, covering every imaginable genre.

"Who *wouldn't* be inspired by living here?" I thought to myself.

First Time Meeting Doris Day

Doris Day was one of those celebrities the deputies looked out for, each elected sheriff made sure she felt secure. Long since retired from acting, she was still being sought after by media outlets and her legion of fans.

I first met Doris while I was on duty. It was at the Crossroads Center at the mouth of the valley, just outside Carmel. I had some sort of detail to attend to and I pulled my patrol car into a parking place. As I started toward the sidewalk, I walked beside a parked Jeep Wagon with about four barking dogs inside. I saw Doris talking to someone outside of a pet store. She must have noticed my uniform because she ran over to scold her dogs. Shaking her finger at them, she said, "*Stop*, you're disturbing the peace."

Terry Melcher

Not only was Terry Melcher Doris Day's son, he was a prodigious producer of records and bands, including The Beach Boys, The Byrds, and Paul Revere & the Raiders. He was also a solo artist in his early years calling himself Terry Day. It led to a teaming with Bruce Johnston and together they recorded, "Hey Little Cobra." There was so much more to Terry than his public image. In later years, I was proud to call him a dear friend. As a deputy, I was aware of Terry, especially when he produced his mother's syndicated television show *Doris Day's Best Friends* (1985–1986). Many of Doris' co-stars were being brought to Doris' Cypress Inn and Carmel Valley to shoot the show, names like Rock Hudson, Kay Ballard, Howard Keel, and even neighbor Joan Fontaine. One episode featured Angie Dickinson and Doris having lunch on the patio of the Quail Lodge, with Ed Haber (the owner) serving them. The comedy plot entailed the girls forgetting their wallets and tried to explain it to Haber, who called them "deadbeats." Responding to the call was Deputy Pat Duval, our own "singing sheriff." Doris and Angie played it straight, but Deputy Duval purposefully played it up, to great comic effect. He said, "This is my chance to break into show business," before belting out one of Doris Day's hits, "Secret Love."

More Celebrities

- Merv Griffin owned a ranch in Carmel Valley that he would frequently visit. He and his friends would fire rifles at targets on the property, generating countless complaints from the neighbors.
- Jean Arthur lived in a cottage near Carmel Point, which was within walking distance of the Pacific Ocean. I often saw her on my beat; her hair was white and she always seemed to be in her garden. I used to wave to her as I drove by, but I never imposed on her. She lived mere steps away from poet Robinson Jeffers.
- The late Robinson Jeffers (1887-1962) built his Tor House and tower on Ocean View Avenue right on Carmel Point. The facility has since been run by the Robinson Jeffers Foundation, a non-profit organization. I passed by this structure many times when I was on this beat. One day while on duty, I drove up the pathway and met someone from the foundation. She allowed me to enter the tower made of polished river rocks and I climbed the very narrow staircase to the top flight. Jeffers was also famous as a playwright having penned (among others) "Tower Beyond Tragedy," first acted out by Judith Anderson and Henry Brandon at the Theater in the Forest in the heart of Carmel (1941).
- Kim Novak used to have a house right at the edge of the Pacific Ocean; it was treacherous to respond there for alarm activations. She later made her home off of Aguajito Rd., where she and her husband raised llamas.
- Betty White is another celebrity that I never met, although I knew where she lived.
- Paul Anka had a fantastic private residence in the Carmel Hills area overlooking the Monterey Bay. Outside of the residence,

I met Anka's bodyguard, who was a bit spiffed. I heard that when John Lennon was killed, this bodyguard allegedly told Anka, "They're shooting all the singers." If this was his form of "job security," I had no respect for the man.

- Reggie Jackson, the baseball legend, also had a home in Carmel Hills. I met Reggie during an alarm activation at his house. I talked to him, but only in my professional mode. Reggie owned a breakfast restaurant in Monterey with a baseball theme, "Reggie's Place." It was filled with artifacts from his career.

- Mike Nesmith, the former Monkees actor and musician, lived across from Jackson, another local celebrity I never met.

- Dean Stockwell, the former child actor who now lived in Carmel Valley, was involved in television when I was working the beat. I met him on Christmas night when a couple of my fellow deputies were outside of a Safeway in the valley; he drove up to us and while smoking a cigar, sincerely thanked us for our service. "You guys do a good job!" he said. The other deputies didn't know who he was until I told them.

- Allen Funt, the host of radio's Candid Microphone and television's Candid Camera, was a regular at area restaurants. Mr. Funt lived quietly on a huge ranch south of Carmel going towards the Bixby Bridge. Sadly, Mr. Funt suffered a debilitating stroke in the 1990s, requiring twenty-four-hour care at a family member's house in Pebble Beach. There was an impropriety that I was called in to investigate, a fraudulent nurse. The district attorney's office sorted it all out after I submitted my report.

Sons of the Desert

Groucho Marx once said; "I refuse to join any club that would have me as a member." I was involved in plenty of non-profit organizations, but not a fraternal one—at least, not until I joined the official Laurel & Hardy appreciation society, better known as the Sons of the Desert. Stan Laurel & Oliver Hardy made over 100 films together and one of their features depicted them as members of a mythical fraternal organization called *Sons of the Desert*. Prof. John McCabe, the authorized biographer of the renowned comedy team, asked Stan Laurel for his blessing to start up an appreciation society celebrating Laurel & Hardy. Stan wanted assurance that it wouldn't be a "fan club," but a loose organization of film buffs, with a "sort of half-assed dignity to it." There would also be featured toasts ("To Stan," "To Babe," "To Fin," and "To the ever popular Mae Busch and Charlie Hall"), and the showing of one of the team's films, followed by a discussion.

A charter was made up and the organization was founded in 1965. The only rules were that there *weren't* any rules. This was my kind of society. I had been aware of the organization since I bought a pocketbook version of Prof. McCabe's *Mr. Laurel and Mr. Hardy*[42] for my dad years ago.

There have been many chapters—known as tents—of the Sons since its inception, each tent was named after a Laurel & Hardy film. The closest tent to us was in Santa Clara, and my patrol partner, Tom Crompton, and I drove to a meeting on an off night and had the best time. What had we been missing? Phil McCoy was the grand sheik and he presided over the "meeting" with a joyful spirit mixed with a sense of dignity. Phil had built his house to incorporate a stage, a bar, and priceless musical antiques. To say the McCoy's were musically inclined would be an understatement; at the meetings, they had live music, supplied mostly by the Monterey Classic Jazz Band and sometimes augmented by old jazz singers.

Two of my colleagues, Dave Allard and Tom Crompton, became interested in helping me to start our own tent, but with a law-enforcement theme. Our tent based on the cop characters Laurel & Hardy played in their 1933 short *The Midnight Patrol*. We identified with them since we were all working the midnight shift. We were aided and abetted by two of the Dixieland jazz musicians, one of whom was Frank Goulette, a trumpet player originally from San Mateo, who just happened to be a high school friend of Merv Griffin. They formed a band and started to play professional gigs, such as playing live on a San Francisco radio station.

Frank was a dedicated lover of all things Laurel & Hardy; he actually met the famed duo when he was a boy. It was at the World's Fair in San Francisco's Treasure Island in August of 1940 during the Golden Gate International Exposition. Frank's mother was one of director John Ford's secretaries; the three of them shared a dinner table with Stan and Ollie during one of the functions. Frank was in awe of those kind and humble men.

---

42. Published by Doubleday & Co. Inc. in 1961. The paperback version was published by Signet Books in 1968.

Our other Dixieland musician was Dave "Whoopie Fingers" Cotter, a collector of records who had worked as a disc jockey during the 1950s. He was heavily influenced by the banjo-playing style of Freddie Morgan.[43] Dave announced that he was qualified to help us establish a tent in the Monterey area because he had sat through a Laurel & Hardy marathon screen event.

It came to be that Tom Crompton, Dave Allard, Frank Goulette, Dave Cotter, and with the approval of Professor John McCabe, (The Exhausted Ruler) our own tent was founded in 1984. During those first couple of years I hosted our meetings in my home in Monterey, then graduated to a banquet room at a Carmel restaurant. We had some great times.

Searching for Edgar

It was from reading Leonard Maltin's landmark book *The Great Movie Shorts* that I learned that one of Laurel & Hardy's co-stars, Edgar Kennedy, was born "somewhere in Monterey County." From then on I studied every Edgar appearance I came across and wondered about his family history. Where *exactly* was he born? No one seemed to know, and there were no birth records. For the members of the Midnight Patrol tent, Edgar became our special project. As a middle-aged, balding, and an inept public servant, he delighted us in *Night Owls* and *Leave 'Em Laughing*. Earlier in his career he was one of the original Keystone Kops.

Sometime in 1985 there was a banquet in San Francisco hosted by the Call of the Cuckoos tent. The event had a hospital theme, "Laughter is the Best Medicine." Everyone who attended was asked to come in some sort of hospital garb. Many of the females came as nurses, some of the guys were doctors of dubious distinction, and then there were the patients. I was a little different; I came in a clean coroner's jumpsuit. It was all meant in the spirit of fun. Speaking of spirits, this was the first time I met some of the movers and shakers of the "Sons," so I bought some of them drinks from the portable bar in our banquet room. When I offered to buy one of the female dignitaries a drink, she asked for something exotic that they didn't serve at the private bar. That meant that I had to go into the crowded main bar of the hotel and order the libation. I wasn't aware that every eye was on me as I picked up the floral lined cocktail until the

43. Freddie Morgan was a member of the Spike Jones and His City Slickers band. He performed as a mute. His wild expressions sometimes resembled those of Harpo Marx.

bartender (noticing my coroner attire) said, "Must be a bad one, huh?" It was at this banquet that I met Lois Laurel, Stan's daughter, and her British-born husband, Tony Hawes. They were so endearing and Tony was such a riot that it didn't come as a surprise when I learned that he had been a professional comedy writer on both sides of the Atlantic. By the end of the evening, Lois and Tony invited me to visit them in Los Angeles. That opportunity came soon after when Chris Hubrig of the Way Out West tent arranged a visit to the Hawes' home. After touring some notable Laurel & Hardy filming locations (such as the steps up which Stan & Ollie delivered the player piano in *The Music Box*), I was driven to their home. Tony greeted me at the door with a Corona beer and some nuts.

I was somewhat awestruck by the one-of-a-kind artifacts on display throughout the house. Tony brought out one of the dozen or so Stan Laurel scrapbooks and placed it on my lap to peruse. As I did so, Tony said, "Did you ever see this?" and put on a tape transferred from film on his VCR. They were Stan Laurel's home movies. Tony kept piling scrapbooks on my lap before I could even turn a few pages.

The chair I had been sitting on had a low-hanging lamp above it. Even though I was warned to "mind the lamp," I nevertheless hit my head on the base when I stood up. I immediately heard a ringing sound in my brain. I was so embarrassed that I pretended the contact didn't hurt, and sat right back down. I also assured Lois and Tony that I was now aware of the lamp.

After a lively conversation, I eventually started to stand when I heard Lois say, "Look out for the—!" It was too late: I collided with the lamp again. After hearing the hollow sound of my head making contact, Lois and Tony looked greatly concerned. I tried to laugh it off, only this time I was not so sure I would retain consciousness. Tony gave me another Corona for my nerves. "It's the iron in it," he said, knowing I would recognize the line from the Laurel & Hardy short *Them Thar Hills* (1934). They also offered me another chair to sit in, but pride made me politely refuse it.

Eventually, it was time to go. I stood up to address my host and, sure enough, banged my bean again. This time Lois said, "Well, you broke the record. No one has hit their head on our lamp *three* times before." I tried to convince them that I had intentionally hit my head for comic effect. At least I was assured that I left an impression on Tony and Lois—and the lamp.

In 1986, I invited Lois and Tony up to Monterey for our tent's second anniversary. "We'd love to come," they said. I picked them up at the airport while I was on duty and transported them in the back seat of my patrol car to their hotel. Tony and Lois just laughed about it and took pictures.

The Midnight Patrol anniversary was held at the California First Theater, which had been built in 1850. It was a small venue that sat about 100 people, but it had a stage. I was the emcee and got to introduce not only Tony and Lois, but Henry Brandon and Phyllis Coates. The evening was made complete by the showing of Laurel & Hardy films and special toasts.

Henry Brandon

In December of 1984, I met Henry Brandon,[44] who played the villainous Silas Barnaby in the 1934 Laurel & Hardy feature *Babes in Toyland*.[45] A veteran actor in film, television, and the stage, he was in town to be the guest of honor for San Francisco's "Call of the Cuckoos" tent for the 50th anniversary of the release of *Babes in Toyland*. I recognized Henry from some of his films, most notably as Chief Scar in John Ford's *The Searchers* (1956).

It was arranged that I would pick up Henry at the train station in San Jose. He wore a suit and tie and was about six-three, about an inch taller than me. I was struck by his remarkable, almost military, bearing. It was hard for me to believe that he was actually seventy-two years old.

Henry and I hit it off right away and had a good chat. I drove north on El Camino Real through the cities in Santa Clara County[46] and stopped for lunch in Palo Alto. I had in mind to surprise him at one of my favorite restaurants, Dina's Shack. This landmark eatery had been established in the 1920s. As soon as we arrived, Henry said, "Dina's Shack? I haven't been there since I was at Stanford!" He was referring to his time in college, during the years 1929–1931.

We arrived in San Francisco for the evening's program, which was led by Grand Sheik Gary Cohen. There was, of course, a screening of "*Babes*," as well as a serial chapter of *The Drums of Fu Manchu*, featuring Henry in another sinister role. With my new professional quality portable camera, I recorded Henry Brandon filling us in on his recollections of working with Laurel & Hardy, and his acting career.

---

44. In 2018 Richard S. Greene and I co-wrote a book about the man: *Henry Brandon: King of the Bogeymen.*

45. Also known as *March of the Wooden Soldiers.*

46. Now known the world over as Silicon Valley.

Sons of the Desert Convention

The summer of 1986 was a memorable one for me. I went to my first Laurel & Hardy "Sons of the Desert" Convention. It was held in Philadelphia and was attended by film buffs, collectors, celebrities, and Sons members from across the globe. It had been wonderfully organized by the host committee. Entertainment was constant: Vince Giordano and his Nighthawks band played live music from the 1920s and '30s. There were raffles, toasts, jokes, bus trips, lunches, a Laurel & Hardy archive displays, and dealers' tables. There was even a recreation of the *Babes in Toyland* set, with members in costume as Mother Goose characters. I went as "The Pie-man."

The evening was capped off by a recreation of the wedding scene from the movie, with original cast member Henry Brandon reprising his role as Barnaby. The scene was a surprise to those in attendance as we watched Henry, with great comic flair, playing opposite Laurel & Hardy lookalikes. Tony Hawes officiated.

International conventions were held every two years, and after my first experience, I rarely missed another event. They continue to be hosted by different tents in their respective cities: St. Paul, Minnesota; Seattle, Washington; Las Vegas, Nashville, Tennessee; Cincinnati, Ohio; St. Petersburg, Florida; and New York City. One of the conventions took place on a cruise ship to Cozumel, Mexico, and Ulverston, England (the latter of which is Stan Laurel's birthplace). I made many dear friends during these sojourns through the years. They're almost akin to family reunions. While in New York, I could not pass up the opportunity to visit Ellis Island to pay respects to my grandparents who ventured through this facility.

Washington, D.C.

After the Philadelphia convention, I took advantage of the close proximity to visit my cousin, John Cassara. He lived in the greater part of Washington, D.C., and was a Secret Service agent assigned to the White House during the Reagan era. I had a high clearance rate, so John was able to escort me through the White House. And since the president was out of the building, I got to see the Oval Office. The next day I took the opportunity to tour the Smithsonian, where I could easily have spent a week! Cousin John was a career federal employee who later worked for the Treasury

Department and the C.I.A. A career law-enforcement professional, he went on to write three books.[47]

Lois' mother (Lois Sr.) was living in Santa Cruz, on the north side of Monterey Bay, in the house Stan had built for Lois Sr.'s mother, at 120 Rathburn Way. At the time (1986), Lois' mother was a frail ninety-one. Lois and Tony decided to bring her to live with them in Tarzana. I was assigned by Lois to help close her banking accounts in Santa Cruz and to bring the legal documents to her. Before meeting Lois Sr., Tony admonished me, "Whatever you do, *don't* mention Laurel & Hardy." I had to smile at that one.

Lois Sr. passed away in 1990.

---

47. *Hide and Seek* – Intelligence, Law Enforcement, and the Stalled War on Terrorist Finance (2006)
Demons of Gadara (2013)
Trade Based Money Laundering (2016)

Dirty Harry

Chapter Ten

Mayor Clint and the Pope

THERE WERE MANY "ECCENTRIC" people of the street in and around Carmel, the kind that might inhabit a Steinbeck novel. The first one that comes to mind was Albert, who called himself "Triple A." He lived in a beat up van, bright with American flags. An older, scrawny man, he always wore a white construction hat. He was a self-described "doctor" and talked a few women into his van for free examinations. On a quiet Christmas day, Albert called 9-1-1 for an undisclosed "emergency." When I arrived on the scene he told me, "Safeway is throwing away heads of cauliflower into the dumpster" and wanted me to help fetch the produce to take to his friends in jail. I admonished him for abusing the emergency line, but he retorted, "This *IS* an emergency."

Another odd individual was "Dogman." He and about a dozen dogs lived just off Highway 1 in a broken-down, purple school bus. Dogman was huge, about six-eight, and when he got angry, he could throw people around. He was gentle when I approached, however. I asked him if he would help me if he ever saw me being attacked. He proudly voiced his support.

Dogman had a goofy girlfriend who was half-crazy—make that *all the way* crazy.[48] She was known to walk the foggy highway at night and throw herself in front of traffic, scaring motorists half to death. We took her to the hospital many times, but they kept releasing her.

---

48. The cop vernacular for "crazy" is section 5150 of the Welfare and Institutions Code of California.

103

Dogman had a mother who was a fine citizen of Carmel. She had a nice home but didn't allow her son access to it. She eventually died and left the house to him. Dogman, now a proud homeowner, naturally threw his hat in the ring for the mayoral election. If dogs could vote, he would have been elected. Speaking of eccentrics, there was a guy who called himself "The Greek." He was a medium-sized man with a beard and a noticeably deep groove on the bridge of his nose. And, oh yeah, he had been convicted for killing someone with an axe. When he was released, he rode the rails to Southern California and somehow talked his way onto television's *The Gong Show*. His "talent" involved balancing the blade of a heavy knife on his nose (I guess that noticeably deep groove came in handy). After his fifteen minutes of fame, The Greek went into retirement, living under the Carmel River Bridge in a nest of transients. The thought of an axe murderer living within walking distance of Carmel would have freaked out the residents had they known. He, like so many others, fled the area after the great flood of 1995.

The Feriozzis

Like all officers of the law, I handled a lot of routine details that do not bear remembering. An exception was a nice elderly Italian couple who became friends of mine. Mr. Feriozzi was a jewelry crafter and owner of Feriozzi's of Rome, a shop next to the Hog's Breath Inn in Carmel. He and his wife were residents of Carmel Valley, they were victims of a burglary.

When I arrived to take the report and investigate the scene, I introduced myself. Hearing the name Cassara made them practically throw their arms around me—I was a *pizano*! With the formalities aside, Mr. Feriozzi told me about himself. He was a jeweler by trade from the old country. It was hard not to notice the huge, framed painting of Benito Mussolini over his fireplace. He saw me looking at it and expounded that he had once, long ago, been a general in Mussolini's army. He said, "It's a free country, no?"

After wrapping up the investigation, I received a cordial invitation to join them for dinner on some evening when I was off duty. I politely declined, citing that it would be unprofessional on my part to accept. Mr. Feriozzi explained that, where he came from, it was an honor to host an "official." The more I tried to sidestep the issue, the more pleasantly he persuaded me to relent. I told him I would be in touch and, after thinking it over, I decided to take him up on his kind invitation. There is, after all, no reason to insult someone's culture. I made a commitment to them for dine on one of my off days.

Mrs. Feriozzi was also an Italian native and *could she cook*! It was a superb dinner, complemented by vino. Mr. Feriozzi opened a bottle and, in his wonderfully thick accent, proudly announced: "It's a wine from-a Big-a-Sewer [Sur]." I adored this charming couple and kept in touch with them throughout my career.

Another interesting person of Italian heritage I met was no eccentric; he was a successful businessman/restaurateur/golf course designer/developer by the name of Nick Lombardo. He was the proud owner of the Rancho Canada golf course and resort in Carmel Valley.

I was detailed to his office concerning a vandalism report that needed to be taken. I was very professional in meeting Mr. Lombardo and introduced myself as Deputy Cassara. We were in his private office and he inquired, "*Cassara*? What's that, some half-assed Sicilian name?" I looked up and saw Lombardo with a big smiling face and a hand extended. I knew this wasn't a character assault and it certainly wasn't a racial taunt, not when we were both of Italian heritage. I found myself shaking hands with him like an old friend. Only Nick Lombardo could pull off a cheeky stunt like that. He had a secretary who was married to one of our detectives, so he must have been very comfortable dishing out some good-natured "homeboy" gibe. This wouldn't have worked well if, say, I had pulled him over on a traffic stop.

Carmel

Carmel has a reputation as a bohemian colony that attracts artists, musicians, photographers, painters, poets, writers, and actors. And those are just the mayors! This quaint village-like setting is only one square mile and dotted with fairytale shaped homes and businesses. The roughly four thousand residents have always had a love/hate relationship with tourists.

In 1986, Carmel was in the international spotlight when Clint Eastwood was elected mayor.[49] Clint won by a landslide. The *San Francisco Chronicle*, of course, gave it front-page bold headlines. Mayor Eastwood dutifully—and seriously—took on the position. He certainly didn't need the publicity.

---

49. Triple A put himself in the spotlight as well. We all let out a collective groan when national news stories referred to him as a "typical Carmel resident."

As a routine, the mayor would sit down with staff at the *Carmel Pine Cone* once a week and go over the city's agenda. It was always printed in the weekly newspaper. One of those weeks I dropped by their office to share a copy of an British tabloid newspaper with the headline, "Clint Eastwood is Stan Laurel's Son." I left it for one of their reporters and she was reading it when Clint walked in. Clint spied the headline and repeated it aloud, then just shook his head. The article went to great lengths to point out that Laurel had a son, who died a few days after his birth in May 1930. The writer of the article pointed out that Mr. Eastwood was born in May of that same year. There were also comparison photos of Clint and Stan.

In preparation for advanced publicity for Pacific Grove's annual "Good Old Days," I brought a press release for the newspaper to run. It was a promotional item detailing our tent's forthcoming Laurel & Hardy film marathon to be held at the local elementary school. It was then that I was filled in by one of the journalists about Clint's reaction to the tabloid headline.

I often saw Clint Eastwood in and around Carmel; he never had an entourage with him and he was all but unrecognizable in his oily gray baseball cap that covered his eyebrows. I saw him stride into a juice bar in the Crossroads center during the summer when it was packed with tourists. He simply ordered a beverage and walked out without anyone looking up. He avoided attention as much as he could. When someone did recognize him, they would say dumb things to him; "You really made my day."[50]

Clint could be seen around town driving his 1961 GMC pick-up (The same one used in his 1995 film *The Bridges of Madison County*). Once, while on patrol, I saw him pull into a gas station, lift the hood of his car, and tinker with the engine. When not in use, the truck was parked at his Mission Ranch restaurant. The locals really appreciated Clint's personal attention to the place; it was on the threshold of being sold and demolished to make room for condos when Clint, without fanfare, bought the property. Clint often told of the connection he made with the old landmark when he frequented it while stationed at nearby Ft. Ord in the early 1950s. He wanted to keep it the way he remembered it.

---

50. This is part of the catch phrase: "Go ahead, make my day," famously said by Eastwood's character Dirty Harry Callahan in *Sudden Impact* (1983).

A Papal Visit

Father Junipero Serra (1713–1784) was a Roman Catholic Spanish priest who founded a string of missions along the coast of California. He died at the Carmel Mission[51] from tuberculosis and is buried under the sanctuary. The mission is located off the Carmel River, where it meets the Pacific Ocean.

In 1987, Pope John Paul II made the trek to the Monterey Peninsula to beatify Father Junipero Serra. Mayor Clint Eastwood dutifully met the pope for a photo session at the Carmel mission. The cameras clicked away at this unique pairing and the resulting photos bore the caption: "Dirty Harry Meets His Holiest."

It was a gigantic, logistical endeavor to maintain safety and crowd control during the pontiff's visit. Fortunately, there was a large enough venue for him to hold a communion service at Monterey County's Laguna Seca Park and racing speedway. This is a huge outdoor, unseated facility surrounded by rolling hills.

As expected, the historic event attracted a wide variety of humanity, from the young to the old, the lame and the blind. I was one of the many regional officers assigned to help ensure everyone's safety.

The pope was helicoptered into the area and motored around the race track in his "Popemobile." It was a vehicle especially built so he could safely give blessings to the faithful. For this once-in-a-lifetime spiritual event, an estimated 100,000 people had congregated from all over the central California region. Most had already traveled in the pre-dawn hours to make the trek to Monterey by either church-sponsored or public buses.

After that inspiring afternoon, Pope John Paul II was whisked away in his helicopter. The multitudes of people prepared to board the buses in which they arrived. Suddenly, there was a crush of people trying to leave at the same time. The situation was compounded by the fact that many were confused as to which bus they should board. There was some panic in the crowd as it grew late and the skies darkened. Many of the elderly individuals needed to take their medicine, and all needed food and water. This went on all evening, with the buses spewing carbon monoxide fumes from the incessantly idling engines.

People became separated, sick, and exhausted. There were incidents of folks boarding *any* bus just so they could sit down. Some of the buses

---

51. Also known as Mission San Carlos Borromeo de Carmelo

took off without a full load to all points in California, leaving those left behind in anguish. It was a mess that would not be sorted out for several days. As a result, whenever I smell diesel exhaust, my mind takes me back to that day of exhilaration and despair.

Pebble Beach

Samuel Finley Brown Morse, commonly referred to as S.F.B Morse, became president of the Del Monte properties in 1919. Three years later, he supervised the design and landscaping of the Pebble Beach Golf Course. It has since been hailed as one of the most spectacular and challenging courses in the world. The property encompasses eleven square miles, and Morse generously donated a great deal of the land for the betterment of the community. Morse oversaw and approved special homes, golf courses, and the Monterey Peninsula Country Club; one of the most exclusive private golf membership clubs in the world.

I remember a detail I had at M.P.C.C. during the Crosby Pro-Am during which there was always outside seating for members. On this particular day, a bearded fellow on a bicycle rode in and sat down on one of the exquisite patio chairs and pulled up to a table. The staff had been carefully trained not to challenge people and risk insulting them. They must have thought this guy was Howard Hughes, as he was presented with a luncheon menu. He ordered lunch to his heart's content. When the bill arrived, all that was required was for the gentleman to write down his identifying club number. No identification was necessary. He wrote down some numerals, then calmly took off on his bike. When the waiter returned to process the billing, he realized the numbers did not correspond with those of any member. I came to take a report, but the mysterious bicycle rider had long since disappeared into the forest, a little less hungry.

Crosby-AT&T Tournament

The Bing Crosby National Pro-Am Golf Tournament has been a staple in Pebble Beach since 1947. Bing owned a home there and his backyard led to the Pebble Beach Course on the fourteenth hole of the fairway. He wanted his buddies to come to the Monterey Peninsula to enjoy the beauty of the location, the camaraderie, and the challenge of the game.

In the beginning, the competition had the champion receiving a trophy cup and $10,000. courtesy of Bing Crosby. The novelty was that Bing paired the professionals with amateur golfers; the latter were all of Bing's friends or fellow celebrities.

Prior to the tournament, Bing hosted a "Clam Bake" for all the volunteers, featuring entertainment by many of the performers in attendance. In the early years, the Clam Bake was held at the California State Theater on Monterey's Alvarado Street. The stage was put to good use.

On each succeeding day, the golfers would compete at the Del Monte Golf Course in Monterey (the first golf course built in California), Cypress Point (an exclusive and private course in Pebble) and ending the tournament at the famed Pebble Beach course. One *San Francisco Chronicle* columnist of the time reported there were 150 participants, including Bing, Bob Hope, Johnny "Tarzan" Weissmuller, Edgar "Slow burn" Kennedy, Richard Arlen, Bob Crosby, and New York Yankees owner Del Webb. The tournament drew large crowds and local charities were the biggest benefactors; this proved a winning formula and was repeated every year in January or February until Bing died in 1977.

The contest continued in the Crosby name until 1985 when AT&T wanted to sponsor the tournament. Apparently, Bing had anticipated this and left instructions for his wife, Kathryn, not to let the corporations in. Though the tournament generated its own non-profit funds over the years, the rumors were that the professionals wanted a bigger purse. There was a board of directors with Crosby's son Nathanial an active member, but Kathryn held out for the intimacy that Bing had established. She eventually moved the Crosby name and tournament out of state.

In the years immediately following Bing's passing, Kathryn took over as the perfect hostess. In the forest there is a huge picnic area where the tournament held a barbeque for all the volunteers. Kathryn helped serve and even sat down to eat with them, far away from the celebrities. She was a lovely person and before marrying Bing, her name was Kathryn Grant. I remembered her from her role in the 1958 film, *The Seventh Voyage of Sindbad*. I would have liked to have met her, but the opportunity never presented itself.

There were some great stories associated with the Crosby Pro-Am over the years; it was just like one big party. The Crosby tournament had the name and draw, but everyone knew that S.F.B. (Sam) Morse was the president of Del Monte properties until his death.

One legendary incident that took place at the Crosby occurred in January 1964. One headline in a San Francisco newspaper read: "**Sinatra Wants Snack, Settles for Smack**." It began when Sinatra, accompanied by fellow Rat Pack member Dean Martin, approached the desk clerk at the Del Monte Lodge at 1 a.m. and demanded something to eat. The kitchen was closed, but Sinatra insisted on service.[52]

The desk clerk tried to appease the recalcitrant Rat Packers, but they had been drinking heavily and could not be reasoned with. Frank, a man to whom no one dared say "no," became belligerent. The employee summoned Mr. Morse's right-hand man, Richard Osborn, to handle the dispute. Osborn was awakened and, as a gesture of appeasement, grabbed a bottle of champagne and brought it to Frank's room. Unfortunately, Osborn did not bring food.

According to the paper, "Osborn never got the chance to pop the cork, Sinatra did the popping."[53] A more apt description was Sinatra started flailing his fists, knocking the champagne to the floor. He also gave Osborn a black eye, along with other injuries. As a result, Osborn had to go to the hospital. Unbeknown to him, Sinatra went to the same hospital.

Another newspaper picked up the story: "Doctors found that [Sinatra] had fractured the little finger of his right hand—the finger which, in polite company, is extended when one is drinking tea. It was not believed that the injury would be any great handicap to Sinatra, who is not much of a tea drinker."[54] Once Sam Morse found out about the incident, he issued orders to kick Sinatra out, bag and baggage, and banned him from Pebble Beach forever. As the years passed, the story had morphed to where it was Morse who had corked Sinatra.

Sam Morse, the "Duke of Del Monte," died in 1969, but his legend lives on.

In that gentler time, etiquette was strictly adhered to, and volunteer field marshals were put in charge of crowd control. Most of the attendees were golfing enthusiasts and displayed common courtesy while each golfer set up their shots. No photographs were allowed during play as it upset the players' concentration. Unfortunately, the celebrities sometimes drew people who were not respectful of the game. One such occurrence involved some tourists taunting James Garner, the actor who played

---

52. *San Francisco Call-Bulletin*, January 20, 1964.

53. Ibid.

54. *San Francisco Examiner*, January 20, 1964.

Maverick on television. After putting up with this abuse for a time, Garner went over and punched the guy in the face. Also in that "gentler time," this incident was not reported by the press, nor were attorneys consulted.

I worked many of the tournaments during the Crosby and there was only one extra sheriff's unit assigned during the event. Pebble Beach had its own security and plenty of volunteers. When AT&T became the sponsor and host, it became bigger than ever and needed a larger law-enforcement presence. This was another "outside employment" opportunity. We had three posts in and around the Fairway One House, right off the first tee. The sponsor used the old house to host all the V.I.P.s during and after the games. Top chefs prepared gourmet foods, bartenders served drinks from the open bar, and beautiful ice sculptures were on display for guests.

To be allowed access to the Fairway One House, V.I.P.s had to be preapproved by corporate with the appropriate name tag identifier. It was our job as deputies to ensure the safety of the guests inside and to make sure that no one sneaked in from behind the facilities. Working the rear post requires some tact and diplomacy as some very important people enter this venue. During many of those years I took a week's vacation just so I could work there. I sat on a chair opposite where the gallery was watching the action. Clint Eastwood usually acted as host and it was a treat to see him and Tom Selleck shaking hands, a "Dirty Harry meets Magnum P.I. moment." I saw Tommy Smothers, President George W. Bush, Charles Schwartz and many professional athletes. When Kevin Costner came to the tournament, he attracted many female fans. There was a line of them just outside his hotel room.

A perennial favorite of the tournament was one of Hollywood's true gentlemen, Jack Lemmon. He had been coming to this event for many years and never made the final cut, but that never discouraged him from trying, and the crowd loved him for it. One of those years we had a deputy assigned to the rear post that did not know who the players or celebrities were and couldn't care less. Later that day, up came Jack Lemmon to gain entrance and our deputy demanded to see his identification badge. He didn't bring it, but offered, "I'm Jack Lemmon." The deputy said, "I don't care if your name's 'Jack Grapefruit,' you're not coming in without a proper name badge."

The next year I made it a point to work that detail and, as usual, I was standing out in back of the entrance. After play, I saw a man in a red sweater approach, and then he stopped suddenly and turned around. I recognized him and yelled out, "That's okay, Jack, come on in." Mr.

Lemmon had forgotten his badge and wasn't going to challenge a deputy again. He was thankful I called him in and that he didn't have to go back to his room.

In the mid-1980s, retired San Francisco Giants Willie Mays and Willie McCovey came to Pebble Beach for a "Celebrity Shoot Out" at the Spyglass Hill golf course during the AT&T. Mays and McCovey put on an exhibition at the driving range. Their powerful drives made those little golf balls disappear into the sky. It made me remember the old Candlestick Park days when they were in their prime, hitting baseballs into the stands.

The tournament took all year to prepare for and, frequently, the weather was a factor. Huge television towers were built over the Pebble Beach course at the seventeenth hole to cover the action. Advanced TV crews recorded any number of things, to include going out to the ocean in a rig to record the frolicking whales in migration. The footage was carefully edited in to coincide with the TV broadcast as though these events were happening right at commercial break. To viewers around the world, Pebble Beach was symbolic of a magical place and no one can deny it. It is somewhat of a mecca to play golf at, second only to the ancient and royal St. Andrews golf course in Scotland. I could never afford to play there but that's O.K., I don't play golf.

Photo Section

Wishy Washy Window Cleaners

"We'll Wash Your Panes Away"

W. J. CASSARA
294-6700

C. H. THORSELL
269-2041

Wishy Washy Window
Cleanersbusiness card

Rookie Football card for Dan Pasterini

Charlie, Randy and me (as Chico)

With guard dog, Rocky

At Candlestick Park

As a young administrator for the San Jose
Missions baseball club

College graduating photo

Swearing-in ceremony for
the Santa Clara Co.
Sheriffs Office

Just starting with the Monterey
Co. Sheriffs Office

At the site of the old
Hal Roach studios

My baseball card

With our robot, Deputy Mac

In crime prevention

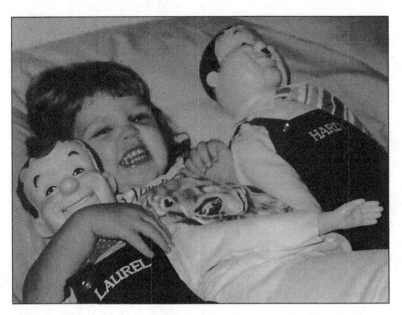

Daughter Diana

Visiting my daughter's 2nd grade class

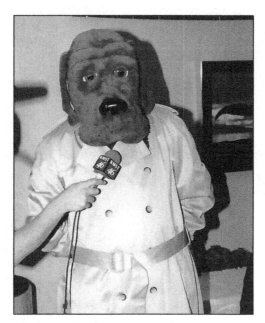

Being interviewed as McGruff

At the Sons of the Desert convention in Las Vegas (1992)

Dad and I in Las Vegas

On patrol in Pebble Beach

Art Carney

Doris Day

DORIS DAY PET FOUNDATION
NEWSLETTER
P.O. BOX 8509 • UNIVERSAL CITY, CA 91608

"THANKS FOR CARING"

AUGUST, 1994

Dear Friends,

We're all having a wonderful summer here in Carmel and the weather has been absolutely spectacular. I've had lots of good friends visiting during the past couple of months and it's been fun spending time together. My four-leggers are all well and happy and my greatest joy is "doing" for them. They're a constant source of pleasure and they bring so much to me and my home.

What a response we've had for information about our next DDPF fundraiser! We have literally dozens of pre-addressed envelopes to mail when we have made our plans. My daughter-in-law, Jacqueline, was in charge of putting the event together last year and she did such a terrific job, we've asked her to help us again. She's busy going through her notes and lists, making telephone calls and renewing contacts. It will take several more weeks before we have anything definite with regard to dates but as soon as we do -- you'll know!

Earlier this year I was thrilled to be presented with the Laughing Gravy Award -- and I know that requires an explanation! Admirers of Laurel and Hardy have formed an appreciation society called "Sons of the Desert." Each chapter (or tent) is named after a Laurel and Hardy film. Ten years ago our very own Monterey County deputy sheriff Bill Cassara founded the Carmel chapter, appropriately called the Midnight Patrol Tent. This chapter was based on the film of the same name where the boys are portrayed as cops working the midnight shift.

Since Laurel and Hardy were animal lovers, it occurred to the Midnight Patrol Tent to honor the DDPF by presenting me with an award based on one of their films. "Laughing Gravy" was a little dog they rescued from the snow when the landlord banished it. A still from that film was beautifully framed and matted and presented with a lovely inscription.

So here I am with the Midnight Patrol Tent, clockwise from top left: Anne Cassara, Duon Zeroun, Gloria Hughes, Jim Maley, Dave Cotter, Bill Cassara, me, and Bob Zeroun. I wish you could see the award, it's really lovely.

Our next newsletter will be mailed in November so we're offering our holiday greeting cards at this time. We have our original design that everyone asks for year after year, and a new design as well. We hope you like them.

Enjoy the last days of summer, have a happy and safe Labor Day and Halloween, and we'll be back again before Thanksgiving. By the way, don't forget the Cypress Inn when you visit Carmel. We welcome your pets with open arms, so come and see us!

Doris Day

Doris Day newsletter

Doris, Terry Melcher and I

Doris hold up the "Laughing Gravy" award

Calamity Jane night in Carmel

With Tony Hawes in San Jose

Sheriff's Public Information Officer

With Edie Adams

With Virginia O'Brien

With Hal Roach

With Henry Brandon

With Suzanne Somers

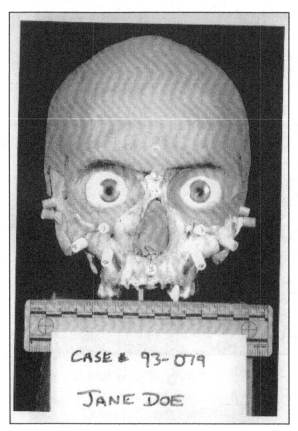

Dep. Neil Shaw's early stage
of the "Skullpture"

Neil Shaw's drawing of Laurel & Hardy w/ Edgar Kennedy

Edgar Kennedy Celebration in Monterey

**Weissman and Faversham
as "Laurel and Hardy"**

Jeffrey Weissman and Bevis Faversham

With author Raymond Daum

39. With Tom Hanks impersonator

Play Misty for Me
DVD

Clint and his wife, Dina
at the Misty gala

Monterey

MOVIE TOURS

Experience Monterey's Movie Magic

Home
About Us
Tours
Directions
Reservations
Groups
Media
Contact Us

"PLAY MISTY FOR ME" GALA

SEPTEMBER 15th, 2001

The "Play Misty for Me" Gala was held on September 15th at the Crossroads Community Room and the movie was presented at the Resort Theaters immediately after the Gala.

Clint was very gracious and gave a little talk on making the movie and his experiences of first time directing. Wonderful decorations from "Illusions of Grandeur" and delicious food and wine donated by local restaurants and wineries. The committee worked very hard on this event - special thanks to Chair Bill Cassara and all committee members. The committee also decided to donate the sale of the limited edition DVDs of the movie to the California Professional Firefighters Foundation in response to the September 11th terrorist attack. We raised nearly $900 for this cause.

The "Magical Misty Bus Tour" was the brainchild of Bill and our great 'friend' Doug Lumsden made it all possible. We had an advance copy of the DVD and committee member Heather Arnold worked with Full Steam Marketing to edit the DVD so it could be shown at the various stops on the tour. Doug donated his "Monterey Bay Scenic Tours" bus and all his high tech video equipment to make this a wonderful and unique outing for the community. We hope to do this again as a 'friends' event. Watch out for news.

Clint Eastwood poses with Bill Cassara (left) and Doug Lumsden (right) at the "Play Misty for Me" DVD Premiere.

Don't forget, this is the first of a series of films that highlight Monterey County locations. Any suggestions for future films would be greatly appreciated.

Misty flyer

Citizen's Academy

On a recruitment
mission w/ the LA
Laker girls

With Tommy Butch Bond

With newly elected Sheriff Gordon Sonne

As President of the Monterey
Co. Peace Officers Assoc.

Sheriff Kanalakis giving
me an award

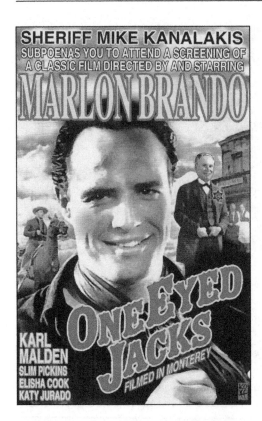

One-eyed Jacks fundraiser

Promotional photo for Sergeant

Michelle

Our wedding invitations

Wedding day (take one)

Wedding Day with my children, Doug and Diana at Joan Fontaine's house

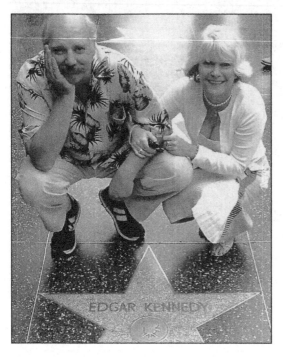

Michelle and I at Edgar Kennedy's star

Bill Cassara, author

With Joan Maurer (Moe's daughter)

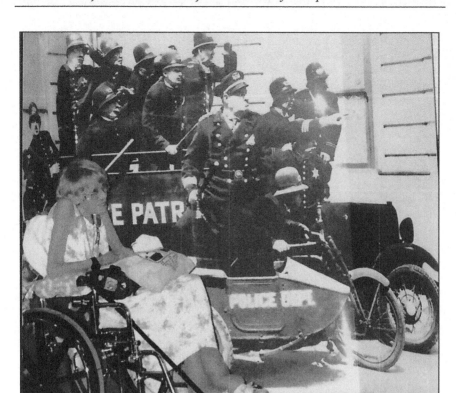

Dorothy DeBorba's last photo

With my wife, Michelle (2018)

𝕸onterep County 𝕭oard of 𝕾uperbisors

𝕽esolution

Resolution No: 07-061

Adopt a resolution commending **Bill Cassara,**
Monterey County Sheriff's Sergeant, upon
His retirement from public service of over
26 years...

WHEREAS, Sergeant Bill Cassara was hired by the Monterey County Sheriff's Office under the command of Sheriff D.B "Bud" Cook on February 9, 1981 as a Deputy Sheriff. Sergeant Cassara spent 26 years of his law enforcement career serving during the terms of Sheriffs David "Bud" Cook, Norman G. Hicks, Gordon Sonne, and Michael Kanalakis. His duties included assignments in the Enforcement Operations Bureau and the Administration Bureau; and

WHEREAS, Sergeant Cassara was born in San Jose, California on August 18, 1951. After graduating from Willow Glen High School in San Jose, he attended San Jose City College where he earned his Associate of Arts Degree. Sergeant Cassara went on to attend San Jose State University where he earned his Bachelor of Science Degree in Administration of Justice; and

WHEREAS, Sergeant Cassara is a 1979 graduate of the Santa Clara County Police Academy where he was assigned jail duty. Sergeant Cassara was hired with the Seaside Police Department and assigned to Patrol from 1979 to 1981. Sgt. Cassara was then hired in 1981 by the Monterey County Sheriff's Office, where he was assigned to the Enforcement Operation Bureau. As a deputy, Sgt Cassara had a multitude of different assignments to include Field Training Officer, Corporal, Crime Prevention Officer, Background Investigator-Recruiter, Citizen's Academy Coordinator and was the Public Information Officer for 5 years. On June of 2003, Deputy Cassara was promoted to the rank of Sheriff's Sergeant by Sheriff Kanalakis and worked in that capacity until his retirement. As a sergeant, he was also assigned to the Professional Standards Division and was also the Department Historian; and

WHEREAS, Sergeant Cassara was recognized with the following awards during the course of his career: Outstanding Young Public Safety Officer by the Salinas Jaycees, Outstanding Young Public Safety Officer by the California Jaycees, Resolution from the California Assembly as one of five top cops in the State, Outstanding Service Award for Crime Stoppers fundraising and the North County LULAC Award for Outstanding Service in Law Enforcement; and

WHEREAS, Sergeant Cassara is the author of the published book: "Edgar Kennedy-Master of Slow Burn." He has also authored numerous professional articles for law enforcement journals; and.

WHEREAS, Sergeant Cassara throughout his distinguished career has contributed countless hours in support of community groups and service organizations to include the following: President of the Monterey County Peace Officers Association, Board of Directors for Arts Habitat and the Monterey County Film Commission. He was also a member of the Monterey County Historical Society; and

NOW, THEREFORE, BE IT RESOLVED that the Board of Supervisors of the County of Monterey on behalf of the County and all citizens thereof, hereby acknowledges, commends, and thanks Sergeant Cassara for his 26 years of outstanding service to the citizens of Monterey County and to the Monterey County Sheriff's Office.

BE IT FURTHER RESOLVED that the Board of Supervisors wish him success, health, and happiness in all future endeavors and joy in this well deserved retirement.

PASSED AND ADOPTED this 13th day of March, 2007 by the following vote, to wit:

_____
Dave Potter, Chair

_____
Fernando Armenta, Vice Chair

_____
Supervisor Louis R. Calcagno

_____
Supervisor Simón Salinas

_____
Supervisor Jerry Smith

Resolution of my career accomplishments

Chapter Eleven

Deputy Field Coroner

FROM 1984 THROUGH 1988 I was not only a training officer, I was a corporal and a deputy field coroner. There was a transition in the office when the board of supervisors decided to do away with the coroner's division as a separate entity and meld it with the sheriff's responsibilities.

My duties required me to be available while I was on duty as a deputy to respond to any death call, including the cities. My orders were to stand by and freeze the scene until the coroner investigator responded. Most people would be surprised how many relatives come over to help themselves to items "promised to them" by the deceased. Many of these calls were routine. If the decedent was under a doctor's care for at least thirty days and the doctor was willing to sign the death certificate, the body could be released to a mortuary without an autopsy. The suspicious ones were only released to the coroner investigators. If the decedent lived alone, we had to seal off the house with coroner's tape to secure property inside until it was administrated.

During my years as a deputy field coroner, there was no central morgue. During this time there was construction to build a long-needed brand-new sheriff's office in 1988. The county morgue wasn't completed until a few years later. Up until that time, autopsies were conducted by a medical examiner/pathologist at the various private mortuaries in cities through Monterey County. Much time was lost by just travel alone.

Another problem with mortuaries was that possible evidence could be lost. With a new central morgue out of our office, things were more

in control. It was first class all the way, with X-ray machines to more thoroughly examine the bodies for evidence. It was also set up so internal organs could be harvested and preserved as donors.

One of the worst duties of anyone in the business is death notification. In cop jargon, it was called, "dropping the dime" and it was never pleasant. I did it many times but I only remember one instance distinctly. It was Thanksgiving and I got word from a detective sergeant from St. Louis that a named female was murdered and they needed to talk to the decedent's mother ASAP.

I drove up to the very nice home in Carmel Valley and knocked on the door. A large family was present and they were naturally surprised to see me. I explained that I must talk to the mother in confidence and was invited in. One person remarked that someone must have "an overdue library book." Then, the temperature dropped twenty degrees as they led me to the bedridden mother's bedroom. She motioned me to come closer and I told her the bad news while the whole clan stood at the doorway, listening. I remember this one because of the family holiday.

There was an occasion when I was assigned to attend a class, Death Investigation, put on by the FBI. The course attendees were made up of other law-enforcement professionals whose job description included investigating deaths. Pupils were assigned by their respective agencies on a "need to know basis."

That week-long course included details and examples of deaths in every category: accident, homicide, justifiable homicide, natural causes, sleeping baby syndrome, and suicide. Although the "taking of one's life" and some of the other categories were not in the jurisdiction of the FBI, it was essential for the course. The FBI accumulated all the annual statistics from agencies around the country and then broke them down in categories. They were *the* source for serial killer modus operandi.[55]

They told us what to look for and to be *aware* of the families. Out of remorse, financial gain, or social stigma, there are many situations where family and other loved ones are motivated to contaminate the death scene. Some hide suicide notes, some dispose of medications, and some even move the body in an effort to avoid correct interpretation.

We were informed on the history of the autopsy as medical science. It is an expensive and time-consuming operation. Because of this, most Western cultures relied on a civil jury in the form of a "coroner's Inquest."[56] This procedure introduces witness, circumstantial and real evidence, which is then admitted into court records. Expert witnesses are essential to deconstruct the death. It includes the testimony of the official who first came upon the body and who took charge of the deceased.

Over the years, the roles of civilians who make up a coroner's inquest have mostly been replaced with the trained experts of coroner investigators and pathologists. These professionals have a better understanding of medical terminology and the science of death than most laymen.

The instructors informed us that the prevalence of the autopsy was an evolution in legislative law. One stated example was the "George Reeves case." This caught our attention. All of us had heard through the years that George Reeves (the actor who played Superman on television in the 1950s) was murdered and that, somehow, Hollywood "covered it up." The instructors introduced the autopsy photos by saying, "Classic suicide."

One of the functions of the death investigator on the scene is to do a preliminary profile of the person, including a description of their demeanor just prior to death. They talked specifically about Reeves and mentioned his higher than highs and lower than lows, which might have been the result

---

55. A method of operation or distinct pattern of a single multiple killer.

56. Coroner's inquests are very rare nowadays with the advent of scientific advances and expert witnesses.

of a chemical imbalance. The instructors told us of his stresses in life and his self-medication of alcohol and illicit drugs. Reeves was described as "euphoric" in the days before his tragic end—also a sign of suicide. Then there was a unique term that I had never heard before: "hesitation shots." They showed photos of the scene and explained that this is a common phenomenon to those who plan to use a gun. People who choose this option frequently test out the gun just to feel its power in previous days. There were two such shots near Reeves' bed. Also covered were the angles the deadly shots and the matching paths exhibited in the autopsy photos.

The uniqueness of "Hollywood Deaths" were much discussed in clinical terms. It was important to point out how much attention there is when any public figure suddenly dies. This is especially true between the time of death, the autopsy, and the toxicology reports. Rumors and myths overlap in the public's thirst for knowledge. **Pebble Beach Fire**An inferno was started by transients in late May of 1987, leading to the destruction of more than thirty homes. Smoke was billowing over the forest area for some time and it was thought that other homes were out of danger. At some point, the wind picked up in a canyon and the fire raged again.

I was working swings and the whole shift responded to initiate evacuations; my sergeant told me to go door to door for personal knock notices. It was nighttime by then and all the power was out. Sensing imminent danger, residents were evacuating. That fire was breathing down my neck as I drove up a windy road and knocked on the door. The residents had left by this point and I was almost trapped. The fire, heat, and smoke had reached its apex. I had to back out of that long winding driveway fast and I almost got stuck.

In some pockets of Pebble Beach, residents were refusing to leave their homes. A directive was issued by Patrol Captain Chatterton, who went on the air and ordered us to "arrest anyone who doesn't comply." I always had a fondness for Chatterton; he was passionate about patrol and cared deeply for his deputies. He typed his memos in all capital letters and it would read like the voice of God.

In the Line of Duty

We all know the dangers inherent to law enforcement when we sign up for the job, but we can never prepare for one of our own to die on the job. I was still with Seaside PD when, in June of 1980, deputies Jerralee Jacobus and Craig Knox were killed while responding to a burglary call. It was nighttime and they were hit head-on by a drunk driver whose headlights were off. On September 1996, Deputy Tony Olson was killed when he plunged off a cliff while responding to an in-progress domestic call.

Car accidents are a leading cause of death in law enforcement. Officers are also subject to being murdered in the performance of their duties. Suicide, sadly, is prevalent as well. I had a former trainee who took his own life when he was off duty.

Another tragic incident involved a colleague, Deputy Bob Shaw. On a weekend in April 1988, the Laguna Seca Raceway drew a crowd of thousands of people, who spent the night on the grounds inside tents or RVs. There was plenty of liquor and drugs going around and the crowd built a huge bonfire, using destroyed property. There were only a few of us on patrol that night and we made frequent drive-throughs as we tried to discourage lawlessness. Our presence agitated them, however, and we were taunted. It escalated to the point that they started throwing liquor bottles at us.

Mob rule was evident as the pack turned their anger into a dangerous uprising. A call was put out to summon our special unit for crowd control. Approximately thirty deputies arrived in riot gear and presented themselves in formation. Bottles continued to be thrown and the crowd beckoned the deputies into the crowd. Before deployment, Deputy Shaw collapsed. Captain Chatterton instantly began life-saving measures and continued while fire and ambulance was called. Deputy Shaw died instantly of a heart attack, causing the crowd to roar its approval. I had become acquainted with Bob a few years earlier when we roomed together for an officer safety school. He was a fun guy. Cop funerals are sobering, necessary rituals, and this one was heartbreaking. The eulogy was delivered by Bob's brother Neil, who was also a deputy with us. The bagpipes triggered deep sorrow.

Monterey County Film Commission

The Monterey County Film Commission was established in 1987 as a non-profit, with only one person to administrate it. The predecessor to this organization was the Monterey Peninsula Motion Picture Association (1927) headed by Jean Juillard, then associated with the newly erected Hotel San Carlos. Juillard was formally associated with the Hotel Del

Monte[57] and was in touch with all the Hollywood studios. It was big business to lure production crews and actors to the hotel. Juillard provided logistic assistance as part of the hotel service.

Hollywood films were being shot on the Monterey Peninsula, and curious locals showed up to gawk. Sometimes they were allowed to be extras in crowd scenes. One such film was Eric von Stroheim's *Foolish Wives* (1922), which had been shot mostly on Point Lobos, just south of the Carmel Highlands and, now, a state beach. There was a huge set constructed in the bedrock with the Pacific Ocean behind it also serving as the faux Monte Carlo of the French Riviera.

A crowd of onlookers were put to good use as extras. When the filming was done at this location, all that was left was a huge pile of garbage and shoddy facsimile buildings.

The peninsula learned a lesson from this. From that point on, the community demanded oversight and discouraged pre-publicity, so as not to attract hordes of tourists during shooting. The locals genuinely kept their distance from film stars, a sign of deference to the art of movie-making.

To ensure cooperation, local ordinances were passed to authorize commercial filming on the public roads. If it was a state highway, it fell into the California Highway Patrol's jurisdiction; if filming encroached into county roads, the Monterey County Sheriff's Department issued the permits (the incorporated cities had their own similar ordinances). This did not apply to private property where film companies could shoot without impacting traffic. The ordinance specified that law-enforcement agencies were needed to stop traffic when crews are actually filming. Normally, the shoot would hold up traffic in both directions for five to ten minutes at the most.

There would be a communications specialist from the company who oversaw the interval between "action" and "cut." He had a walkie-talkie to communicate with the officers on each side of the road, telling us when it was clear to release or to hold the traffic. The company had to pay fees to the county to secure law-enforcement personnel and vehicles. The deputies were hired by the hour as "outside employment" on our days off. It was a money maker for the county as they charged the companies for all expenses. The funds were distributed, not to the Sheriff's Department, but to the general fund. I worked quite a few of these voluntary off-duty assignments and the only stress involved was

---

57. Hotel Del Monte is now part of the Navel Post Grad.

holding up the cars. One lady voiced her objections when I gave her the go-ahead.

She rolled down her window and yelled: "So *this* is what we pay our taxes for!"

"No ma'am," I answered politely. "Tax payers don't pay for this, the film producers do." Stuck for an answer, she rolled up her window and sped off.

There were untold car commercials and photo shoots over the years on the Monterey Peninsula. Up until 1987, no one was keeping track of the number of feature films that were made all or in part in Monterey County. The subject was casually brought up in a longstanding column inked by Professor Toro of the *Monterey Herald*. In reality, there was no journalist by that name. The weekly column listed oddball incidents, history, or gossip that took place in the region. One of Professor Toro's columns appealed to readers to help him compile an accurate list of all the commercial motion pictures that had been shot in Monterey County. There was an update every week on its progress from the readers who might have remembered or experienced a particular film being made. The Monterey library had some clippings, but it was a grass-roots effort to compile and verify a filmography that approaches 200.

The list of movies started in 1897 and, through the decades, familiar sites have been identified. Most prominently identified is the Cypress Tree in Pebble Beach and the Bixby Bridge on Highway 1 in Big Sur. Spindrift Road in the Carmel Highlands was often used, much to the chagrin of its residents. The road is off Highway 1 and curves around the ocean front, featuring a short rock formation border. It was used by Alfred Hitchcock for a major scene in *Suspicion* (1941), simulating a European road and sea vista.

In 1986 the original cast of the *Star Trek* crew set up shop behind the Monterey Bay Aquarium to shoot the highly anticipated feature film, *Star Trek IV, the Voyage Home*. This time, the crew to save the whale species in the Pacific Ocean. The Monterey Bay Aquarium stood in for the city of San Francisco, but most moviegoers didn't realize it. Word got out that William Shatner, Leonard Nimoy, DeForest Kelly, and the other familiar names were shooting in Monterey, causing a horde of "Trekkies" to show up. I stayed away.

1988 Banquet

At our 1988 Midnight Patrol banquet in Monterey, we had as special guests Tony Hawes, Henry Brandon, Our Gang (a.k.a. "Little Rascals) member Dorothy DeBorba, and Anthony Caruso. Anthony was the present harlequin (president) of the Masquers.[58] Tony, Henry, and Anthony were all members of the Masquers. Henry and Anthony had worked together and separately playing bad guys, good guys, romantic leads, and Native Americans. Anthony has over 250 screen and television roles from his fifty years in the business. Baby boomers remember him from one *Star Trek* episode,[59] and *The Adventures of Superman*.[60] He often was cast in films that starred Alan Ladd, but his most famous role was as an Italian mobster in *Asphalt Jungle*.

The banquet again took place at the California First Theater in Monterey, with Tony Hawes as emcee. All the traditions of the Sons were carried out and, prior to introducing our celebrity guests on stage, I had a special edited vignette from *The Joe Piscopo New Jersey Special* (1986) that depicted a mid-1950s *Godfather*-type restaurant scene. In the sketch, Anthony Caruso played Tony Danono, (A tribute to *Asphalt Jungle*). His character becomes irritated when a cheesy doo-wop number is performed on his birthday. Of course they get knocked off.

After the banquet, Tony, Henry, Anthony, and I went to Clint Eastwood's famous restaurant, The Hog's Breath Inn, in Carmel. As we ate and drank, we all celebrated the success of the program. The highlight for me was just listening to these distinguished actors tell stories about their careers. At one point, Henry leaned over to me and asked: "Ya know what put Carmel on the map? The Aimee McPherson case." He did not elaborate, but when someone like that says something to me in that way, I make sure to seek out more details when time allowed. That didn't present itself for another fifteen years.

Preventing Crime

In 1988, I was appointed the Sheriff's Office Crime Prevention Officer. This job required me to wear many hats, Neighborhood Watch program

---

58. The Masquers is a fraternal non-profit organization made up of professional actors. Their motto is: "We Laugh to Win."

59. *Star Trek* (1968) "A Piece of the Action," as Bela, a 1930s gangster.

60. *Czar of the Underworld* as Luigi Dinelli.

developer and alarm administrator, among others. I had a civilian partner, Shelly Milliman, and together we performed "Stranger Danger" programs at the schools, wrote environmental impact reports, and conducted business safety programs throughout the county.

Sheriff Bud Cook took a special interest in this position. When he first told me that I was his choice for the job, he took me out to lunch and explained his philosophies. "Politics is not a dirty word," he said. I got the point immediately. He also said that he wanted me to write articles on his behalf. So I became a "ghost writer" for him in a few articles in the *California Sheriff Magazine* and some other crime-prevention literature provided by the office. It was because this man had faith in me that I blossomed (somewhat) into a writer using my own name.

One of those articles pertained to the first publicly funded jail in California, which just happened to stand behind Monterey's Colton Hall. It was a historical look of how the jail came to be, but I added a Hollywood connection. The jail was used as a set in the 1942 film *Tortilla Flats*, based on the novel of the same name by Salinas-born John Steinbeck. The film had a top-flight cast, including

Spencer Tracy, Hedy Lamarr, John Garfield, and Frank Morgan. The location shooting in Monterey was essential. Since the story is a novel, no one can really pin-point where the Tortilla Flats are, although many theories have been presented. Incidentally, the original calaboose is preserved as a relic of the past and opened to the public.

Chapter Twelve

World Series Earthquake

PHYLLIS COATES

Known the world over for her portrayal of Lois Lane in the first year of television's *The Adventures of Superman* (1952), Phyllis is another actress who found her way to the Monterey Peninsula. It was at her elaborate Carmel townhouse in 1986 that Lois Laurel Hawes introduced her to me. Lois and Phyllis had both been enrolled at the Bliss Harden School for Acting in the late 1940s. A fellow classmate was a then-unknown Marilyn Monroe. I later learned that Phyllis had moved to Carmel from Big Sur following her divorce from Dr. Howard Press. Phyllis' son by a previous marriage, David Tokar, a young man in his twenties, lived with her. Phyllis did not had a happy life, but you wouldn't know it from her demeanor. Phyllis and I became good buddies and in later years confided in me. At the age of sixteen, Phyllis was the main breadwinner in her family. She said of her mother: "I think she was a prostitute," and her grandmother was a "falling-down drunk." They left the state of Texas (where she was born) and headed to Hollywood. It was at one of those drug store lunch counters that Ken Murray discovered her and put her in his long-running vaudeville show, *Ken Murray's Blackouts.*

In later years, after she had landed the role of Lois Lane, columnists would ask about her background. In typical Hollywood fashion, the story became that Phyllis was a high school cheerleader who went west to attend the University of California at Los Angeles.

Virginia O'Brien

Our Midnight Patrol Tent had annual banquets and 1988 was no exception. I hosted a small gathering at my house the night before the banquet. Our special guests, including Tommy Bond and his family, dropped in for the evening to relax a bit. Tony Hawes came every year and, this time he brought Virginia O'Brien and her husband. I liked Virginia immediately, she told me when she was growing up, her father was a captain in the Los Angeles PD.

Virginia brought with her a newly pressed LP record of her favorite recorded songs from her MGM days.[61] As the evening wore on, we coaxed her to play the record, and in the relaxed atmosphere, she was in the mood to entertain. In the movies she was known for keeping her face expressionless when she belted out songs, a quite unnatural act, but she was famous for it. On this night she had her producer (Alan Eichler) put her record on the turntable and we were regaled by hearing her recorded voice. It only took a few more seconds until Virginia began to sing along with herself, without the restrictions of keeping her face frozen. Virginia was seventy years old at the time, but that night it was as though she had never left the 1940s.

---

61. *Virginia O'Brien Salutes the Great MGM Musicals.*

The next day was our big banquet and it was held at the California First Theater[62] in Monterey. The theater was packed with our Sons of the Desert members and guests. I had the pleasure of introducing Tony Hawes, who emceed the event. I then took a seat in the audience, next to Virginia. I had previously video edited scenes of our celebrity guests and wanted to see and hear their reactions. Author Robert Strom, Virginia O'Brien's authorized biographer, recounted what happened next.

> Bill Cassara created a brief montage of film clips to introduce the guests of honor. Clips from Tommy Bond's career were screened first. Cassara was seated next to Virginia when the image of Kirk Alyn flashed on the screen. "Nooo!" Virginia moaned loudly. When the shocked audience turned to see what was wrong, she explained, "…that's my first husband." The scene that caused her amusing outcry was from one of the *Superman* films in the Columbia series. Standing next to Alyn was Tommy Bond as Clark Kent's protégé Jimmy Olsen.
>
> Film clips from Virginia's career included her rendition of "Rock-A-Bye-baby," *The Big Store*. Perceptive film historian Cassara remembered the conclusion of the "Sing While You Sell" production number when Virginia, the Marx Brothers, and others end up on the floor of the elevator. Knowing that Groucho says something to Virginia just as the elevator doors are closing, Cassara grabbed the opportunity. "What did Groucho say to you?" he asked Virginia. She thought for a moment before answering. "It was probably something dirty."

Years later, I overheard my aunt Rose talking with her friend while we were all at a picnic. They were reminiscing about Virginia O'Brien. At the end of their conversation, I matter-of-factly told them that Virginia O'Brien had once sung in my living room, after which I waited for their response. It was one of silence, of course. They glanced at each other in disbelief, and I couldn't blame them. I was not about to fill in any more details to try and convince them. My aunt called me "movie crazy," which was a big demotion from Robert Strom's description of me as a "perceptive film historian."

---

62. It really was California's first theater built by Jack Swain in 1848

Clayton Moore

It might have been only a short phone conversation, but I got to talk to Clayton Moore, better known as *The Lone Ranger* (cue the William Tell Overture). This occurred in 1988, when I was assigned to the Crime Prevention Unit. One of my duties was to represent the sheriff as part of the California Rural Crime Prevention Task Force.

My partner, Sam, and I were assigned to put on a fundraiser to benefit the task force. Sheriff Cook and I proposed the event to be held at the Sheriff's Posse Grounds outside of Salinas. This non-profit organization has been in existence since 1939 and supports the Western heritage in Salinas Valley. They have their own clubhouse and rodeo grounds. They also host an annual event, the Junior Rodeo.

The sheriff and I proposed the fundraiser to the members at large during one of their monthly meetings. It was a lot of work to put on a rodeo and they were skeptical of the whole thing. I convinced them by letting them know that they can have all the fun and my partner and I would administrate the event. With the sheriff's backing, the posse reluctantly agreed. They didn't know I had no experience whatsoever administrating a rodeo.

To make money, we would have to attract a crowd as registration fees for the participants alone wouldn't do it. I shared my dilemma with Lois Laurel Hawes, who had once been married to cowboy actor Rand Brooks. They had been invited guests to the big California Rodeo in Salinas back in the early 1960s, so she was quite aware of the Western culture in this area. She suggested I call Clayton Moore, a neighbor of hers in Tarzana.

Lois provided his home phone number and I promptly dialed the number. I wasn't sure what to expect, but Clayton Moore answered the phone in his unmistakable voice. I told him of the event and he was very polite; he told me his wife handled all the business and passed the receiver to her. I introduced myself as a deputy sheriff and friend of Lois Hawes and informed her of the non-profit state task force event. Mrs. Moore had a quick answer: "We'd love to come; we can drive up, so that's no problem. We just need a place to stay and $3,000." It actually sounded very reasonable and I let them know that I'd get back to them. I could have probably found a sponsor to put them up, but it was doubtful that we could raise $3,000. We didn't want to go in the hole for a fundraiser, so the idea of Clayton Moore attending was, regretfully, dropped. No one else knew of the omission of a special guest, so no one was disappointed. The event was a financial success and plenty of good will was shared, not to mention a rousing good time.

Turner and Hooch

Turner and Hooch (1989) is a fun film starring Tom Hanks as a small-town police detective who has a love/hate relationship with his slobbering dog, Hooch. The story takes place in a fictional, scenic waterfront town, which, in actuality, is Pacific Grove. There is a murder to be solved and Hooch is the only "witness." More of a comedy than a mystery, there are some heartwarming and dramatic moments, despite the presence of a rather clichéd murder suspect character.

Tony Hawes and I saw a part of this film being made. We were among the people lined up on the sidewalk, out of camera range. There was a full hour of takes of the dog being filmed in the passenger side of a car as it drove back and forth. It was just another movie shot on the Monterey Peninsula.

By all accounts, Tom Hanks was most gracious to the people of the community. If you ever have the chance to go inside the lobby of the Pacific Grove Police Department, there is a huge blown-up photograph of the PGPD officers with Tom Hanks. The photo has the gorgeous backdrop of Lovers Point by the Monterey Bay.

As a side-note to this production, Terry Melcher told me that originally, the location was supposed to be Carmel and the Cypress Inn. Ultimately, the residents voiced their displeasure over the likelihood of blocked streets and the interruption of other businesses. The city council denied the filming permit in their city. Their loss was Pacific Grove's gain.

WE Tip

WE Tip was a successful non-profit organization in Southern California, which provided anonymously donated rewards for tips leading to the arrest of crime suspects. Sheriff Cook administered monies from the asset-seizure funds and redistributed them to buy into the sponsored program. The sheriff paid for the rest of the cities in the county so they could all be on board. This resulted in Sheriff Cook being recognized as the "Law Enforcement Agency of the Year" at the annual convention. The sheriff could not attend, so I was assigned to go.

The venue for the convention was at a plush hotel in Rancho Cucamonga, in the Imperial Valley of Southern California. All of the police chiefs in the region were present, along with the organization's board of directors. At the ceremony, I accepted a plaque on the sheriff's behalf. The honorary president of that year was entertainer Steve Allen, who did a couple of his old bits at the piano. There were a few other celebrities that night, but I was most interested in meeting Chief Iron Eyes Cody.[63] He was seated at the head table in his full Western Indian attire of buckskin and other regalia. I introduced myself and mentioned that Henry Brandon was a friend of mine. The chief brightened considerably and gestured with his hand in an upward sweeping motion, then, clenching his right hand into a fist, he gave three pats over his heart. In halting "English," he said, "Henry Brandon . . . *my brother.*" I thought it was the ultimate Native American compliment from one actor to another. They had worked together in three films.

It wasn't until after Iron Eyes died that I learned he wasn't Native American at all. His real name was Espera "Oscar" DeCorti, and he was of Sicilian ancestry! He grew up in Louisiana, moved to California in the 1920s, changed his surname to Cody, and became an actor. In retrospect, he might have been the greatest actor who ever lived to pull that off.

World Series Earthquake (1989)

I had never been to a World Series game before. My team, the Giants, played the New York Yankees in 1962. I was determined to witness the my first game in San Francisco, so I bought advanced tickets. My wife and I arrived early to enjoy the atmosphere at Candlestick Park; we were seated in the first row of box seats in the upper deck in left field when the earthquake hit at 5:04 p.m. The quake felt like a train was roaring through, and then a sharp jolt thrust us forward. The concrete moved like an ocean wave. I held onto the rail of our box seats and was immediately concerned with the structure of the stadium. It was conceivable that chunks of the upper deck would fall on the spectators.

---

63. Chief Iron Eyes Cody (1907–1999) portrayed Native Americans in over 200 film and television roles. He is perhaps best known as the Indian with a tear running down his cheek from a 1960s ad campaign to beautify America.

Most of us were stunned at what happened and I was naively hoping this little ol' quake wouldn't interrupt the game; we Californians were used to this sort of thing, after all. After the shock had rolled through the stadium, we Giants' fans roared our approval. We actually thought that we had created the rockin' and rollin'. It wasn't until I overheard a San Francisco police officer's radio that the Bay Bridge collapsed that the magnitude of the earthquake dawned on me.

There was no panic in the ballpark and we had no idea how far reaching the impact was, but trying to get out of that ball yard and onto the freeway took hours. It was like a scene from *Panic in the year Zero*[64]as we inched along Highway 101. With the Bay Bridge down, the residents on the East Bay also had to go south to San Jose to return to their homes, further clogging traffic. It took us eleven hours to reach home; our poor dog was so relieved to see us. Though the power was out in the whole region, we were in pretty good shape.

In an emergency like this, it is an unwritten responsibility to call in for duty. I worked twelve-hour days, six days a week, until the need subsided. **Public Information Officer 1991–1992**

By this time, we had a new sheriff elected, following a bitter campaign. I had my hands full with my regular crime-prevention duties, but one day our captain came in and told me: "The sheriff wants someone to handle the media; here's your first one." He handed me a phone message to call back a newspaper reporter about a case we were investigating. No one asked me to come into their office to tell me their expectations; it was just another duty to add to the pile. I didn't ask for the job but it was one of those "Yes sir," kind of appointments. I was now referred to as the P.I.O., and learned by the seat of my pants.

To do the job properly, I had to be informed. When the media wanted details, I had to find a report on the matter and determine what facts I could give out. It is imperative that if a case is under investigation it must not be compromised, unless a release from our department is seeking help from the media/public. Under such circumstances, I would first let the primary investigator and his supervisor in on the details released.

This necessitated my presence at every detective morning roll-call meeting. All active cases were discussed, starting with murders, home-invasion robberies, drug raids, escaped inmates, etc. It was here that strategies were mapped out in strict confidentiality. I usually kept my

---

64. *Panic in the Year* Zero (1962) is an American-International film starring Ray Milland.

mouth shut at those meetings unless I was asked for advice pertaining to when it would be advantageous to share details with the media.

I handled all the on-camera interviews for the television stations, sometimes at the scene of the crime. I saw a lot of young reporters come and go; one was Dina Ruiz,[65] a field reporter for KSBW TV.

Though the title of P.I.O. meant I was involved in all the high-profile cases, I can only recall a few. Actually, I've been trying to forget. In 1991, our office had to deal with an especially notorious case. It was a home-invasion robbery that turned into a killing. Thankfully, justice was served on that one, but it still impacted everyone involved. The victim's widow thereafter dedicated herself to the non-profit Restorative Justice program. Later, she married the detective sergeant who was supervising the case.

Another one I remember occurred in 1992, when one of the San Francisco 49ers was arrested for allegedly raping a cocktail waitress in Monterey. The whole sordid story played out over time, but as soon as our investigation established probable cause for charges (forwarded to the D.A.), the 49ers' front office released the player. He was eventually acquitted, but many lives were ruined in the process.

When our office pressed charges against the player, I received an untold amount of inquiries from all over the country. What I remember most about the situation were the questions concerning our "targeting name athletes." In the same vein, other reporters accused us of "giving breaks" to professional athletes. The answer is, we did neither. Just like anything else, we respond and act as the situation and the law calls for.

Also in 1992, we had a mass shooting at a nursery in North County. In the early-morning hours, a gunman in camouflaged clothing and armed with a shotgun and pistol, started shooting. He killed at least four people, including the owner of the nursery and some laborers. The shooter then turned the gun on himself. Apparently, he had a vendetta against the family for injuries sustained in a car accident. He was subsequently awarded monies and that were settled in civil court. Despite this, he felt he deserved a bigger settlement from the insurance company once his funds ran out. The family, meanwhile, was absolutely blindsided by the attack.

This incident naturally turned into a big media event. As investigators were on scene, I set up a media staging area nearby and answered questions with a preliminary press conference. As other representatives from news outlets outside the area arrived, I repeated the details.

---

65. Dina Ruiz later became an anchorwoman for KSBW TV and, in 1997, married Clint Eastwood.

The hours ticked by as our detectives and physical-evidence team processed the crime scene. My bald head was getting baked out there in the fields, nevertheless I had to return to the office by 5 p.m. to give an update press conference. What sticks out in my memory is a slickly dressed television reporter from the Sacramento region who asked in a condescending tone, "Is this the *biggest* mass murder Monterey County has ever experienced?"

"No," I answered. Of course there were follow up questions to elaborate. When I look back on press conferences, I think of Willie Mays and how he answered tough questions from reporters. He was once asked how his latest circus-type catch compared to his other ones. Willie's answer was truthful and succinct, "I don't compare 'em, I just catch 'em." That remark was eminently quotable, just how the media likes it. And as a P.I.O., if you can wrap up a complicated presentation and Q&A with a short sound bite, it makes everyone's job easier. It's those short responses that actually make the television news that night, especially when they all get their respective one-on-one interviews after the press conference.

I knew what the journalists wanted and needed, I respected the profession. At the newsroom, they all work at their computers to write and update their stories. They have a police scanner chattering away in all local jurisdictions and their ears pick up when something juicy is going down. Often times they head out to the scene so they can get a story while it is developing. I remember I received a phone call from a reporter who had just heard a "shots fired" call on the air. Deputies were en route to the scene and did not know what they were getting into. The reporter asked me what the call was "all about"? I reminded him that our deputies weren't there yet and I certainly wouldn't know before their arrival.

Chapter Thirteen

A Murder Most Foul

IN 1990, A STRANGE and haunting unsolved murder case was re-opened, attracting international interest. On January 10, 1959, former silent movie actress Clara Eloise Mohr was sexually assaulted and brutally murdered in her home on Taylor Road in the Hatton Field's area outside of Carmel. A new lead presented itself by Markliann Johnston, who claimed to have witnessed the crime when she was just three years old. It seems the child wandered over to her neighbor's home at the time of the mutilated homicide. So traumatized was the little girl that her memories were repressed, only to resurface during "Imaging" procedures with her counselor. Witness statements garnered through hypnotism are considered unreliable and are therefore inadmissible. However, the new technique of imaging is not considered hypnotism. The challenge is to develop new leads in corroboration with evidence to lead to a logical conclusion beyond a reasonable doubt. In this case the physical evidence was long gone, only the original report existed. The cold case caused a media sensation when the witness filed a lawsuit against an eighty-two-year-old woman whom Johnston claimed was involved with the murder. Reporters scoured the original newspaper editions covering the crime, including one with the sensationalistic headline, "Deputies Hunting a Sex Sadist in Mutilation of Former Actress."[66]

The victim, who appeared in a few films as Clara Delmar, was born on December 30, 1898. During her career, she co-starred with Rudolph

---

66. *San Francisco Examiner*, January 12, 1959.

A Murder Most Foul (1959)

Valentino, Ronald Colman, Al Jolson, and Erich von Stroheim. She was married to cameraman Hal H. Mohr from 1926–1934. Von Stroheim, the famous Austrian-born director,[67] also served as best man at their wedding. She retired from Hollywood and was working as a nurse, assisting mentally ill patients. The newspapers of the day divulged that she was stabbed twelve times, from the neck to the waist. Investigating officer Captain Darrel Smith shared the fact that the sixty-one-year-old victim had been hit on the head with a heavy instrument while outside her home, and then carried to her bedroom.

The *San Francisco Examiner* ran a photo of the outside crime scene, with Deputy David Case and Investigator James Matney. They gathered evidence as best they could, but this preceded DNA testing and the standards for preservation of evidence in 1959 were lacking. The place was, however, fingerprinted on every conceivable surface.

The people living on the peninsula at the time of the incident went into a frenzy of panic. Could another Jack the Ripper be on the loose? There were no similar incidents that occurred in the Monterey area, but there was a theory that the suspect might be a soldier stationed at Ft. Ord. The Army base was highly transitory, so there was a concern to find the killer before he left the area.

During the original investigation in 1959, a soldier in the U. S. Army approached investigators to offer his own version of "help." He volunteered to be interviewed, under the condition that he be given a shot of sodium pentothal. This powerful hypnotic drug was used during

---

67. Eric von Stroheim is famous for his epic silent films, including *Foolish Wives* (1922), which was shot at Point Lobos on the Monterey Peninsula.

World War II as a "truth serum" when interrogating prisoners of war. It is very unreliable and the results are certainly not admissible in court. However, the soldier was seemingly sincere in his desire to help the case. All channels were cleared by the military to intravenously administer the serum by Army doctors. It turned out that the worldly soldier knew all about the experience of being under the influence of that drug and sought it out to get the incredible "high" state of relaxed consciousness. He knew nothing about the case.

The open case was given new life in 1990. The original reports pertaining to the case were still in existence and pored over by the lead investigator, John Hanson, one of the best cops on our department. He was supported by a crack crew of Monterey detectives and given unconditional support by his supervisor, Detective Sgt. Bill Freeman.

The investigation took over six months to complete while Hanson conducted interviews in Mexico, Arizona and in Colorado where the witness lived. In the meantime, the media bombarded the witness, who cooperated by giving interviews. Naturally, the story was a boon to the media, it had all the sensational dynamics:

1. A cold case murder.
2. The victim was once a Hollywood starlet.
3. A Carmel killing.
4. After 30-plus years, a woman comes forth with a suppressed memory regained only after psychological treatment.

The case advanced through 1991 with more twists and turns developed. The leads pointed to a suspect who lived out of state. An interview was held, during which the suspect lied about a number of details; she finally asked for an attorney to represent her.

As the department's public information officer, I too was impacted. Television newsmagazine shows such as *Inside edition, 48 hours,* and *Behind Closed Doors* kept their viewers percolating with anticipation. After an almost one-year investigation, Detective Hanson developed solid probable cause to forward the recommendation of homicide charges against the suspect, whose name had not yet been made public.

The case was reviewed by the Monterey County District Attorney's office and, in the many months that the case was "upstairs," the media was champing at the bit. A reporter for the syndicated tabloid news program *A Current Affair* came to our office unannounced and camped out with a crew, waiting for me. I explained "off camera" that the case was investigated and that it was now up to the D.A.'s office to make the decision for prosecution. And, no, I wouldn't be able to speculate or share facts of the case.

The reporter was not discouraged; he asked "Can you repeat what you just said, this time on the camera?"

"Is that *all*?" I asked.

"That's *all*," he assured me.

I invited the reporter and his crew into my office where, for about an hour, they busily set up the cameras and lighting equipment. They were escorted by me through the Salinas Investigations Bureau and were under the watchful gaze of the division's captain and lieutenant. I expected to simply repeat what I had told them, but right away, he asked me specific details on the case. I stopped him flat, saying sharply, "I *told* you outside that I couldn't talk about the case and I have tried to accommodate you." I was about ready to throw them out when the reporter apologized and said, "Well, it was worth a try; the home office wanted me to ask that question on camera." The next question stuck with our original agreement.

The D.A.'s office finally sent out a press release on October 12, 1991, announcing that they would not seek charges against the now-named mid-eighties suspect. The release, which was faxed out simultaneously to the many media outlets, did not include the lead investigator. One reporter decided to call Detective Hanson at his office in Monterey and surprised him when he was told of the decision not to file charges. The reporter asked him for a quote, and he got what he wanted: the detective spewed out all of his frustrations with the case not being prosecuted.

According to policy, only authorized personnel may be cleared to answer questions to the media unless special permission is granted by a supervisor. The D.A. was not pleased with the detective and was no doubt worried how the public would perceive the non-filing of the case. An internal investigations case was ordered by the sheriff for non-compliance of policy.

Once the case was dropped, my job as the public information officer became easy; I simply referred all media to the D.A.'s office. I felt bad for Detective Hanson, whom I considered a close friend, we had worked together on patrol. This was Detective Hanson's self-described "career case" that after retirement he wrote a *fictional* book about it.[68]

---

68. John Hanson, *Images of a Murder-A Cold Case Murder Mystery based on a True Story* (Baltimore: Publish America, 2009).

All the details were recounted, but the names were changed to protect all involved.

This case is but one of many that has challenged and frustrated members of law enforcement. If all the elements of a crime are prevalent, it is sent upstairs to the D.A.'s office. A determination is then made as to whether the case is prosecutable. In this instance, the suspect was a sick little old lady who, if arrested, would have to be extradited to Monterey from Arizona to stand trial. The D.A. must weigh the inherent costs as well as being duty-bound. Further, they must consider, in this case at least, if any jury would convict an elderly female, regardless of the heinousness of the crime? The official reason the D.A. did not prosecute was "lack of evidence." Given this, it is understandable—even inevitable—that investigators become disillusioned by the criminal justice system. This is why it is so important for those in law enforcement to have close family members, friends, and hobbies. Even during the hiring process, oral boards are partial to applicants with outside interests.

In February 1992, I received a piece of mail from "Empty Chair Productions." They wanted to produce a show with recreations of the murder and its aftereffects. They asked my help in supplying them with physical details about the deputies involved. I reproduced an old photograph of Deputy David's case and sent it to them along with patches from our department. They asked about the lead investigator and I told them, "He's a real handsome guy; just find someone who looks like Tom Selleck." The program was shot with the narration and action described by the witness. The reenacted piece was included on an episode of *People Illustrated*.

Chapter Fourteen

Phyllis Coates/Lois Lane

To most of the world, Phyllis Coates is best remembered for the role of Lois Lane in the first season of television's *The Adventures of Superman*. She and I became good buddies. Unfortunately, she was having serious problems with her son, David Tokar. He was a heroin addict and would steal items of value in order to buy drugs. Phyllis called me once when I was off-duty to ask for advice, I came right over. This time, David had stolen her car and she was afraid he would sell it. One option was to report her car stolen. Her son might be taken down with a felony car stop, with a shotgun pointed at him. That scenario might have seemed appropriate under the circumstances, but Phyllis simply could not authorize it.

Phyllis seemed to spend a lot of her time trying to keep David out of jail. She even sought out the judges presiding in cases involving her son to convince them that David needed to be sent to some rehabilitation program. At times, she was successful in these interventions. I gave her an unusual option: she could hire a private investigator. I recommended a P.I., a retired Sheriff's detective who was already familiar with David. Phyllis hired him, and the car was almost immediately found in Salinas' Chinatown. The P.I. jumped in the car and, using Phyllis' extra car key, turned over the engine and drove it straight to her driveway.

I was still at the house when David returned. With a sheepish grin, he said, "Sorry, Mom."

Phyllis and I at the Cinecon

Phyllis could not be appeased: "Your mother is *drugs*," she said sharply.

David was no longer welcome in her home. He died in 2006, at age fifty of an overdose.

In happier times, I invited Phyllis and her close friend, actor Bart Williams, to my house for dinner. For entertainment afterwards, I showed my guests an episode of *The Abbott and Costello Show*. This particular one featured Phyllis as a gangster's moll, doing the old "switch the drinking glass with the poison" routine with Lou Costello.

Phyllis told us of the time she met up with Abbott and Costello in Las Vegas. They were there to perform, but this particular evening they were at the craps table, drunk and betting heavily. There was quite a crowd around them as they bet up to $22,000. They were overjoyed to see Phyllis, which prompted both of them to, as Phyllis described it, "Pinch my boobs." She expressed her disapproval at their throwing away so much of their hard-earned money, to which Bud Abbott replied: "Don't worry, it's not our money; it's the house's money. We're entertaining the crowd." Phyllis just shook her head in retelling the story. She said, "What I could have done with that money..."

For the main feature, I showed my guests a laserdisc version of *Superman and the Mole Men*, co-starring Phyllis and George Reeves. Although it was not intended to be funny, we laughed continuously through the whole movie, especially Phyllis. She said she had never seen it before. Near the end of the film, both Lois Lane and Superman look up at the sky, where some poignant message had been superimposed. Phyllis commented, "So *that's* what we were supposed to be seeing."

When the book *Hollywood Kryptonite* came out in 1996, I read it and then loaned it to Phyllis. She hadn't been in touch with the show's former cast members for some time. The book prompted her to seek out Jack Larson,[69] who had already read it. He dismissed it as, "Hollywood Kraptonite" for its many falsehoods and sensationalistic details.

Phyllis and I had the opportunity to compare notes inspired by reading the book. She was bewildered by much of what was written.

I asked her a direct question: What do you think happened to George Reeves?

She answered: "I always thought he was murdered."

I didn't try and pin her down, because I didn't wish to pry. Opportunities eventually presented themselves over time that allowed her to elaborate on some things. She always said that George had "a beautiful face," gesturing with her right hand as if she were stroking his cheek. Even so, I received no other indication that she had been romantically involved with her handsome co-star. Phyllis said that Toni Mannix (the wife of Eddie Mannix, a former executive with MGM) always showed up during lunch, carrying a paper bag containing a liquor bottle for George. Phyllis said that Toni liked her and often treated her to lunch and/or took her clothes shopping. She respected Toni and George's relationship, illicit though it may have been. Phyllis said she got the role of Lois Lane because she had worked for the producers before, and "they knew what I could do." During that time in her life (1951), she was on her second marriage, and had a child with physical disabilities. George, Phyllis said, always insisted that she join him for a drink after the day's work. This became a routine. Phyllis mentioned that she was starting to gain weight and realized the potential harm that would do her career. The cast had no idea of the show's success. As she told me, "No one knew what we were doing would even be looked at, much less cared about fifty [60] years

---

69. Jack Larson (1928–2015) played the part of Jimmy Olsen on *The Adventures of Superman*.

later." When the time came, Phyllis had no problem walking away from the show. While appearing as a regular on *Superman*, Phyllis was in many other television shows and science fiction films. She was even in one film for which she was never paid. Phyllis was trusting to a fault.

There was a time where I mentioned the FBI class I had taken in which the instructor specifically referred to George Reeves' death as a "classic suicide." I had seen the black and white autopsy photos, which were used in the class as visual aids. I respected Phyllis' personal feelings in that I did not go into graphic detail about them. I do remember that she didn't flinch when I told her of the confirmed suicide.

I don't think we talked more about the delicate subject in the succeeding years. I later became aware of an interview that Phyllis gave to a sci-fi magazine. The writer directly asked her what she thought about the George Reeves case. I can't remember the direct quote, but Phyllis said something along these lines: "A good friend of mine, Bill Cassara, who is in law enforcement out in Monterey, told me George committed suicide. He saw the pictures."

On one occasion, a photographer for *People* magazine went to Phyllis' home to take some photos. They were out all day shooting photos of her walking the beach, with her dog, etc. When the shoot was done, the photographer asked for a personal favor. He had brought with him a Superman shirt and asked her to put it on, "as a favore." A picture was snapped and, of course, *that* was the one that made the magazine. It looked as though she was taking off her shirt to reveal the Superman logo. The image wasn't particularly flattering, but it showed what a good sport she was.

Shortly after the release of my first book, *Edgar Kennedy: Master of the Slow Burn*, I received a sparkling letter of appreciation from Bart Williams. He was enthralled with the book and said he had talked to Phyllis about it. (I had sent both of them complimentary copies upon the book's release).

Bart said that Phyllis was looking for someone to help her put a book together about her life. He said they both agreed it should be me, for several reasons. I took the letter as a supreme compliment, but I was hesitant to accept. Phyllis had since moved to Sonoma County to be near her third child (now grown and a teacher at a local school). She didn't do emails and talking on the phone would be difficult for long durations as we both suffered from hearing loss.

Nevertheless, I started trying to build up Phyllis' family background for her genealogy. Some of the spellings were very unusual, and I always had to call Bart to confirm. I still couldn't match up with the census with much of what I was told.

Bart once told me in hushed tones, "I think Phyllis went with Toni Mannix to the Reeves' house the day after. I think they discovered the bloody sheets." That was a new one on me, but it was very plausible. Phyllis confirmed that Toni called her to come over to the house, "But there was no way *I* was going to. I think she got Jack Larson to come."

The subject of a biography began to be a strain on all three of us. I valued their friendship and I told Bart (Phyllis' confidant for many years) that *he* was better suited than I to write the book. I was afraid that if I wrote the Phyllis Coates story, it would evolve into the George Reeves' story. It would have been a distraction, but I couldn't ignore what I knew about the case. It is a pity in a way; I would have built her up as "television's first female role model," which is what she was. The Lois Lane character, as portrayed by Phyllis, was a consummate professional, a feminine presence but still willing to compete with male reporters to get "the story." She played the part realistically and with restraint. As she once told me, "They never would let George and me look like we were 'playing around.'" She also remembered that the coat she wore on the show was like a "horse's collar." She explained, "We all wore the same clothes so it would match in editing. The shows were not shot chronologically. As Phyllis said, "We'd shoot all the indoor scenes for all the scripts for the season. No one knew what was going on [regarding the plot].

Phyllis was always polite and down to earth. She never thought of herself in an exalted way, but fans admired her. One afternoon at San Francisco's KGO radio station, she was a special guest and the host not only engaged her in conversation but encouraged listeners to call in. A lot of those calls came from females, professional ladies who would give Phyllis credit for inspiring their own careers. The callers were fawning over her, but Phyllis kept her cool, speaking deliberately in that distinctive voice of hers.

A couple of years ago there was some sort of sci-fi convention held in New York City. The guy who put it together had convinced Phyllis to come; offers of travel fare and an appearance fee were discussed and agreed upon. Phyllis made the trip with a friend and was as usual, a good sport. She posed with the organizer, who just happened to be wearing a Superman costume. "Lois Lane" was next to him, arm-in-arm.

I met up with Phyllis in Sacramento for the international Sons of the Desert convention in 2010. She was not an announced guest, so no one knew she was coming, but Bart Williams had clued me in. They came up for one special World War II–themed evening that featured live "big-band" era music. Everyone was dressed in period clothing and wore forties hairstyles. Bart and Phyllis arrived and stopped the show: Bart was dressed as Franklin D. Roosevelt, and Phyllis was Eleanor. I got close to her and smiled, for she was speaking in the low tones associated with the beloved first lady. I hadn't heard that voice in a long time, but Phyllis nailed it.

The last time I saw Phyllis was on September 2, 2012, during the Cinecon[70] in Hollywood. Phyllis and I had a great reunion. She was a featured guest of the festival and, on one of the afternoons at the Egyptian Theatre, she was the subject of a question-and-answer session. As she climbed upon a stool to face the audience, she confessed that she had vertigo, and then asked, "Have you ever heard of such a thing?" The audience was made up of film buffs from around the world and, naturally, they were all familiar with the term, associating it with the 1958 Alfred Hitchcock film of the same title.

Sitting alongside Phyllis was Richard Bare,[71] the director of the Joe McDoakes comedy shorts that co-starred many during the series run. The surprise for most of the audience was that Phyllis and Richard had once been a married couple, in 1948.

Phyllis was asked, "How long were you guys married?"

The answer: "About six months." Her deadpan delivery induced laughter from the crowd. It was a wonderful moment.

70. Cinecon (cinema convention), a festival of classic films, is held annually on Labor Day weekend in Hollywood.

71. Richard Bare was a well-known television director for every episode of the popular Green Acres, Twilight Zone episodes, and many feature films.

Chapter Fifteen

Doris Day and Terry Melcher

I **ALWAYS WANTED TO BE** a dad and I was grateful to my wife for having brought two beautiful children into the world: Diana (1991) and Douglas (1993). I was a doting father and spent all my free time with them going to kid parties, the movies, and played T-ball. I even took the family to Australia for a once-in-a-lifetime vacation. My children are my life's blood.

Back at the office, my public information duties had expanded to include my participation in Crime Stoppers, a national non-profit organization with the motto, "Crime Doesn't Pay–Solving Does." Affiliated chapters in designated communities are run by a volunteer board of directors, who provide law-enforcement agencies with confidential information on crimes or suspects without identifying the tipster. Informants were identified by number only and, if the case was solved, the caller would be eligible for a reward. With a new sheriff, the We-Tip organization was replaced by Crime Stoppers, a different but similar goaled non-profit agency.

The Monterey County chapter was formulated and operational in 1992; with our first president, Gloria Dial. Mrs. Dial was passionate about this organization; she was motivated for all the right reasons, including a highly personal event in her life. Her sister had been murdered some time before, and the perpetrator was never brought up on charges. Since Gloria never saw justice prevail, she sought the next best thing: to start a Crime Stoppers chapter where she lived.

The sheriff appointed me to be the law-enforcement liaison between the other departments and the board of directors. This was a new concept

With my children, Diana, Doug and Oliver

in Monterey County. Through the efforts of our records personnel, we devised a system to set up an unaffiliated phone number to be answered at any time. The information was gathered, the caller was given a classified number, then the details were forwarded to me to relay to the board.

One of my first responsibilities was to tie in the other city police agencies in Monterey County. I was put on the agenda for the monthly chief's meeting to explain how this could help with hot leads or even revive cold cases. One of the chiefs said, "You mean all we have to do is provide cases for you to put out to the public? All in favor?"

My second task was to get the local newspapers involved. They were most receptive in offering a "Crime Stoppers' Crime of the Week," with details released from the respective agencies and vetted through our board of directors.

We were very fortunate to secure a big sponsor: local television station KCBA, the managers of which agreed to produce a featured crime on a weekly basis. This was most welcome. The board selected each installment based on the details given by the respective agency, and the on-camera person would be a representative of the jurisdiction in which the crime originally took place.

The first selected case to profile was the unsolved murder of Linda Perkins. That homicide was committed outside of Carmel in the county area in 1989. The victim was walking to her car when she was struck with a baseball bat from behind. There was outrage in the community and a suspect was found, but a prosecutable case could not be made. The cold case was brought to light in the form of a reenactment at the scene of the crime; it featured the victim's sister, who gladly participated.

The Perkins case was aired in 1993 and started a meaningful relationship between the public, the media, and law enforcement in Monterey County. The board members helped with the production, selection of the cases, allotment for tipsters, and—very importantly—fund raising.

Calamity Jane: **An Evening with Doris Day** (April 17, 1993)

This was a non-profit event to raise money for Crime Stoppers of Monterey County and for the Sheriff's advisory board. It was held at Carmel's Golden Bough Cinema, where Doris Day's Technicolor musical *Calamity Jane* was shown. The 1953 film, a box-office smash, featured Doris as the storied frontier woman who was associated with Wild Bill Hickok and, later, Buffalo Bill Cody.

The idea came about at one of our Crime Stoppers meetings to raise funds for the local chapter. It should be noted that seemingly *every* non-profit sought out Doris for their fundraising ideas, she was firmly retired by this time. As the law-enforcement liaison, I volunteered to write a letter to Doris' son, Terry Melcher. I hadn't met Terry at this point of time, although I regularly saw him participate as a volunteer in the Sheriff's Rescue Team. He had a strong but silent interest in helping others and participated in this volunteer assignment when needed. Terry was one of the founding members of the Sheriff's Advisory Council, a non-profit group of citizens who raise money to support the operations of the sheriff's office.

Terry and Doris talked over the proposal for the film event and agreed conditionally if the proceeds were split between the two non-profits. Doris had one more provision; that she could honor her friend and owner of the Quail Lodge, Ed Habor on stage. All parties were in agreement; it was a GO!

Doris had never done a public event like this before on the peninsula, it was the opportunity that the politicians had been hoping for. Since it was going to take place in the city of Carmel, the mayor set in order a resolution to salute her on the day with a resolution making the date, "Calamity Jane Day."

There was no staff to assign the administration duties of the program, but fortunately one of our records clerks, (Jackie Gash) volunteered to help out during her lunch break. Between Jackie and I, we returned the numerous phone calls and with the Crime Stoppers committee, the monies from the fees were processed.

I wrote a press release on our department stationery to announce the event, and Doris Day gladly signed the memo. I first ran it by Doris' agent, who made sure it was an appropriate event for her client. This was a major fundraiser and a once-in-a-lifetime event; we charged $50 per person for admittance to the screening, and the same amount for an after party event at Doris' Cypress Inn. It was a bargain at the price.

In preparation for the event, I was interviewed by the great Robert Osborne for his column in *The Hollywood Reporter*. In attendance were locals, of course, but people who read about the event came from around the country to attend. The audience was absolutely giddy with anticipation.

Doris arrived dressed in a buckskin outfit, similar to her film character. There was a podium set up on the stage and all the politicians took the opportunity to issue proclamations in her honor, the first such opportunity they had to do so. Doris took the stage and warmly welcomed everyone and talked a bit about the making of the film. Clint Eastwood was in the audience and she called him up to speak. He first gave a shout-out to Crime Stoppers, saying that he supported the organization, and then he really loosened up, reminiscing about taking dance lessons at Warner Bros. "One day they brought in Doris Day and I got to dance with her," he recalled. "I've been in love with Doris Day for many years, just as you have." Clint fondly recalled seeing *Calamity Jane* when it was first released and told the crowd, "The stagecoach scenes are great. It's a fun movie."

After all the introductions, Clint took a seat next to Doris and watched the film in its entirety. In between, they were holding hands and sharing popcorn. It was a "Kodak moment," but, fortunately, everyone respected their privacy. Some people approached me later to let me know it had been a magical evening.

Instrumental in its success was Kit Parker, who supplied a 35mm print of *Calamity Jane*. It was a real throwback evening what one might experience in 1953. Preceding the feature was a cartoon and a newsreel and an Easter Seals pitch by Walter Brennan. The audience loved the feature. They roared their approval at the action and applauded vigorously after every number. Within walking distance of the theater was the Cypress Inn, Doris' unique hotel and bar that caters to tourists and their pets. This night it was filled with many donors who had attended the screening. Wine, food, and music were provided by Terry Melcher (a co-owner), it was all first class. At one point, Terry turned to me and said, "Bill, I'd like you to meet Barry Gordy." The legendary founder of Motown Records and I shook hands. Terry told me that Barry had long wanted to meet Doris, but that no such opportunity had arisen prior to this special night. Doris was the perfect hostess, working the room with her warm grace. Not to be missed was Clint Eastwood, who also engaged in spirited conversations. I dearly wanted Clint to meet my friend Tony Hawes, so I introduced them to each other. Tony said in his very proper British accent, "I happen to be married to the daughter of Stan Laurel." Clint responded in his characteristic deadpan, "Oh, *that*. I don't know where people get that idea." Then he turned slightly away and scratched his head in manner of Stan Laurel. Tony and I looked at each other in astonishment, then he hurriedly went upstairs to his room to call Lois.

Doris Day and her Best Friends (October 9, 1993)

To benefit Doris Day's pet foundation, the Boys and Girls Clubs of America, the Family and Children's Services, and the Monterey Peninsula Outreach, Doris had her team put together a fundraiser never duplicated in Carmel Valley. It was heavily sponsored by corporations and the local Monterey County Bank and KSBW-TV.

The all day and evening event drew guest celebrities; Jane Seymour, Suzanne Somers, Loni Anderson, Vicki Lawrence, Clint Eastwood, and even Oakland A's baseball manager Tony LaRusso (a fellow animal lover). Doris' publicity agent, Linda Dozoretz was responsible for the coordination of all the media shows and sponsors, attracting vast media attention. However, Doris publicly thanked her daughter-in-law, Jacqueline "for doing it all."

Terry Melcher was always a bit nervous in crowds and he went through the proper channels to hire seven deputies and a sergeant to provide security for the events. As he told us, "I want you guys to be in every shot taken of Doris." A couple of TV guys tried to shoo us away, but we stood our ground. Clint Eastwood was there as scheduled, walking around and mingling in that unassuming way of his.

Something was cooking earlier in the day when a crew from local TV KSBW came in to set up. One of the newscasters was walking in and I recognized her right away: Dina Ruiz. She was being *coached* by her female boss (the news director for the station). The ladies walked in separate from the news crew. I knew Dina from my earlier public information duties and I'm embarrassed to reveal that when she saw me, she gave me a big hug, uniform or not. She was exuberant that day. I wasn't keeping track of her, but shortly after this event, Dina and Clint Eastwood started dating and eventually married.

The events all took place at the Golf Club at Quail Lodge in mid-Carmel Valley. Starting at 8:00 a.m., there was a celebrity golf scramble, a children's tennis tournament, a croquet match, celebrity tennis, a silent auction, an awards ceremony, and a catered lunch, topped off with champagne and strawberries.

At that time, Vicki Lawrence[72] was the hostess of a syndicated television talk show called *Vicki*. Because of this, she brought her entire production crew to shoot footage of she and Doris competing in croquet.

Our "singing deputy," Pat Duvall, was in uniform and working this event. He and Doris had known each other personally for many years. During Doris' sit down interview with Vickie, Pat was out of camera range but, just as if on cue for a Hollywood musical, started singing a robust version of Doris' theme song, "Que Sera Sera." The whole crowd joined in. Vicki was startled, but Doris just smiled at Pat lovingly, the same type of look she might have given Rock Hudson in *Pillow Talk*. The cameras caught up to Pat and he took it from there. Doris clapped the loudest and thanked him afterward. Only professionals do that. Pat was so gifted and so naturally charming, he was a great role model and true asset to our department.

Vicki Lawrence was not the only one to interview Doris on a makeshift set on the lawn. Film critic and author Leonard Maltin had brought a camera crew from *Entertainment Tonight* and interviewed

---

72. Vicki Lawrence is best known for her comic support on the *Carol Burnett Show*; she later starred in her own syndicated series, *Mama's Family*.

Doris and Clint as well. This was my first meeting with Mr. Maltin, we later talked privately about our shared friend, Kit Parker. I would meet up with him again a number of years later.

The star-studded event broke up in the afternoon, only to return to a big top–style tent for a dinner dance. Everyone was in fashionable evening wear; one local woman was even wearing a fur coat. This was a faux pas: one simply does not wear a fur coat to animal lover Doris Day's event.

Les Brown and his Band of Renown, the big band that introduced Doris Day as a singer in the 1940s, performed all the music for which they were famous. We were all hoping that Doris would get up on stage to sing, but she begged off, citing that her voice was "hoarse."

Paul Anka had been scheduled to perform for the occasion, but he had to bow out due to a family emergency. Deputy Duval offered to pinch-hit, but the bandleader told him, "I don't work with non-professionals." Doris came to Pat's defense, "He *is* a professional, and he's a wonderful singer." With Doris' endorsement, Pat discussed what song(s) he would sing, and in which key he would sing them. Without so much as a rehearsal, uniformed Deputy Duval belted out some of Doris' best-known songs. Afterwards, Les Brown gave his approval: "You've got a great set of pipes, son. You can sing with me *any time.*"

There was a tuxedo-clad pianist at the affair providing lovely background music. He was an accomplished musician with Les' band. Sensing disappointment that Doris wasn't going to sing, Susanne Somers quietly approached the pianist and suggested that she could sing a few songs. This was welcome news and, to rehearse, she sat on the piano bench. The pianist was light on the keys while Susanne purred the lyrics into his ear. When it was time, she took the microphone and sang about four torch songs with perfection. Susanne was gorgeous in her sequin blue gown and her performance was a highlight of the evening.

Right before the Band of Renown was to play their last set, Les glanced at we deputies and asked for requests. Our sergeant innocently asked, "How about 'String of Pearls?'"

Les' expression changed noticeably: "Oh, a *Glenn Miller* fan, huh?"

As the evening was winding down, people were starting to leave. It was way past our on-duty time, but Terry insisted we stay as long as people were still there. He told us, "Late in the event, that's when things might happen."

The evening was now concluded and, as the lights were lowered, Les Brown sought out Doris, away from everyone. Almost everyone, that is—I was keeping a close eye on her. It's sometimes nice to be a deputy: no one notices you (the proverbial "fly on the wall"), and we see things. Les and Doris went back many years with their hit single, "Sentimental Journey," it was a song that defined a generation. They enjoyed a few moments of closeness away from the crowd. They embraced and passionately kissed each other like longtime lovers (or perhaps a goodbye to each other?)

A lot of nice things were happening in 1994. Our Midnight Patrol Tent celebrated its tenth anniversary at the Monterey Elks Club, and their stage came in handy. We hosted a big banquet for all of our members and celebrity guests, including Tony and Lois Hawes, Tommy "Butch" Bond, Pineapple Jackson,[73] and Buster Keaton's widow, Eleanor Keaton. In honor of her late husband, we showed Buster's hilarious 1921 short *Cops*, with live piano accompaniment by Gary Sage. A surprise guest was Jackie Lyn Dufton. She had been "Eddie's Baby" in Laurel & Hardy's *Pack Up Your Troubles* (1932) and later was a member of Our Gang. She had dropped out of show business at an early age and lived as a civilian lifestyle until the Sons of the Desert and Tony Hawes located her. Lois brought home movies her father had shot of she and Jackie in the early thirties. We had the good fortune of reuniting these lovely ladies, much to the delight of our members.

The year 1994 was also significant in that the California State Sheriffs Association picked Monterey to host their 100th anniversary as an organization. Each of the sheriffs (and their wives), representing the state's fifty-eight counties, was present for a week's worth of training, ceremonies, and celebration at a nice resort. It was a chance to show off the best of what Monterey County had to offer in food bounty and wine. Clint Eastwood put in an appearance, which greatly pleased the law-enforcement contingent.

The sheriff's wife oversaw a committee for a wonderful event known: "A Luncheon with Doris Day." The sheriff asked Terry Melcher if he could bring his mom to the function, but Terry was reluctant to do so because he simply hated such public events. He then suggested, "How about if Bill Cassara escorts her? She's comfortable with him." The next thing I knew, dispatch raised me on the air while I was on patrol. The communication was "Call A-1."[74] I recall wondering what kind of emergency this was. I had never heard such a crisp and succinct instruction to call the sheriff

73. Pineapple Jackson, Tommy Bond, and Jackie Lyn all appeared in "Our Gang" comedies

74. A-1 is a radio command for administration #1, the sheriff.

like that and I couldn't help but think I was in trouble. So did everyone else who heard the radio that day.

I immediately called in and was transferred to the sheriff, who said: "Bill, I have a job for you. How would you like to escort Doris Day to the sheriff's wife's luncheon?" There was no hesitation on my part; I called Terry Melcher and set it up.

Came the day and Doris was waiting for me at her home. She was a bit subdued. (As Terry told me later; "It's hard to be Doris Day.") I was in a coat and tie and drove Doris to the Barnyard Shopping Center in my marked patrol car. Before entering the restaurant, we worked out a signal for when she had enough, then I was to impose myself and whisk her away.

We purposefully arrived a bit late and everyone was very excited to see Doris in person. I escorted her in and there was a VIP table already set up. I got her to her chair and started to sit next to her but I was interrupted by the chairperson, who said, "No, [so and so] is supposed to sit on her left," and the chairwoman had the seat to her right.

"But I'm supposed to sit next to Doris—I'm her escort."

"Oh, you can sit outside and keep an eye out," the chairperson said brusquely. I glanced at Doris and she was clearly disturbed about this. She looked up at me as though to say, "So what are you going to do about it?" Doris had anticipated my being a buffer so she wouldn't be overwhelmed. I could have been assertive and insisted on the original arrangement, but I was representing the sheriff and his wife and I didn't want to make a scene.

The restaurant featured a buffet, but I was not going to let Doris carry her own plate up there and become surrounded. I went with her so she could pick out what she wanted and brought a plate back to her. I did take a seat at an outside table to watch over her as I picked at my food.

Doris—the consummate professional—turned on the charm, to the delight of everyone; this was *Doris Day* after all! There came a point when she looked out at me and gave me a nod. That was my signal. I entered the restaurant and announced that Doris had to leave for another engagement. As I began to help her from her chair, a wave of wives descended on us; some had books for her to autograph, others had pictures, and some even had paper napkins to thrust at her. Hands and arms lunged at her like one gigantic octopus. Doris complied as best she could, hurriedly signing as she walked backwards. I got her out of there as gracefully as I could. Even so, I imagine that some of the wives would complain to their husbands about the "rude deputy" who prevented them from getting closer to Doris. It was better that *I* be the bad guy than Doris. That was my responsibility.

On the short ride back to her home, Doris and I didn't speak at all. I was hoping she wasn't mad at me for being forced to sit outside. Once we arrived, I opened the car door for her and she kissed me lightly on the cheek. Later on, I told Terry Melcher the whole story. He said, "That's O.K., it always happens." Terry was greatly pleased that I had escorted his mom; he really tried to shelter her from crowds. Doris was perfectly happy to be retired and didn't need to be in the public eye—but she made an occasional exception as a sign of gratitude to her many loyal fans.

Another such occasion was a luncheon for her official fan club. Once again, I had been requested to be her escort to the event, which was held at a Holiday Inn outside of Carmel. Doris knew just how to turn on the charm and charisma as I escorted her through the doors to greet the throng. She made a lot of people very happy that day. Fans have never forgotten Doris; she had a P.O. box at Carmel Rancho Blvd., and at a mailbox outside her home. It was always filled with cards and well-wishes, especially on her birthday.

Later that summer, I invited Terry and Doris to receive the "Laughing Gravy Award" from our Midnight Patrol tent. The award seemed especially appropriate for Doris as Laughing Gravy was the name of the little dog Stan and Ollie were trying to protect from a nasty landlord in a funny and touching two-reeler of 1930. Doris professed to be thrilled at the honor, remembering how audiences laughed at Laurel & Hardy when she was growing up in Cincinnati.

The arranged meeting was held at the Cypress Inn during August of 1994. It was a family affair, and Terry brought along his son, Ryan. The hotel was filled with guests and their animals, but they had no idea that Doris was going to appear. When she first came through the entrance doors, she bolted to a guest's oversized poodle and hugged it. She said, "What a *beautiful* dog!" and asked his name. The guests were from Germany and they were absolutely stunned to see this living legend in person.

The following is Doris' own account of the event as it appeared her pet foundation newsletter of August 1994:

Earlier this year I was thrilled to be presented with the Laughing Gravy Award—and I know that requires an explanation. Admirers of Laurel & Hardy have formed an appreciation society called "Sons of the Desert." Each chapter (or tent) is named after a L&H film. Ten years ago our very own Monterey County deputy sheriff, Bill Cassara founded the Carmel chapter, appropriately called the Midnight Patrol Tent. This chapter was based on the film of the same name where the boys are portrayed as cops working the midnight shift.

Since Laurel & Hardy were animal lovers, it occurred to the Midnight Patrol Tent to honor the Doris Day Pet Foundation by presenting me with an award based on one of their films. "Laughing Gravy" was a little dog they rescued from the snow when the landlord banished it. A still from that film was beautifully framed and matted and presented with a lovely inscription.

So here I am with the Midnight Patrol Tent. Anne Cassara, Duon Zeroun, Gloria Hughes, Jim Maley, Dave Cotter, Bill Cassara, me, and Bob Zeroun. I wish you could see the award, it's really lovely.

It was during that memorable afternoon that I asked Doris about Edgar Kennedy, the character actor whose life and career I was then researching. Doris had worked with Edgar in her second feature for Warner Bros., *My Dream is Yours* (1949). Recalling the man who had played her uncle in that film, she became animated and said, "Edgar Kennedy?" She then impersonated his signature "slow burn" mannerism, bringing her hand down over her face and protruding lip.

In later years I would interview her again about Edgar for my eventual book on the man. I was invited for lunch at her home, with Terry in attendance. I showed her a photo of she and Edgar from *My Dream is Yours*. "Where did you find that?" she asked with surprise.

I inquired what she remembered about him, and she replied, "It was only my second movie and about his fifth hundredth. He was kind, sweet, and everything dear. *Everyone* in the business knew he was a *genius*."

When I related this to Edgar's daughter, Colleen Deach, she told me that her dad was smitten with Doris and knew that she'd be a big star. He couldn't stop talking about her. Edgar died in 1948, but Doris never forgot him.

There was a day when I was called at home frantically by Terry Melcher; they had received a piece of mail addressed to "Doris Day—Jew of Carmel." How that hate mail was delivered without a proper address, I couldn't even guess. They were both so paranoid over long-ago threats from Charles Manson, that both Terry and Doris were really shaken up. The irony was, Doris was not Jewish; her real surname was Von Kappelhoff, and she is of Protestant German descent.

Inside the letter was a scribbled message maligning the Doris Day animal foundation. The words were menacing, with the implication that she should be put in a gas chamber "like the rest of the Jews." I wrote a report and submitted the letter into evidence. The individual who had written it had actually included his name and return address on the envelope. Its postmark was that of a small rural town in a northern California county. I followed up with a teletype communication to the agency and a phone call to the respective sheriff's office. They knew the suspect; he was a regular "poison pen" type. My contact also informed me that the guy was a wheelchair-bound paraplegic. I knew that Doris did not wish to press charges, but the deputy assured me they were going to the guy's house and that they would make sure that it "would never happen again." They planned to put the fear of God into him.

Doris and Terry were relieved somewhat that the guy was physically harmless, but old concerns crept up. Just when things died out about the incident, I received a phone message at work to call a reporter from *The National Enquirer*. Uh-oh—how did *they* know about this? I called the reporter and he wanted details, which I naturally would not provide.

He then asked, "Is it true that the sheriff's department surrounded her house?"

"No," I said. "She lives on a bluff overlooking the valley."

I thought I had effectively discouraged the reporter, but sure enough, there was a front-page story in the *Enquirer* about it. Fortunately, they didn't give many details other than to state that there had been some sort of "bomb threat at her home."

Sometime after this, Terry Melcher called again, this time to inform me that Doris had been issued a traffic citation from a California Highway patrolman for driving without a seat belt. In addition, her driver's license had expired. There was much anxiety from Doris concerning this, but I communicated with a supervisor at the local DMV and explained the situation: Doris was nervous at the prospect of taking a written examination in a group setting. I was assured they had a private room for such things. The day of the appointment came. Doris, always prepared, had been studying the practice booklet tests like a script. We went in the back door and met the supervisor, who had been waiting for us. I was crossing my fingers in the hopes that she would pass. When she finally emerged, she was smiling—she had aced the test! While driving her back home, I casually remarked that *my* license was due to expire later in the year and that I should have taken the opportunity to also test. She handed me her test scores and asked, "Do you want to study mine?" Chuckling, I politely declined. Now, looking back, that test, with Doris' signature on it, would have made an interesting souvenir. I really didn't need to study a test. For Doris and Terry, death threats and negative publicity were the stuff of nightmares. The story has been told many times that it was Terry Melcher whom Charles Manson had originally targeted for his slayings in Los Angles in 1969. The fear had never left him; it was Terry, after all, who had to testify in court against Manson.

For some reason, Terry thought it was important that I knew his side of the story. He told me he had first heard about Manson from one of the [unnamed] "Beach Boys" band members; they picked up one of his female followers while hitchhiking and drove them to the camp. The next thing he knew, he was roped into going to see them about their music (Manson fancied himself a songwriter/musician). Terry said, "I knew as soon as I got there that I wanted to leave, it was filthy." Terry tried to appease them by listening to Manson's song, which Terry added, "was horrible." Nevertheless, he bucked up and pretended interest. As the final notes were played on Manson's guitar, awkwardness set in. According to Terry, "I told them they had good harmony and we would have to think about a record deal." When the news broke of the murders at Terry's home, LAPD sought him out. The detectives asked Terry if he had anything "going on" with Manson's girlfriends. Terry was indignant: "Those Manson dogs? *Here* are my girlfriends." At this point Terry actually acted out his movements, Terry whipped out his wallet telling me that he showed the officers snapshots of the beautiful women with whom he associated, starting with Candice Bergen. Terry liked it when someone in uniform came by to check on him, something Deputy Pat Duval and I did on occasion. Terry had a music studio built in his beautiful home overlooking the Carmel Valley, I had reason to drop in that day and Terry said, "I'm glad you're here; I'd like you to see this." He led me upstairs to his studio, where an entire crew was preparing to record a young male singer. Terry had everyone there on salary and he was the producer of the soon-to-be released record album. Beach Boy Brian Wilson was the engineer. After introductions, I watched the young singer attempt a take. It was a wonderful moment, especially because Terry was supplying the vocal backup.

At the conclusion of the song, Terry addressed the young man, emphasizing his approval by pantomiming a French chef touching his thumb and middle finger to his lips, "That was perfect—that was *the* perfect pitch I wanted out of you." Apparently, there had been many unsatisfactory takes made before I showed up. Wilson played the recording back while he had his earphones on and detected something amiss. "I hear something electronic," he said. Then he played it again loud so that we could all hear; it was a very faint sound but the recording picked it up. Just then my portable radio piped up from the lowest volume there was; it was obviously where that "electronic noise" was coming from. I had ruined the whole take! Everyone just looked at me, and I sheepishly excused myself and left.

I liked Terry, his wife, Jacqueline, and their son, Ryan. Terry was a good father, playing catch with Ryan by the pool. When I visited their home, the phone seemed to ring constantly. Terry could get something done in one phone call that would take a multitude of agents and a month's time to achieve. An example comes to mind when I sought out Terry's advice for an idea I had for our sheriff's office. At the time, I served as a background and recruitment officer; I had experimented with making a music video of our personnel to take to recruitment fairs, but it was an amateur production. My notion was to make a new music video to the tune of "I Love L.A.,[75]" only to change the title to "I Love Monterey" and modify the lyrics to fit Monterey County locations.

Terry was intrigued by the idea, although I hadn't expected anything more than his thoughts on the matter. He told me to stop by the following day, which I did. He handed me a piece of paper on which were written new lyrics and said, "The best thing about it is that you don't have to make it rhyme." He was right: there was little rhyming in the Randy Newman version—the chorus, "We love it," was the kicker. Terry changed one of the lines from, "Rolling down the Imperial Highway…" to "Driving down the Number 1 Highway…" I began to imagine the visual of a sheriff's patrol car en route to Big Sur on Highway 1.

In the days that followed, I met with Terry again; he had an update he wanted to give me. It was a faxed communication from his longtime friend Randy Newman. Mr. Newman gave consent to have the lyrics changed and recorded "as long as the singing voice does not try and impersonate me."

Things stalled for a bit when I was transferred back to patrol. Something else was developing as well: Terry had begun drinking in the daytime. It seems he was weighed down with conflicts, including the possible separation from his wife. I empathized with him as I, too, was in a rocky marriage. We both hesitated to take the next step because of our kids, but tensions were building. Terry told me, "I think it's about time we had a deputy living at Doris' house." He was offering me a place to stay at a separate unit on Doris' property, right by the entrance gate. For a

75. Randy Newman's 1983 hit song.

number of reasons, I did not jump at this offer. First of all, I wouldn't have a place to have my children over for visits. And I wasn't sure I wanted to have *two* jobs instead of one. I kept hoping that my marriage would work out. Terry had met someone else, Terese Edwards, a masseuse at the Beach and Tennis Club in Pebble Beach. He eventually moved in with her.

Terry and I would sometimes meet for lunch, although I don't remember asking him specific questions. I don't interview my friends, but he would tell me things of interest without bragging. I didn't know that he was a major influence on the Monterey Pop Festival back in 1967. He said that both Los Angeles and San Francisco were vying for a festival that showcased their respective performing artists with entirely different sounds. Monterey was reached as a compromise and, despite the concern on the central coast, they had full approval from the local politicians and police chief. By then, Terry was an executive with Columbia Records and had already begun signing various acts.

There was a time when Terry had a pretty good relationship with his stepfather, Marty Melcher. This was despite the fact he and his mother had sent him away to military school. When Terry started making big money as a record producer, he bought himself a quarter-million-dollar house overlooking Los Angeles. Terry invited Marty over for dinner with his mom and, afterward, walked out to the terrace.

Terry asked him, "What do you think, Dad?"

Marty responded, "It makes me *sick*, a kid like you."

Marty Melcher, who handled Doris' finances with attorney Jerome Rosenthal, died in 1968. No one had ever bothered Doris with finances; she was too busy working, making movies and records. Terry made an appointment with the attorney to go over his mother's assets and the guy essentially said, "Go away kid, I'm busy."

Terry replied, "*That's* your answer? Well then, you're fired."

It soon became apparent that Doris was under contract for a television series she didn't even know about. It became a five-year commitment for "The Doris Day Show" on CBS.

Doris, now deep in debt due to her late husband's bad business deals, had to go back to work. Terry was looking out for her, working as the executive producer of her television series on CBS. Terry helped her reinvest in property on the Monterey Peninsula, buying exquisite pieces of land with the settlement she was awarded from her lawsuit against Rosenthal.

There was a time in the 1960s when Terry was riding a motorcycle and wiped out, which left him severely injured. Doris finally had a chance to take care of her son, nursing him back to health. When Terry told me such things, he always seemed to have a lump in his throat and a quaver in his voice. It must have been hard to be Doris Day's son and business manager. Terry tried to insulate Doris as best he could, but I remember one day he was especially anxious. He had just been in a lawyer's office and agreed to a non-disclosure agreement pertaining to his mother. Someone who had been working for Doris was going to go to one of the tabloids to share a story about her and it was a nature of great concern. I had no idea what the details were, and I certainly didn't ask, but it was apparent that even Doris Day could be targeted by the unscrupulous. Such is the case with celebrities. Is it any wonder they try to keep out of the public eye as much as possible and keep lawyers on retainer?

Chapter Sixteen

Tragedy, Loss and Goodbyes

IN MARCH 1995, Northern California was hit hard by floods, but it seemed as if the Monterey Peninsula was impacted most. The Pajaro River at the North County line jumped its banks, as did the Salinas River to the east, and most dramatically, the Carmel River. As the volume of water raged toward the ocean, the constant pounding against the Carmel River Bridge caused it to be swept out to sea. Big Sur was effectively cut off from the peninsula until emergency state approval allowed a new bridge to be constructed.

The rivers had been rising for months as a result of rains from the El Niño conditions of the Pacific Ocean. Heavy rainfall started in 1994 and continued into January and February 1995. The whole region was soaked and, when March arrived, it became an intense crisis.

Emergency services were able to determine just when the river would jump the banks, and the deputies set out to warn those living or working in low ground to vacate. I was assigned to evacuate the Barnyard Shopping Center, which was below sea level. It had been raining heavily and there were few customers as it was. I did notify a few business owners to get out while the getting was good, and fortunately, they heeded my warning.

There was one exception. A lady said to me in her haughtiest tone, "This is *ridiculous*! It's just a little rain and everyone is running around, panicking."

Bevis Faversham, Jeffrey Weismann, me, Phyllis Coates and
Mark Kennedy at the Edgar Celebration

I told her, "Ma'am, the river waters are going to turn the parking lot
and businesses into a lake, and if you don't leave now, you won't be able
to drive off."

She waved me off and went about her business. Twenty minutes later,
it hit. The waters jumped the river banks and rushed in. It rose steadily to
a height above the door handles of parked cars. I lost track if she got out
in time or had to be rescued, I had to leave to warn others.

Just across the path was the Holiday Inn. The hotel had the usual
number of tourists staying there, but there was no way for them to escape
the flood. The manager and I decided to hold a meeting for all guests
in the dining room; I also suggested to the kitchen staff that they put
together sandwiches while they could. Through the glass doors I could
see the rain water climbing dangerously high, and ominously rushing in
through the bottom of the doors. We tried to stop the flow by rolling
up the hotel's beautiful, thick carpets and placing them in the doorways.
Though the reinforcements did stem the tide somewhat, I could see that
it was only a matter of time before the rising water would burst through
the glass windows.

We grabbed trays of sandwiches and bottled water and I led the folks
to the hotel's second story. It felt like a scene from *The Poseidon Adventure*.
There was no way to get out, but at least everyone was safe. I radioed the

dilemma to our dispatch and they sent an emergency crew with a raft to pick me up. My duties were just beginning.

The rafts were utilized, evacuating all the homeowners who were stuck by the riverbanks. The homes were flooded with the muck that was flowing downstream. That water was severely contaminated with chemicals from people's garages, dead animals, waste, and poison oak. As I helped push the raft, the now muddy waters were waist high on me, but this is what I had signed up to do, help people. All our deputies and crises personnel were doing the same thing.

There was an emergency command post set up at higher ground at the Carmel Rancho Shopping Center. From there, all emergency calls pertaining to the flood were handled and coordinated by multiple agency representatives. On one of those days, Clint Eastwood came in to lend moral support and observe the operation.

Emergency crews were working twelve-hour shifts, if not more. Our uniforms were worse the wear, but our bodies were truly suffering. We couldn't dry out, and our shoes were soaked. In the days that followed, my feet and legs felt the remnants of chemical burns. My skin was so irritated that it constantly itched, and infection set in. As mandated, we had to report all injuries on duty. This one was filed under "hazard of the job."

Colleen Kennedy Deach

It was because of Lois and Tony Hawes that I met with Edgar Kennedy's daughter, Colleen Kennedy Deach. Tony had been curious about finding the offspring of the "slow burn" comedian since he learned that Edgar had been born in Monterey County. Our Midnight Patrol tent actually started a search of all public records that included Edgar Kennedy's death certificate, which had been issued in November of 1948. The informant was Colleen Deach, his daughter, and that was a revelation. Tony was very excited about this development and he initiated contact with Colleen. They eventually arranged to meet at a restaurant. In attendance that day were Tony and Lois, Colleen and her husband, Ivan.

Lois and Colleen, both being only daughters of the famous comedians, had much in common and the conversation flowed. Tony filled them in on the Sons of the Desert organization and about our tent's quest to learn of Edgar's precise birthplace. They put her in touch with me to follow up.

It was a pleasure to finally have the opportunity to talk to a member of Edgar Kennedy's family. Colleen managed to solve so many of the riddles we had. Edgar, it turns out, was born in southern Monterey County in a now defunct town of Pleyto in 1890. Edgar's parents were homesteaders and school teachers at the area's Veratina School.

Death of Tony Hawes

Tony loved the Monterey area and would ride in my patrol car every chance we had; Lois told me later it was his very favorite thing to do. He was the quintessential English gentleman. On one of those afternoons, we responded to a past-tense house burglary detail. It was a fairly routine call for me, but Tony's heart broke for the homeowner while she tearfully listed her stolen property. After my business was concluded, we got back into the patrol car. Before I had even started up the engine, Tony had an idea.

"Bill," he said, "do you think we should invite her to lunch with us?"

I smiled at that compassionate man and replied, "No Tony, she has important things to do."

I had Tony with me on another occasion when there was a drowning at Monastery Beach. As I explained to him, "The locals call this 'Mortuary Beach' because of all the swimmers and scuba divers who lost their lives here." When family members saw our marked patrol car, they naturally met us in an anguished state. Tony was very uncomfortable watching the victim's families (who isn't?), but he always came back for more. Tony and Lois had planned to retire in Pacific Grove; they had even found a house they liked, which was, appropriately enough, off Laurel Avenue.

Tony was the lynchpin in proposing that our tent host a four-day tribute to Edgar Kennedy to show fellow Sons "what Monterey could do." Tony was like the Pied Piper in that he was so charismatic. He was the one who convinced celebrities to come to Monterey for our annual banquets, and the Sons of the Desert absolutely loved him. Tony lent his considerable talents to several events, ensuring their success. Tony insisted on coming up from Los Angeles to Salinas on the train every other month to compare notes with me. After the requisite stop at the Penny Farthing Pub, I brought Tony to our house for an extended visit.

I was receiving commitments from people, which allowed me to book a block of rooms at the host hotel for the Edgar Kennedy

Celebration. This was done with careful consideration as I had to invest my own money. Success, though, was assured thanks to Tony's lining up his many friends and pub mates from Los Angeles to attend the July event. In early February, however, he called me, saying he had the flu and that, regrettably, he would not be able to come up for our planned visit that month. I told him to focus his energies on getting well and let him know we could proceed, reluctantly, without him. The very next day, February 13, 1997 Tony died in his home. A devastated Lois did not want to be the one to tell me, so she called my wife. I was stunned and grief-stricken when she came home immediately from work to tell me, "Tony's dead." A memorial service was held at the famous Forest Lawn in Glendale, California. I knew Tony would be in excellent company. The place was packed with his friends, family, fellow Masquers, and countless show business veterans with whom he had worked. Lois selected certain friends to help eulogize her husband. To start off, Bart Williams sang a rousing, acapella version of "At the Motion Picture Ball." This was followed by a eulogy by Anthony Caruso, the harlequin of the Masquers Club. Longtime Sons Bob Satterfield, Randy Skretvedt, and I spoke. I walked up to the podium and said, "Looking around at all the important people here, I can't help but think how Tony would have liked to emcee this." It got a laugh and helped to break the tension. One of the speakers was actor Alan Young, best known as Wilbur on the popular sixties sitcom *Mr. Ed*. He informed us, "I had the good fortune to know Tony and his father-in-law, Stan Laurel." Like all of us, he shared some personal memories. As the memorial wound down, there appeared a little six-year-old girl dressed as an angel. She slowly pirouetted up the aisles holding a wand like Tinkerbelle and motioned with it to each row.

There wasn't a dry eye in the house.

Edgar Kennedy Celebration in Monterey (July 3-6, 1997)

In preparation of the Edgar celebration, Terry Melcher offered his support. He knew that I arranged for a video and big-screen unit for one of our banquets. Terry committed to attend and volunteered something I had no idea existed. Somewhere in his mother's house was footage of he and Jerry Lewis. "Could you use it?" he asked.

"And how!" I replied, adding that many of our attending Sons were comedy fans in general and of Jerry in particular.

Terry provided some background on the film. It had been shot in the mid-1950s when Jerry had Doris, Marty, and Terry over for dinner. Jerry had an interest in directing and had a mini-studio downstairs. At one point after dinner, he invited Doris to be interviewed on film, but she politely declined. She then suggested, "How about Terry?" Jerry agreed and put the kid on a chair at the set. Jerry pointed the camera to start filming, took a seat next to Terry, and began to ask the usual questions: "How old are you? Where do you go to school?" And then, calmly, he asked who his parents were. When Terry said, "My mom's Doris Day and—" Jerry raised his "Kid" voice and yelled, "*Doris Day*—now *there's* a name for ya!" It was a fun evening and, when the film was developed, Jerry sent it to Doris.

That 16mm film and canister had been packed away all those years, but where exactly was it? I went with Terry to Doris' house and noticed a little dog running around the grounds with no hind legs. There was a wagon-like contraption attached to the little fellow so he could be mobile. He was quite happy as he scooted about. This dog had been hit by a car and had to have his back legs amputated. I don't know why, but some people felt they could dump their unwanted animals in front of Doris' gate and she would save them. She often did, at great, personal cost. Doris was known around the neighborhood to knock on doors if she saw a dog running loose. If the pooch happened to belong to them, she would bawl them out but good. Doris was expecting us that day and Terry led me into what Doris called "the sun room." I had figured we would be combing through packing boxes, but I didn't realize it until Terry pointed up at the loft where I was assigned to look through some cardboard boxes. I had to climb the ladder to get to them as Terry searched another room. With Terry out of sight, I felt a little uncomfortable with my close proximity to Doris, who was sitting in her chair, reading. She did not look happy.

I opened a few of the boxes and noticed that everything was wrapped in old newspapers. I was looking for a round canister, but instead I came upon some truly amazing artifacts from Doris' career. I only opened a couple of boxes and asked myself, "Now, *where* is that *film*?" My option was to climb down and move the ladder to the other side of the loft, but I chickened out; I did not want to disturb Doris any longer than I already had. Terry finally appeared, but was empty handed. We called off the search, hoping it would show up. It never did.

Our Midnight Patrol tent hosted the Edgar Kennedy Celebration in Monterey in July 1997. I took a week's vacation to help plan and organize the event, which drew two hundred people from five different countries.

In addition, we had Lois Laurel Hawes and Edgar's daughter, Colleen. Also on hand was our friend Tommy Bond and his fellow Our Gang member Dorothy "Little Echo" DeBorba. We also had Harpo the clown along with "Cupid," a local actor who made a living entertaining at weddings and anniversary celebrations.

A year's worth of preparation for the Edgar Kennedy Celebration in Monterey began at The Double Tree Hotel in Monterey. It was steps away from The Custom House[76] and Fisherman's Wharf. The first event started with a special outdoor viewing of *In Old California*[77] and *Perfect Day*[78] at Carmel's Forest Theater (built in 1910). Lois and Colleen then took part in a question-and-answer session on stage between films. The city of Monterey sponsors an annual 4th of July parade, and our group was invited to participate. Among our two hundred members were representatives of Sons from England. We all had parasols and marched in the city parade. The lads had the best time of all, participating in America's Independence Day. I rented a unique bus to transport the celebrities, including a dog I "discovered" that looked like Pete from Our Gang. He was just a white dog I saw being walked by his owner, whom I asked if I could have his permission to put his pet in the parade. All we had to do was draw a circle around the dog's eye. Everyone loved him, especially the old Little Rascals. Many photographs were taken that day.

That evening, we had a banquet and the mayor of Monterey dropped by to read aloud a proclamation making July 4, 1997 "Edgar Kennedy Day." The document was given to Colleen. The balding mayor remarked what a fun group we were, so we beckoned him to do the trademark "slow burn." He knew exactly what to do. In fact, we invited all the balding men onto the stage for a "burn-off."

As the sun was setting, fireworks were launched over the Pacific Ocean. It was a spectacular sight. Afterwards, the attendees were treated to a special "Midnight[y] Patrol" film festival back at the host hotel. To enter, people had to be in night clothes. What a scene! There were hair curlers, face masks, nightgowns, and old-fashioned night caps.

76. Monterey's Custom House had been Mexico's primary port of entry on the Alta California coast. It was the location where Commodore John Drake Sloat first raised the American flag in July 1846.

77. *In Old California* (1942) a feature film starring John Wayne, with Edgar Kennedy as his comic sidekick.

78. *Perfect Day* (1929) a comedy short starring Stan Laurel, Oliver Hardy, and Edgar Kennedy.

The next day, we had a "Perfect Day" barbeque picnic, followed by a softball game, "Laurels vs. Hardy's" (skinniest vs. portliest). Everyone got the biggest kick out of Edgar's two grandsons, Mark and Glenn Kennedy, who got right into the spirit throughout the festivities. Glenn showed off his athletic skills by pulverizing the ball high and deep. Mark clowned around on the infield, once purposely bumping into me when a pop-up was hit, followed by both of us taking a pratfall. Edgar would have been proud.

There was a vaudeville night at the California First Theatre (built in 1850). More than a hundred folks filled the auditorium and were entertained by the "Troupers of the Gold West" performing an old melodrama. It was followed by an olio that encouraged group sing-a-longs of old-time songs.

After the Troupers completed their act, a select number of our Sons took over. We had Tommy "Butch" Bond in the audience and he got to see his son act out a scene from an early Our Gang short, singing, "Just Friends, Lovers No More"[79] Butch Junior was wearing an old-time football helmet, like his dad had worn in Laurel & Hardy's *Block-Heads* (1938).

Tracy Tolzmann was up next, singing "The Curse of a Broken Heart," which had everyone crying with laughter. His wife, Merrie, joined him in a number as well.

The showstopper was a performance by Laurel & Hardy lookalikes, Jeffrey Weissman and Bevis Faversham, straight from Universal Studios. The boys did a fantastic stage act that included audience participation. It's one thing to look like L&H, but these two had their voices and mannerisms down pat. They performed together for twenty years, all over the globe, and our audience embraced them.

Another event during our celebration was "A Pair of Tights"[80] ice-cream drop. We set up a reenactment of the film with our members trying to catch a falling scoop of ice cream from a second-story overhang. Boy, was it messy! The banquet's theme was "This is Your Life," and celebrities were introduced by way of film highlights of their careers.

I rented John Harris' wonderful Dream Theater in Monterey for another screening the following afternoon. It was of one of the most heralded of all Laurel & Hardy films, *Two Tars* (1928, also featuring Edgar

---

79. Tommy Bond originally sang this song in the Our Gang comedy *Mush and Milk* (1933).

80. *A Pair of Tights* is a 1929 two-reel Hal Roach comedy starring Edgar Kennedy, Stuart Erwin, Anita Garvin, and Marion Byron.)

Kennedy as an irate motorist) and the rarely seen *Fra Diavolo* (1933), in a stunning 35mm print generously provided for the event by Kit Parker Films.

Another highlight was a simulated radio broadcast of "The Wedding Night," a sketch Stan Laurel had written for radio in 1943. The original cast consisted of Stan Laurel, Oliver Hardy, Edgar Kennedy, and Patsy Moran; Lucille Ball introduced the skit. Our players were Jeffrey Weismann (as Stan), Bevis Faversham (as Ollie), Phyllis Coates (as Patsy) and Mark Kennedy (as Edgar). The players all read from scripts and acted it out, replicating what a studio audience might have seen in 1943. It was all sewn together by Bart Williams, our producer and sound man.

In the original play, Edgar Kennedy was a justice of the peace with a short fuse. Tony Hawes was going to play Edgar and his untimely death almost caused us to the scrap the play. Who else could play Edgar? Grandson Mark Kennedy volunteered for the part. He had no acting experience, but his very genes allowed him to play the role. He not only had Edgar's voice, looks, and body language down, he knew how to get laughs. A surprise topper was planned for the skit's climax. Mark had spent most of his adult life with long straight hair that went past his shoulders. Prior to the show, he walked to a downtown barbershop and instructed the operator to not only cut his hair but to shave his crown, "a horseshoe do." Despite objections from the female barber, she finally succumbed to his request. Mark wore a hat until the evening's performance. It came as a complete surprise—more of a shock, actually—when, in a state of unbridled exasperation, he pulled off his nightcap to reveal his newly bald pate. His relatives let out a scream!

The final evening of the celebration was a "Cops and Robbers Night," a tribute to the Keystone Cops, of which Edgar had been an original member. Terry arrived, smartly dressed in a suit and tie. He also brought Terese, a strikingly beautiful lady with straight long, dark hair. I had just the table at which to seat them; it was in the back with a couple of true Laurel & Hardy experts, Richard W. Bann and Randy Skretvedt. Randy is also a disk jockey in Southern California and an all-around authority on virtually every genre of music. When I introduced Terry, Randy said, "Oh, the Ripcords."[81] I showed Terry the program I made for the evening and his name was among the other celebrities. Suddenly, he did not seem relaxed.

---

81. Terry Melcher and Bruce Johnston sang the leads for the group during the studio sessions of Columbia Records' "Hey Little Cobra" (1963).

Most everyone who attended that night was in costume. I emceed the evening in my rented Keystone Cop uniform, and I think half the people there had the same idea. Even Colleen wore a uniform in honor of her dad's esteemed association with that famous comedy team. A lot of people came dressed as robbers, convicts, and gun molls.

The days following the celebration, we still had many guests from England. I brought them to Carmel to walk around and inevitably we came to rest at the Cypress Inn. We ordered our drinks and took in all there was to see of the Doris Day movie artifacts that were tastefully on display. Terry Melcher came in and addressed the bartender; "Whatever this party orders, charge it to the house." I never saw Del Kempster smile so wide with the possible exception of receiving a lobster dinner on Monterey's wharf.

One day, I came home and there was a long message on my answering machine from Terry. He was almost hysterical as he related some altercation in which he had been involved. I immediately called him back to tell him I was coming over.

By this time, Terry was living with Terese at a house they were renting in Pebble Beach. Terry was beside himself as he sat rocking back and forth. Half-talking and half-crying, he related the events that occurred the previous day. I did what any friend would do: I listened intently. Terry had an out-of-town musical executive in his BMW as he was driving on Carmel Rancho Road towards Carmel Valley Road. According to Terry, he was rolling to a stop when his car barely made contact with the rear bumper of another vehicle. Terry looked as he passed by and saw no damage. So he drove away, up Carmel Valley Road, only to be closely followed by the other driver. Terry was getting scared again; he was always paranoid about the Manson family. He made a sudden right turn up Rancho San Carlos Road, but couldn't shake her. He then turned onto Valley Greens Drive, where the driver began honking her horn to get him to stop.

There was no way to avoid this now; the young lady from Pacific Grove was angry that he didn't stop his car while she assessed the damage. Terry was certain that there hadn't been any damage, as both cars had rubber bumpers. Terry was ready to exchange driver's license and insurance details with her when she suddenly came closer. As she did so, she noticed a badge in his wallet. She took down the information and promptly deduced that she was dealing with an off-duty deputy sheriff on a hit and run. She made her way to the sheriff's office to file a complaint.

CHP was called out to inspect her car. No damage there. Our commander at the Monterey office was aware that Terry Melcher was a part of the sheriff's advisory non-profit organization and was concerned that he had used his badge to influence the situation.

If there is one thing a sheriff can't tolerate, it's when a volunteer misuses his badge. The commander sent a gruff sergeant to Terry's home. He knocked on Terry's door and demanded the badge back. There was no discussion: Terry fetched it and handed it over. The office certainly knew of my close association with Terry Melcher and they didn't want any complications. I was *ordered* by my sergeant to "keep out of it!" I didn't know how to interpret that. Naturally, I had access to the report and read it. It said there was no damage done to either car. The reporting party thought he was a cop because of the badge. Terry denied "flashing" it and was unaware of it being visible.

Intentional or not, the case was run upstairs to the district attorney's office. They take anything like this very seriously; they originally charged Terry with "impersonation of a peace officer." Everyone is entitled to seek legal counsel and I encouraged Terry to consult a lawyer, it is something I always did when asked for legal opinions.

Terry was running a gamut of emotions: he was embarrassed, in shock, and emotionally defeated. He was also crying when he told me, "I can't take this to court because [the media] will bring in my mother, and the Manson thing. I just can't do that. It's only a hundred-buck fine if I plead guilty." The media never got wind of this quiet solution.

Terry's entire demeanor started to change after that event. He was seeing a psychiatrist and reflecting on his life. He blurted out to me, "My old man shot his brains out." I was deeply concerned for his mental state. He had his mother's affairs and his own family to think of. Terry made a break for it by moving to Southern California with Terese and marrying her as soon as he was legally able.

I heard from him a couple of times following his relocation. At first, he said he was happy again and felt like writing music. He had either bought or rented a studio in Santa Monica; I was hoping he was content. He wasn't, of course. There were legal entanglements pertaining to community property, and the proceedings and challenges were dragging out.

All of this was very unsettling for young Ryan. At one point, he made the effort to visit Terry at his house. He never got past the front door. Terry was now taking some strong prescription medication, which resulted in his being even more paranoid. Terry called me at home that night, saying that he was sick. It was heartbreaking to hear him in his current state. It was obvious he was suffering a breakdown. I tried to remain neutral, but I did not let on to Ryan and his mother that Terry was afraid someone was trying to kill him. The family surmised that his new wife was keeping him paranoid and in confinement. There was nothing I could do. That was the last time I heard from Terry. I felt horrible for the family but hoped Terry had found new happiness with Terese. Unfortunately, I don't think Terry was ever the same after the "hit and run" incident. **John Denver Killed**

On October 13, 1997, the singer most famous for his songs; "Rocky Mountain High, " "Sunshine on My Shoulder," "Thank God I'm a Country Boy," and others met a tragic end when his homemade Long EZ single engine plane crashed into the Pacific Ocean. Denver was trying to land it on the shores of Pacific Grove when his contraption fell with such force, it exploded into the water.

This quickly became international news. All water emergency crews set out to recover the flying machine and its occupant's remains. In the days that followed, the body was transported to our county morgue, where an autopsy was scheduled. By this time there were swarms of media practically camping out in front of our office.

My colleague at that time, Lieutenant Dave Allard, was the public information officer. Fortunately, he had a whole division to help him out, and he needed it. Reporters and photographers were everywhere, giving updates after a press release was issued. Lt. Allard set up a huge press conference, introduced the sheriff, and then explained the manner of death.

In reconstructing the incident, and the inspection of the recovered machinery, experts were able to determine that John Denver had a series of mishaps. Though Denver had a pilot's license, it was risky to fly the plane into the winds off the ocean. During flight, one gas tank emptied, but there was a whole other filled tank. If only Denver had been able to reach the switch in time, he might have made it. A theory developed that panic might have set in as Denver had to divert his attention while trying to find the switch and he was not familiar with the machine.

This was a multi-agency-involved press conference and the room could not accommodate that many members of the media. During the Q&A session Lt. Allard was asked, "Can you confirm that John Denver's head was chopped off"? What a wholly inappropriate question to lead off with! Allard, in his most professional tone, explained that the coroner's responsibly was to identify the manner and cause of death *only*. The combination of plunging into the ocean with speed from a high altitude will result in a hard impact, not unlike hitting concrete.

As the world mourned John Denver, his loss may have been felt in a more personal way by many of Monterey's citizens. Denver had made himself available performing during the AT&T Pro-Am "Clambakes" for the volunteers, held annually on the day before the event. He also participated in four of the tournaments. Doris Day had done a television special with the singer back in 1975. A resident of Aspen, Colorado, Denver had been thinking about buying a house in Carmel Highlands and had buddied up with the singing deputy, Pat Duval. Denver was with Duval the day before his death, posing for pictures in the sheriff's car.[82]

Deputy Pat Duval's Retirement

In December 1997, Pat Duval put in his papers to retire after thirty years of serving the people of Monterey County. No one could replace him; he had reached icon status. Everyone in the county, it seemed, had brushed up against this trailblazing deputy, whether he was on or off duty.

Pat deserved a retirement party, and I volunteered to put one together. My first thought was to have it at Clint Eastwood's place, the Mission Ranch. As soon as we put out a notice, we were overwhelmed by requests for tickets. We didn't want to disappoint anyone, so with the encouragement of Nick Lombardo, the owner of the Rancho Canada golf club, we held the event at that larger venue. Even with three hundred people packing the place, many more were disappointed that they couldn't get in.

I set up this dinner banquet in the manner of a celebrity roast, and most of the deputies were lined up to tell stories. Pat had invited some of his oldest friends from where he grew up (in Florida), and many more individuals whose lives he touched on the peninsula.

Clint Eastwood dropped by following an afternoon of golf and settled right in with the rest of the guests. I approached him beforehand with an idea; I handed him a faux Oscar from one of the Hollywood souvenir shops and asked if he would present it to Pat. I planted it inside the podium so it would be a surprise when Clint pulled it out and handed it to Pat.

---

82. There is a photo of John Denver and the uniformed Deputy Pat Duval on page 106 in Duval's autobiography *From Colored Town to Pebble Beach*.

As the emcee for the event, I kept things moving. I started it off with some video highlights of Pat's screen appearances from Clint's movies and footage of Ed Haber describing Doris Day and Angie Dickerson as "deadbeats." Very few people present had ever seen these clips and they just howled.

The off-duty and mostly retired deputies gave Pat a good roasting. Clint gave Pat an impromptu roast of his own, describing Pat's screen debut, and then presented him with his Oscar. Pat ended the evening with a short speech and a song, "My Way." It was the end of a chapter for many of us.

Chapter Seventeen

Stan Laurel's Daughter, Lois Laurel Hawes

WHEN TONY HAWES DIED, he and Lois were in the process of picking out a house in which to retire in Pacific Grove. Now, with Tony gone, she was more determined than ever to relocate to the Monterey area.

Over the years many people approached Lois to inquire about her father, Stan Laurel, and she always cooperated enthusiastically. When an interviewer pressed too much, however, she became guarded. As she explained to me, "Why should I give away everything I know? *I* may write a book someday."

Lois and I had many phone conversations through the years. Whenever I was in the L.A. area, I sometimes stayed over at her house. She gave me some of Tony's show business books and a couple of his sports coats as we were the same size. She knew how much it meant to me; Tony was like the big brother I never had. Of course, Tony was a big brother to everyone he met.

Sometimes, Lois would share her stories with me and at one point said she wanted me to help write her memoirs. I was only too glad to do so. There was no time frame for this project. I found that Lois tired easily, and a long interview was out of the question.

Most L&H fans know that Lois' husbands were Rand Brooks and Tony Hawes, but she once informed me that her first husband was Don Falconer, a resident of Santa Cruz. Lois spent a lot of time in Santa Cruz growing up, and her mother had a long family history in the area. Lois

told me she met Falconer at a teenage canteen there, when she was with her best friend (and future bridesmaid).

Don Falconer's father was Goldie Falconer, a prominent citizen in Santa Cruz. The Falconers had lived in Santa Cruz for five generations[83] and were close personal friends of Stan Laurel. Goldie (or Golden) and his wife were also family friends of Lois Nelson before she married Stan.

It is more than likely that Lois and Don had known each other from the time they were children. There is a newspaper article from 1932, linking the two families. According to the article, Dr. and Mrs. Golden Falconer returned from a two-month European tour through England, Scotland, and France. They sailed on the *Aquitania* from New York and returned on the *Paris*. The couple traveled with Stan Laurel and Oliver Hardy, who had frequently visited the family at their Sylvar Street home. The comedians were on what was ostensibly a vacation trip, but graciously made appearances in the three countries visited.[84]

One day, when Lois was in Monterey for a visit, we passed by St. John's Church. She pointed out, "I was married there to my first husband." The little Episcopal place of worship was adjacent to the Del Monte Golf

---

83. *Santa Cruz Sentinel* September 10, 1946.

84. *Santa Cruz Sentinel* September 8, 1932.

Course, the first one course built in California, in 1897. She said it was written up in the Santa Cruz newspaper. I later tracked down the item in question, it reads:

Lois Laurel Bride of Don W. Falconer at Del Monte Chapel

Following a honeymoon in Beverly Hills, the couple are at home to their friends at Capitola. The wedding took place at Del Monte chapel, with the Rev. Theodore Bell officiating August 1st. A light blue suit with matching hat and black accessories was worn by the pretty young bride, and she carried an orchid bouquet. She was given in marriage by her father, Stan Laurel.

There were more than 100 guests who attended the reception following the ceremony. Quantities of beautiful white tuberous begonias from the Vetterie gardens were used in the chapel decorations and graced the bride's table at the lodge. The just-weds left for a honeymoon in Beverly Hills following the reception.

The bride is the daughter of Lois Nelson Laurel and Stan Laurel of Beverly Hills. Her father is the well-known member of the Laurel & Hardy comedy team. She attended Westlake school for girls in Los Angeles and was later graduated from Beverly Hills high school She also attended Santa Monica city college for a year.

Mr. Falconer is the son of Mrs. George Cooper of Santa Cruz and the late Golden Falconer.[85] He was graduated from the New Mexico Military Institute at Roswell, New Mexico, and following that he entered the U.S. Navy and served overseas. The two well-known families have been united in this marriage. The Laurel and Falconer clans have been friends for many years, [and] they toured Europe together in 1932.

Lois divorced her husband in 1948, charging him for "failure to provide." Ironically, Don Falconer had a long life as a bank executive in Santa Cruz, with a second marriage and a child. He died in 2000.

Lois had told most interviewers that she began her career in show business as a dress extra in Laurel & Hardy's *Swiss Miss* (1938). In a 1971 interview with columnist Jeannette Mazurki, Lois described herself as a "Danny Dare Girl"[86] in the 1930s. She also took to the stage in the summer

---

85. Golden Falconer died in 1936 after a tragic accident while playing polo.

86. Danny Dare was an actor, choreographer, director, writer, and producer of the stage and screen.

of 1939 and played on the same bill with her father in Steubenville, Ohio, Dean Martin's home town. "If I ever meet Dino, I'll tell him I broke into show biz at his birthplace."[87]

As it happened, Lois never did move north. Instead, she lived with her granddaughter Cassidy and doted on her two great-grandchildren. She passed away in 2017, at the age of eighty-nine.

Search Warrants

I was lousy at search warrants at first. The places suspects would hide things I would never have thought of. Then I caught on to a few such hiding places: the vegetable bin in the refrigerator, contraband taped to the backs of drawers in a dresser, holed out walls, etc. There are numerous, creative ways of hiding guns, drugs, money, and other evidence.

Some of the big busts are coordinated with a team, which divides up the areas assigned them. Other times, the search is limited to a particular area for something specific. There was the time I assisted Pacific Grove PD in a search warrant to a small apartment. The first thing to do is survey the area and try and think like a crook. In other words, look for the unlikeliest places to stash something.

At this particular place I thought I'd hit the jackpot. It was a round woven hamper with a blanket draped over it and heavy books on top. Surely, *this* was the hiding place. The suspect just watched me and didn't say a word. I removed the items on top and when I opened the lid, my eyes didn't immediately grasp what was in there. Suddenly, a huge coiled boa constrictor snake, thick as a human leg, raised its head out of the container. I was lucky to have had the presence of mind to slam the lid back on and secured it with the same books. I saved a few bullets that way.

At one of the offices at Pebble Beach Security, one of the security personnel, Mac, was stationed at one of the gates during the midnight shift. Mac was a sketch artist and we enjoyed his talents. Sometimes the deputies clued him in to some of the embarrassing mishaps and Mac caricaturized the incident and deputy. I was victim to a few of those, including the snake-in-the- basket-caper.

---

87. *Naples Daily News* (Florida) June 18, 1971.

Impersonating a Police Officer

Sometime during my career an incident was called to my attention that my co-workers thought was humorous. This could have happened to anyone, but in this case some creep obtained one of my business cards and used it unlawfully. Not only unlawfully—he used the card to identify himself as Deputy Bill Cassara and convinced a female in his apartment unit in Salinas to cooperate in a free security inspection.

The guy gained entrance, but the female was suspicious and called Salinas PD. They wound up arresting the suspect with my business card on him. They booked him into the county jail, but what frosted me was that the suspect was also entered into our computer system with an a.k.a. of "Bill Cassara." I just *knew* this would complicate something down the road. My colleagues had fun with this, especially when a Salinas officer said he knew it wasn't Deputy Cassara because the suspect "had too much hair."

Unusual Calls

Over the years I had my share of nutty details. There was one early morning when the Pacific Ocean was as calm as a lake. This meant that sound could carry quite well. On this night, the seals perched on Bird Rock in Pebble Beach were being noisy. This caused a resident to call 9-1-1 because of the "loud barking dogs" and wanted the noise to stop *at once*. Another time I was called because "someone has stolen my garbage cans!" The reporting party was furious that she had been "targeted." I didn't argue with her; I just drove down the street and found them. It had been a windy night and the garbage cans had simply blown away.

Raccoons are not uncommon on the Monterey Peninsula, and the residents have learned to live peaceably with these wild creatures. They live everywhere they can find shelter, and that includes trees. I don't know how many times I've been called to a "burglary in progress," only to find that the culprits were raccoons. One evening, my partner and I were called to a Pebble Beach residence which had reported "someone breaking into the house via the roof." The reporting party was a sixteen-year-old girl who was at the house, babysitting. She was terribly frightened and my partner and I checked the exterior and found raccoon activity in and around the garbage cans, with their paw prints all over. We explained how common the raccoons were and that breaking into a roof by a burglar was *not* common. Once we left, she called back for the same thing. The poor girl—she was so frightened that we decided to stay with her until we got our next call. Sometimes, movies and TV shows can create such macabre images that it affects the imagination, especially at night.

I got a call during the morning hours from an irate party who lived in "Pebble." He insisted that "kids are climbing my twelve-foot-high fence and tormenting me by making little mounds of dirt at the base of the fence." This guy was a corporate C.E.O. and highly educated but was devoid of common sense. He was still agitated when he showed me the "damage." I looked closely at the mounds and poked it with a stick. They were gopher holes. I explained that the gopher burrowed up. The reporting party was incredulous at this discovery.

I was dispatched to a call in Pebble Beach when neighbors complained that a retired doctor always chucked his morning urination void out his kitchen window. Over a period of time, the stench had become unbearable; it also killed the plants and was attracting flies. The neighbors were anxious. I made a welfare check on the doctor (who lived by himself). He calmly explained that when he got up in the morning, the first thing he did was to make coffee and then pee in his special designated sauce pan, the contents of which he catapulted outside. This wasn't exactly an "emergency call," but you can't say he didn't have a pot to piss in.

While working the midnight shift as a double unit, we were called down to the Ventana Inn at Big Sur regarding a furious domestic dispute. This resort is world famous for its graceful décor, so perfectly blended into the natural beauty of God's Country. The hideaway is complemented by a four-star restaurant and exquisite views.

Upon our arrival, this discrete lover's nest of a hotel room was in chaos. The manager was in a panic and explained that a woman showed up with her two kids and confronted her husband, who was there with another woman. She found him with the aid of the new technology of a global positioning system on her husband's car. She drove up, saw the car, marched into the lobby with her kids, and demanded to know what room he was in. The honeymooning folks weren't bothered, but the commotion caused many couples who were involved in similarly illicit rendezvous to put on their clothes and beat a hasty retreat. It reminded me of the last scene in Laurel & Hardy's *Block-Heads*.[88]

---

88. *Blockheads* was a feature film starring Stan Laurel and Oliver Hardy (1938) in which the last frames of the film show errant husbands jumping out of apartment windows after

I remember once taking a call out in an obscure area of Carmel Valley. A local masseuse wanted to report that one of her customers skipped out on her after services rendered. She was a very lovely young lady, who operated this business out of her home, attracting clients by word of mouth. She was professionally trained and an expert in her field. The guy did not identify himself and, without paying, took off his car. The suspect got away, but I remember something the victim said that she thought might be helpful in our search: "While massaging his feet, I could tell he has kidney problems and will die shortly."

Then there were the habitual callers of little to no merit. One lived in Pebble Beach and used to call 9-1-1, seemingly on a weekly basis. The "emergency" I remember most from this older lady was a "burglary in progress." When I got there, she was calmly sitting down and asked me to sit as well.

I asked, "Where's the burglary?"

She said, "Everyone's gone," and insisted I sit (I remained standing). She then began her story: "I was born a poor Nazi child . . ."

I said, "Okay, why did you call 9-1-1 today?"

Irritated, she answered, "I'm *getting* to that . . . I married a man who was no good." She was now on a roll. "I met him in Germany when he was a professor and we moved to this country."

Again I asked, "What happened *today*?" She spoke slowly and deliberately and I realized there wasn't an emergency at all. She exaggerated the fact that her ex-husband met up with her son (who lived there) and removed a sleeping bag from the garage without her permission.

Then there was the woman who lived in the High Meadows area (outside of Carmel), who frequently called 9-1-1 to report that "a bear is looking at me through the window." Deputies were dispatched there frequently and the whole thing was absurd: she was just an older lady suffering from minor delusions. I was a sergeant during this time and I responded to one of those calls myself. She showed me where the bear would look at her, but (of course) there was no bear. This is where law-enforcement officers have to have patience and help solve the problem. In this case, I advised her that the next time this bear looks at you, take a picture of it and *then* call us. We weren't bothered by her for a while afterwards.

I had a lot of fun whenever I went to training classes put on by the Police Officer's Standard Training (P.O.S.T.) of California These out-of-town classes were taught by grizzled veteran cops who were experts

hearing the ominous sound of a shotgun blast.

in their field. The classes were made up of law-enforcement personnel from all over the state, and, of course, we would exchange stories when appropriate. They all wanted to know what it was like working for Monterey County, and I led them on for a while that we are busy taking reports from victims who suffered misguided golf shots through their windows. I could see in their faces that they wished *their* beat was the Monterey Peninsula, and I'd play it up. Then I would wake them up by informing them that our county also includes the cities of Salinas and two state prisons. Crimes are proportionate with population.

Everyone was familiar with Salinas, but it was not common knowledge that we also had beats in King City, or how big the county was. Unlike the cities with street lights to aid their visibility, the rural areas of the county are pitch black and backup may not be close. We tell our rookies on patrol that an emergency response might take up to an hour to get to, "so be diligent." We are called for all kinds of problems to areas that don't want us there. People skills to defuse tempers are a must.

Jamesburg Earth Station

When I went to work for the Sheriff's Department, I had no idea that an Earth Station existed in the farther reaches of Carmel Valley, high in the mountains outside of Cachagua. It had been built and maintained by scientists to help track the progress of the moon landing in 1969. The satellite dish is over ten stories high and in a remote location. With the pristine white buildings and white lab coats the engineers wore, it looked like a spot that James Bond might find himself. Of course, what was considered the most sophisticated technology in 1969 slowly became obsolete, but it was still operational in the 1980s. Engineers were only too happy to welcome deputies to the facility. They even showed us what they could pick up via satellite.

Chapter Eighteen

Joan Fontaine

JOAN FONTAINE, THE LEGENDARY MOVIE star best known for her roles in two Alfred Hitchcock films (*Rebecca* [1940] and *Suspicion* [1941], lived in the Carmel Highlands at 229b Lower Walden Road; her mailbox identified the property as "Villa Fontana." Ms. Fontaine was receiving harassing phone calls from a past associate, prompting her to call the sheriff's office. I drove to her home, rang the doorbell, and waited. These aren't social calls, the reporting party usually experience some uneasy tension about the predicament, they worried about what their neighbor's think [of a patrol car] coming onto the property. "Good afternoon, Ms. Fontaine," I said in my most professional delivery, "I'm Deputy Cassara." (I think I even clicked my heels together). "What can I do for you?"

She told me she was a victim of harassing phone calls from a prior friend and business associate. I listened attentively and took a report. I assured her that I would communicate with the other party to end the unwanted calls. It was a pretty routine detail and I was happy to help her out. When I finished taking the report, I said: "I've known for some time that you lived up here; I'm very glad to meet you."

She gave relaxed and noticed that I glanced at a framed lithograph in the room. "Oh," she said, "these are contract players for RKO in the 1930s," and pointed to herself. She then began to identify a few others, but stammered and snapped her fingers to jump-start her memory. I couldn't help myself; I walked up to the lithograph and named the others: "Jack Oakie, and Wheeler & Woolsey."

She said, "You know your stuff."

Joan Fontaine

With that, she insisted that she show me around her gorgeous home. She put her arm around mine and walked me through every room in the house. Standing on a platform in a room of personal keepsakes was her Academy Award for Best Actress for her unforgettable performance in the Alfred Hitchcock–directed *Suspicion* (1941).[89] Before taking my leave, I did something unprecedented: I wrote my personal phone number on

89. Joan has the distinction of being the only actor in a Hitchcock film to win an Academy Award. In addition, Joan and Olivia remain the only siblings to have both received Academy Awards.

the back of my business card with instructions for this American treasure to call me at home if she ever required my assistance.

As promised, I contacted the party with whom Joan was having problems and the harassment stopped. I can't recall the time frame, but Joan did call me at home in order to invite me to lunch on my day off. There was something she wanted to discuss, we met at one of her favorite restaurants in Carmel. She had brought with her a copy of her autobiography, *No Bed of Roses*[90] What's more, it was already inscribed: "To Bill Cassara, may your life be a bed of roses." Joan handed it to me and said, "This is me. I want you to read it."

Joan then relaxed and wanted to know more about my personal life. We had quite a chat and it livened up when I told her I was born in San Jose. Joan had been raised in Saratoga, a beautiful community a few miles southwest from where I grew up.

I was familiar with Joan's career and I knew that her sister was Olivia de Havilland, but that topic did not come up, at least not then. She told me of the time when her mother was recently divorced and came to California for her health. Joan was born in Tokyo and was a sickly baby. Her mother took her to the Vendome Hotel in San Jose and struck up a conversation with her future husband, George Fontaine outside in the gardens. He was the manager of Hale's Department store downtown.

Joan shared some of her favorite memories of visiting downtown San Jose in the early 1930s; she remembered fondly O'Brien's Candy Store on First St. I told her that my grandfather owned a barbershop on San Fernando St., just around the corner from Hale's. I let her know that my grandfather took pride in shaving all the business men in the district prior to their work. Could it be that her stepfather had been one of my grandfather's customers? She smiled at the thought.

After reading her book from cover to cover, I let her know that I had done so. She promptly invited me to lunch again on one of my days off. Joan surprised me by filling me in on her sister Olivia de Havilland, whom she absolutely despised. Joan's biggest fear was that she would predecease her and that Olivia would come to her home and steal items that had once belonged to their mother.

I listened, but I was skeptical. After all, Olivia lived in Paris and was older than Joan. I didn't know what she was leading up to until she blurted out, "I want you to be at my house when I die." I wasn't sure if she was addressing me as a friend or as a deputy sheriff. Joan assured me

---

90. Joan Fontaine, *No Bed of Roses* (New York: William & Morrow Co., 1978

that, with my cooperation, she could now contact her attorney and have him put in writing that I was to be at her house. I patiently explained that when death comes, the coroner freezes all the assets and tapes off the house. I drove home the point that it is the same procedure for anyone, and that attorneys have no jurisdiction until the property is released by the public administrator. It is then that the legal machinery releases assets to the heirs according to the terms of a will.

Joan could not be comforted and I did not want to be in some legal entanglement. She gave me her attorney's business card and said that he would be expecting my call. That's the first thing I did when I got home. The attorney reassured me that he was just, in effect, humoring her and not to worry about it. He sent me some duplicate documents that she specified for me to have, one of which was a list of individuals she wanted notified of her death. I couldn't take any chances; I immediately briefed the sheriff to ensure that I wasn't caught in some conflict of interest.

Joan was settling her affairs not only because of her advancing age, but because she was scheduled for hip surgery. She was horribly afraid that she would die on the operating table. Joan had been the victim of a fall when she was in her cherished rose garden. One of her three dogs had jumped up on her unexpectedly and she rolled down the incline, over the many rows of thorny bushes. No "bed of roses," indeed. While Joan was in the hospital, I dropped off a bouquet at the nurse's desk to give to her. I awaited word from her that she was released and recovering at home, but to my surprise she only had a physical therapist drop in for a brief period during the day. No one lived with Joan; she enjoyed her solitude and did not wish to surround herself with staff. But, in her current condition, how was she to eat? That's where my Italian heritage came to the fore. I made a big pot of homemade spaghetti sauce with meatballs over a bed of cooked noodles. Joan was most pleased in accepting the dish, along with French bread and wine. She remarked, "My neighbors would *never* have done this for me."

Some say that, in her later years, Joan was a recluse living in her multimillion-dollar home overlooking Pt. Lobos and the Pacific Ocean. She had a Bentley and a Mercedes-Benz in her garage, but the only time she drove was to her church (St. John's Chapel) in Monterey on Sundays. She also drove a short distance to the cinemas in and around Monterey. She was, after all, a voting member of the Academy of Motion Pictures Arts and Sciences and wanted to be up on all the new releases.

Though Joan only drove a few miles from home and back, she was once stopped by the California Highway Patrol. The officer observed some driving deficiency and held on to her license pending a new DMV test. The fact of the matter was that her advanced age, (eighty-five) was now becoming a problem for her. Joan was quite upset over this situation but committed herself to shine during a written and driving test. There was one more phase she had to complete: she had to face a DMV officer in private and record an interview.

When that date came, Joan insisted I accompany her. I did so as a friend, not in my official capacity as a deputy sheriff. I was able to bring up a contradiction to the officer's actions and Joan pleaded her case; she only asked that she be allowed to continue driving short distances. After a few weeks, Joan received written notification that her driver's license had been reinstated. She was thrilled.

Gordon Sonne elected Sheriff June 1998

It was a happy day for me when Gordon Sonne won the election for sheriff of Monterey County. He ran against the incumbent on a platform that he was not a politician but an experienced detective. He was a professional of long standing who really made a name for himself as a street cop. I had seen him in action and had great respect for his talents.

Sonne was that rare flatfoot who jumped to the top position without any supervisory or administrative experience—and he never forgot where he came from. Once he became sheriff, each Christmas he would come down to the Salinas office roll-call room and take the place of a deputy who had been assigned the shift. It was always a family man who received this "gift." There was never any attention to this, and the media never caught on.

Sonne was overwhelmed by the responsibilities inherent to the position, but he had a good heart. He surrounded himself with people he had worked directly with and trusted. Most people in that position make it known that they will be running for office after their term is up; it eliminates the lame-duck perception others might have. Not this sheriff. He made it known he was there for one four-year term only. I became heavily involved in Sonne's campaign for a number of reasons. I was at a standstill with the previous sheriff, and I felt overlooked. I was hoping to be promoted and advance through the ranks, but I was held back for eight years. When Sonne became sheriff, he and his undersheriff took me out to lunch. His idea was for me to return to duties as the public information officer and act as a buffer between him and the media.

I agreed to return to my previous title to help with the transition. At least this time I didn't have to prove myself to investigators, whose best interests I had in mind. They asked for my input when the department needed the public's help.

Quite honestly, I didn't want the job; I had already done it. But, still, I made the best of it because the sheriff trusted me so much and gave me the freedom to perform the job as I saw fit.

My unofficial workday actually started by watching the local televised news at 11:00 p.m. to see if any arrest, fatality, or other such incident had occurred when I was off-duty the previous day at 5 p.m. Arriving at the station the following morning, I was usually greeted by a stack of phone messages pertaining to media inquiries.

Joan Fontaine was interested in this new sheriff; she always had her ear to the ground in politics. In 1962, she was accompanied by Adlai Stevenson,[91] at a special dinner at the White House. At some point, I arranged for Joan and Gordon Sonne to meet over lunch. Sonne was a handsome man, standing six-four, with an athletic build. Joan actually swooned when she met him.

Christina Williams Case 1998/found 1999

I responded to in-progress shootings, mass homicides, home-invasion robberies, suicides, and run-of-the-mill murders. However, it was the Christina Williams' kidnapping and murder case that was the most heartbreaking of my career.

It began when a thirteen-year-old girl took a walk with her dog on the old Ft. Ord territory and didn't come back. Her leashed dog did return home and it was hoped the child would show up as well. An alert went out right away; a missing child, after all, is one of the top emergency responses there is in law enforcement. A search immediately took place in her home, her neighbors' homes, the schools, and parks. But when she was missing overnight, a greater concern kicked in. A call went out to the FBI. Technically, this was their jurisdiction because most of the base was still the property of the federal government.

---

91. Adlai Stevenson was the Democratic candidate for president in 1952 and 1956. In 1962 he was the chief U.S. delegate to the United Nations (1961-1965).

A command post was set up and over fifty FBI agents were assigned to work the area. The staff was augmented by agencies from the Monterey Peninsula and each given certain tasks. The media helped when they could, providing front-page print news and wide exposure over the airwaves. We were hoping for a call from the suspect or a witness, pinpointing where Christina was.

I went to the command center often to interact with two of my supervisors, and our own search-and-rescue team had the daunting task of looking for a crime scene and/or the body of the child. A vigil was kept for signs of vultures circling the vast area.

Every morning there would be a briefing held by the FBI, sharing any new information from the hundreds of tips that poured in. We were reminded that, in similar cases, even volunteers could be suspects. One psychic reached out to the command center, claiming that she could communicate with Christina's dog, who had "witnessed" the crime. The FBI was interested in hearing from anyone who could help and this person was no exception. People did want to assist in any way possible, even if their theories proved wildly illogical.

In our office we had a very skilled deputy, Neil Shaw, who was also an FBI trained police sketch artist. Law enforcement appealed to the public to report any suspicious persons in and around the area of the abduction. Deputy Shaw sat down with one informant who had seen two male suspects driving a car during the same time frame. Shaw captured the essence of the two persons of interest and the sketches were released to the media. This resulted in hundreds of additional calls coming into the command center.

The case quickly became national news, and received bigger play the longer it remained unsolved. A large sum of money was raised for a reward leading to the arrest and conviction of those responsible for the crime. This case was the focus of many network magazine television programs, including *America's Most Wanted*. Celebrities such as Joe Montana, Clint Eastwood, Reggie Jackson, and Mariah Carey, made on-camera appeals to the public to come forward with any helpful information. One of the female FBI agents wanted Doris Day to appear on camera. Doris offered her sympathy and said, "I wish I could do more." Pleas by the famous was not going to flush out this kind of murderer. The law-enforcement agents were cognizant that, at any time, the suspect may call in and give himself up, or a tipster would lead us to a person of interest. The case dragged on for days, weeks, and months, with no impactful breaks. Nearly seven months later, the remains of Christina Williams were found approximately three miles from the area of Ft. Ord where she had been abducted. This area had been thoroughly searched before, so the probability was that the body had been dumped there. Coroner investigators took control of the body while the area was combed for evidence.

This case lingered for years without an identified suspect. FBI and Monterey County detectives were doing due diligence in going over all the registered sex offenders in the area. There was one suspect in whom they were especially interested, Charles Holifield, a twice-convicted child rapist who preyed on the former Ft. Ord. Holifield had been interviewed before, but had family members supplying alibis for him on the date Christina Williams was abducted.

Holifield, a registered sex offender, made the move detectives were waiting for: he relocated from his registered residence without informing the sheriff's office within the legal time frame. I was the lucky one who was selected to accompany the dicks to his place of business. It is always better to have a uniformed deputy make the physical arrest as opposed to someone in street clothes. Holifield worked at a machine shop in Sand City and, judging by the detective manpower, this guy was pretty important. It was in the morning hours when we announced ourselves at the shop, and all the other men working there just froze. Holifield was surprised as well. I gave my verbal commands to maintain control and grabbed his belt from behind. He had his fingers interlaced on top of his head as I told him, "nice and easy." Holding his belt gave me an advantage if he had tried to spin around; he was, after all, a big dude, easily six-three, with a muscular build. I could feel his whole body tense as I hooked one of his hands and brought it around. If he was going to do anything, it would be at that moment. I've been in those situations countless times before, and could tell he was weighing his options to turn on me. The trick is to secure him fast. Once handcuffed, he was given off to the detectives.

Once Holifield was in custody, he was booked into jail and held to answer for other crimes against women in other counties. It wasn't until March, 2020 that this horrific predator was finally convicted in court for the Williams murder. DNA saved the day and everyone who lived through this experience could now turn the page. Still, there always remains a pit in one's stomach of every law-enforcement officer who had worked the case.

Raymond Daum

I first met Mr. Daum as a victim of a crime that had just occurred. He waved me down frantically at the Crossroads Center, saying that someone had just stolen his car. He filled me in on the details. The day before, he had picked up a male hitchhiker who was heading south. Daum offered an opportunity for him to "crash" on his sofa for the night. The next morning, the guest offered to drive Daum back to the Crossroads to do some shopping. As Daum exited the vehicle, the thief took off in the car. There was a lapse of thirty minutes when all this happened.

I had Duam jump in the front seat of my patrol car and we headed to his home. I was hoping to catch the suspect burglarizing the place. When we arrived, there was no car, but inside the place was ransacked. The suspect stole Daum's checkbook and valuables but left some of his own belongings. I put out a B.O.L. status on the car as stolen and later had the plate numbers entered into C.L.E.T.S.

I couldn't help but notice that the walls were decorated with framed photographs of Hollywood celebrities: Alfred Hitchcock, Penny Singleton, Ginger Rogers, Bette Davis, Gloria Swanson, Joan Crawford, and Art Carney, to name a few. They were all personally inscribed to Raymond Daum. I was especially looking at the image of Art Carney when he said, "Art's a good friend of mine. I'm going to tell him about you."

A few days later, I got a break in the case. Phoenix PD had arrested the suspect while he was trying to cash a check at a bank; they recovered the car and other stolen valuables as well. I went over to Daum's house to inform him of the update. He was thrilled with the outcome. As I started to leave, he insisted that I wait for a few minutes, "Art Carney wants to talk to you."

Daum dialed a long distance phone number and there was a pick-up on the other end. "Art, it's me, Raymond. I have that nice deputy here." Then he handed me the phone. It was a bit awkward, but I was relieved when I heard Carney's recognizable voice. He said, "I just wanted to thank you for helping my friend out." We chatted a bit and I asked him about something that had long been on my mind. "Do you remember being in a band and playing in San Jose in 1938? I saw a snapshot of you when I was a docent at the San Jose Historical Museum."

He had instant recall. "Oh, that's when I was in the Horace Heidt Band. That was my start in show business."

About a week later, a large envelope arrived at the Sheriff's Monterey office addressed to me; inside was a picture of Art with a nice note, thanking me. The image depicted Carney as his "Norton" character from *The Honeymooners*, and it was signed too!

I kept tabs on Raymond, who was then in the final stages of life with cancer. I invited him to do a "ride-along" with me while I was on duty. He was fascinated with the opportunity and I got to ask him questions. I came to learn Raymond Daum was a retired film professor from the University of Texas, and had been a combat cinematographer for the Army during the Second World War. He filmed the rediscovery of Beethoven's piano, which had been hidden somewhere in France. He also shot footage of the Battle of the Bulge and was a Purple Heart recipient.

Professor Daum wrote a book, *Walking with Garbo*, in 1991, and it soon became a *New York Times* best seller.[92] He had been in charge of television production at the United Nations during the late 1950s when he met the reclusive Greta Garbo. After an introduction, he invited her for a tour of the building. This marked the beginning of a long friendship. Garbo confided in him during their many walks together on the streets of New York City.

After a stint of teaching at the University of Texas, he started having health problems. He did what other authors had done: he moved to Carmel. I took a special interest in Raymond; he was so upbeat and interesting. He told me of the time he took Shirley Temple out on her first date and, sometime later, set out to meet Judy Garland. He put on his high school varsity sweater and rang her doorbell; it was answered by one of her sisters. Raymond introduced himself as a representative of his high school and said, "We just voted Judy as our favorite movie star; may I interview her for our paper?" Of course, Judy cooperated fully.

Raymond attended the University of Southern California to study filmmaking. In 1939, Laurel & Hardy were shooting *The Flying Deuces* at General Service Studios in Los Angeles. A gathering of staff and students of the USC cinema studies arranged to meet Stan outside the studio. He addressed the class along with producer Boris Morros, who talked about the film in progress. A group photo was taken, one that Raymond framed and kept as a souvenir. Before Prof. Daum succumbed to cancer, he handed me the framed photo as a farewell gesture. The image can be considered a "one of a kind" photo that has never been circulated publicly.

---

92. Raymond Daum, *Walking with Garbo* (New York: HarperCollins Publishers, 1991).

I introduced Raymond to my dear friend Kit Parker of Kit Parker Films. Kit invited us to meet some old veterans of the movie trade at a restaurant in Monterey. They called themselves "The Dinosaur Club," and the group consisted of Ralph Senensky, True Boardman, Don Hanmer, and Lamont Johnson. Kit hung on every word those guys uttered, and wrote pieces on Ralph, Don, and Lamont for his blog.[93] Those guys loved Raymond and his many wonderful stories about old Hollywood, he fit right in.

Kit Parker

I knew of Kit Parker Films, but I didn't have a chance to meet the man until 1985. He had made a name for himself with his unbelievable collection of films that he loaned or rented out. Kit was a local lad who had grown up in Carmel Valley. His father was a contemporary artist and a good friend of Hank Ketchum,[94] the nationally syndicated cartoonist who gave the world "Dennis the Menace." Kit is one of the most interesting people I have ever met. When he was still in his teens, he shot film footage and sold it to KSBW television. He is a big fan of the old comedians and had even corresponded with Stan Laurel during his youth. Kit reinvested his money to buy more film and gave back to the community by holding weekly, nominally priced screenings.

I invited Kit to one of our banquets, where he got to meet Stan Laurel's daughter. He even volunteered to provide the film prints for the evening. Kit and his wife came to every banquet we hosted and once brought along character actor Aldo Ray. At the time, Kit's office was on 10th Street in Monterey, where he had a small office staff and a large inventory of film. He oversaw the construction of a new facility in Sand City, adjacent to Seaside, and expanded his business nationwide. We became fast friends and had lunch together at least once a month.

There were many times when Kit rode with me in the patrol car on his days off; he later attended one of my citizens' academy courses. Kit had a growing family to take care of and eventually relocated to Arizona; I notified my former sergeant, Chief of Police Mike Klein, of Sand City,

93. https://kitparkerfilms.wordpress.com/2012/05/17/the-dinosaur-club-part-2-lamont-johnson/

94. In later years, Hank Ketchum lived in Pebble Beach and had an artist's studio in Monterey.

and he arranged with the city manager and mayor to present Kit with the ceremonial key to the city.

U.S. Open with Tiger Woods

Sergeant Chris Pascone and I were assigned as special security officers to follow Tiger Woods for the PGA golf tournament in June of 2000 held at Pebble Beach. Chris took the front area to discourage the gallery from interrupting Woods, while I took the back end. Tiger Woods was like Superman that day. His long strides were interrupted only when he stopped to size up his shot. I could barely keep up with the man, but I was there through the 18-hole course and stood by him when he was proclaimed the winner of the U.S. Open that year.

Film Commission 2001

I had always followed the progress of the Monterey County Film Commission. It was established by the Monterey County board of supervisors in the mid-1980s. The board subsidized this new non-profit, recognizing that drawing in film, professional photographers and support crews brings revenue and provides employment opportunities for local citizens. In 2000, I became a member of their volunteer board of directors. Their longtime administrator, Karen Nordstrand, is someone with whom I really enjoyed working with; she is a vivacious lady who has arranged for production crews to shoot on location at various venues in the county. Once I committed myself as a board member, the director, Richard Tyler, told me, "We have an assignment for you, Bill. We'd like you to head a new committee that showcases films that were made in Monterey County and show them to the public as fundraisers."

I had previously been on the board of directors for the "Arts Habitat" for Monterey County, and worked with Richard Tyler who was also on the board. As a fundraiser, we secured the right to show The Beatles' *Yellow Submarine* feature cartoon at an independent cinema in Monterey. It was a great draw. Mr. Tyler recruited me to be a part of the Film Commission.

Imagine being the chairperson of a committee to screen for the public any movie that was shot in Monterey County! Our committee narrowed it down to ten titles and debated the merits of each. Clint's directorial debut from 1971, *Play Misty for Me*, was the obvious choice, especially since it was shot exclusively in the greater Carmel area. I remember a close second was Doris Day's *Julie* (1956), with scenes in Carmel, Pebble Beach, and the police department downstairs at Colton Hall in Monterey.[95] It was a dramatic plot with Doris saving the day, this time as an airline stewardess. I also recall that we considered Disney's *The Parent Trap* (1961), which featured scenes of the airport and Carmel Valley. Unfortunately the then juvenile star, Hayley Mills, was residing in England.

Another possibility was *Clash by Night* (1952), starring Barbara Stanwyck, with Marilyn Monroe in a supporting role. It took place in Monterey's Cannery Row and had some good scenes on the wharf. It didn't make the list, but one of my favorite films partially shot on the peninsula was Bob Hope's *My Favorite Brunette* (1947), with scenes in Pebble Beach and at the Crocker Mansion.

Another possible title: *The Edge of Darkness*, starring Errol Flynn, Ann Sheridan, Walter Houston, Ruth Gordon, and Judith Anderson was considered. In that one, Monterey stood in for a small Norwegian village taken over by Nazis. Two additional choices: *A Summer Place* (1959), is a wonderful showcase of the peninsula, including Colton Hall standing in as a private girls school, and the Frank Lloyd Wright house on Carmel Point. Throughout this film the haunting violin theme permeated this soap opera. John Steinbeck's novel turned film, *Tortilla Flats* (1942) was also considered with shots of Spencer Tracy leading his *pisanos* with scenes at the old Monterey Jail and the Carmel Mission.

The legendary Sam Karras was entrenched in Monterey history as a county supervisor, teacher, and musician. He was one of the leaders of the non-profit Monterey Jazz Festival (founded in 1958). The success of the jazz festival paved the way for The Monterey Pop Festival (founded in 1967). Sam told me that George Harrison was in town and holed up at the Carmel Highlands Inn with his wife during the festival. No wonder there were rumors of a Beatles performance! *Monterey Pop* was filmed at the county fairgrounds. Our committee considered the filmed documentary for us to showcase, but the final choice, naturally, was *Play Misty for Me*.

---

95. Colton Hall is the place where, in 1849, California's State constitution was signed. The downstairs portion contained the Monterey Police Dept. during the time of the film shoot.

The Caddy

After the great success of showing *Play Misty for Me*, the next year our committee decided to screen the Dean Martin/Jerry Lewis film, *The Caddy*. It was filmed in 1953, with scenes shot at Pebble Beach's Fan Shell Beach, near Cypress Point. The film was also notable for Dean Martin's singing of one of his signature tunes, "That's Amore."

Our committee secured a 35mm print from Kit Parker and screened it at The Golden State Theater, Monterey's crown jewel of a cinema. We had as our special guest Christopher Lewis, one of Jerry's sons, in attendance and to say a few words to the audience. Like all male Boomers, I grew up watching Jerry Lewis movies. I asked Christopher if his dad knew we were playing this film. Christopher confirmed that he did, and Jerry had asked him to let him know of the audience's reaction to it. It was as close as I was ever going to get to thanking Jerry personally for the joy he had given me as a child.

An Evening with W. C. Fields

I have known Ron Fields since 1987, when I met him at the W. C. Fields festival held in Lompoc, California,[96] and I kept in touch with him over the years. We had Ron as a special guest at one of our tent meetings and at a banquet, so it was easy to invite him to give a talk about his famous grandfather. It was unanimously decided by the Film Commission to host, "An Evening with W. C. Fields" at the Monterey Convention Center. The house was packed to hear what Ron, an author and lecturer, had to say. It was a rare treat to watch *W. C. Fields: Straight Up*, an outstanding documentary featuring Ron as one of the presenters. We also showed two of W. C.'s funniest Mack Sennett shorts, *The Dentist* (1932) and *The Pharmacist* (1933), to unbridled laughter.

Monterey Movie Tours®

I first met Doug Lumsden when he established a business called Monterey Bay Scenic Tours. He had a special bus rigged with monitors, and took groups (mostly tourists) to prominent sites on the peninsula. He was

---

96. Lompoc is the city where W.C. Fields' *The Bank Dick* (1939) supposedly takes place.

a board member of the Monterey Film Commission and volunteered to assist in our "Magical Misty Tour" in 2001 by offering his specially designed bus. Doug was one of the reasons our "Misty" fundraiser was so successful, a truly nice person.

After the success of the fundraiser, it was obvious there was a tourist market for people wanting to see the landmarks from the many films shot on the peninsula. As the demand for tours grew, Doug refitted his business and renamed it, "Monterey Movie Tours." He edited scenes from the various films to illustrate his insights, matching the locations seen by the passengers on the monitor. Doug has tie-ins with the hotels and has captured the imagination of everyone interested in film history.

Bandits (2001)

The Film Commission administrators played a huge role in attracting the production for *Bandits*, starring Bruce Willis and Billy Bob Thornton. The major scenes were shot in downtown Salinas at a defunct bank. The commission invited the members and public to a special evening to dine at a restaurant in Salinas the week of the shoot. The event attracted quite a few people, one of whom was on the hunt for Billy Bob Thornton. She was a red-haired beauty and was visiting from out of the area. Everyone was in a jovial mood—almost everyone, that is. This lady said, "I thought Billy Bob Thornton was going to be here." No one on the planning committee expected the stars to show up, especially when they were in the middle of filming.

I was always ready to assist the film commission. On one occasion, I learned that an independent film crew was in town, shooting a crime-drama. They were looking for a facility to shoot a police interrogation scene. I suggested our office's interview room, pending approval by the sheriff, of course. Permission was granted and it was arranged to allow the crew access to the investigation's wing of the department during evening hours (when no one was in the building).

It took a couple of hours to build a track to glide the camera, set up lights, and shoot outside the door of the interview room. Beside the table was a one-way mirror and an adjacent video monitoring/recording room. The scene would depict a female homicide suspect being interviewed by a detective. I was there on my own time, trying to accommodate the film crew, and I was surprised when they had no actor to play the detective.

Then the director asked, "Would *you* like to do it?" Fortunately, in the event of a spontaneous news-related interview related to my PIO duties, I always kept a spare sports coat and tie at the station.

They handed me an artist's contract to portray Detective Anderson in *Gentle Hands*, which I signed on June 22, 2001, waiving any kind of a fee. I wanted to avoid any kind of conflict of interest. Prior to shooting the scene, I filled a file folder with blank pages. I made it as thick as a telephone book to create the illusion of a case file. Before I sat down at the table, I plopped the file down emphatically. The camera shot the scene at the victim's back while she talked; the camera was focused on me and my reactions. I knew that once they got back to their studio, they would edit the scene with the female suspect being full faced and another actor would be in my place from behind.

After the scene, they reset the track to extend outside the door of the monitoring room. They wanted a shot of me coming through the opposite door, closing it, and asking if they "got it?" [the recorded confession]. As one of the actors remarked, "Yeah, we got it," he then (no kidding) handed me a donut and coffee in a Styrofoam cup. I must have looked surprised, I actually thought they were playing a joke on me.

Gentle Hands was screened in L.A. for a small group of potential backers. I was invited to attend, but could not. The president of our commission went instead and reported back to me later. The whole thing was legitimate, apparently, but I don't think it ever reached the distribution stage, at least not under its working title.

There was another time I thought I was the victim of a joke. I responded to a detail at an Albertson's market at the mouth of the valley. I was unescorted and walked to the administrative area in the back. As I did, I passed the produce section. In the middle of the wide aisle there was a huge display table with an unusual promotional gimmick. It featured individual napkins with a very large ripe strawberry on each. Each strawberry had an asparagus shoot inserted with the ends sticking out of each side. I stopped in my tracks, thinking what a horrible combination it was. I entered the back of the store, only to find a camera crew setting up to film an episode of *Candid Camera*.

Chapter Nineteen

The Great Skullpture Mystery

WITH THE ELECTION OF a new sheriff, my career took a new direction. I had wanted the opportunity to go into investigations and set a path for promotion, but it hadn't worked out that way. The sheriff wanted someone to handle the media so he wouldn't have to. This was an assignment I had done before so I didn't think my career would be enhanced by going this route. In truth, I was flattered that the sheriff wanted me in there; I knew I could be of assistance.

This time, I had the full cooperation from the staff and, even more important (to me, at least), was the cooperation I received from the detectives. I was ten years removed from when I was first P.I.O. and there had been almost a 50% turnover in the Investigations Division since then.

My predecessor was a lieutenant who was supported by a sergeant and two civilians. Their positions were dissolved and personnel was reassigned by the new sheriff. I was on my own again without staff.

I was in on every detective roll call and sat silently when the cases of the day were carried out. On many of the high profile cases, I was fully involved. My job was to answer media inquiries all day that were based on a previous arrest or circumstances. At some point, I would go downstairs to the Coroner's Division and peruse the list of names of the decedents scheduled for autopsies. Some of these were of interest to the media because of who they were or if the death had been a result of a particularly tragic circumstance. It was usually my job to put out the press releases and/or press conferences. With the distribution, I was sure to be ready

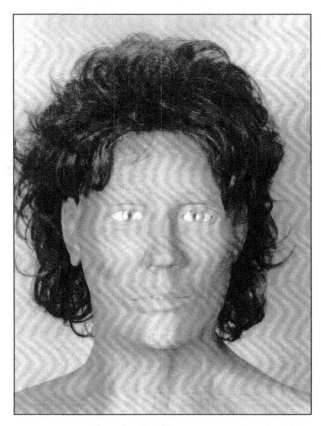

Jane Doe

for follow-up questions or to make myself available to be the on-camera spokesman. Usually, they took those shots at the front of our office, but if it was a murder or a drug lab bust. I would go to the scene to be filled in and disseminate the releasable information.

The patrol deputies were required to type into a station report log a short synopsis of the reports they had written for that shift. I remember one such report well. Deputies had responded to a house behind Carmel High School, where a woman reported that her son and a friend had been "beaten up." They made themselves sound like the victims when, in fact, they were the perpetrators.

Deputies went to the scene and noticed that a car, containing two sleeping men, was parked alongside of the parking lot. Upon being awakened by a deputy, the men explained that they were from New Zealand and, following a hard day of driving, had pulled off the road to get some sleep. In the darkness, they heard someone trying to steal something stowed atop their vehicle. The two tourists burst out of the car and caught the culprits before they could make off with their property. Those teenage thieves were given a lesson in street justice, "New Zealand style."

One of my favorite deputies, Neil Shaw, was exceptionally skilled at drawing. He was encouraged to become a police sketch artist and took a specialized class put on by the FBI at their headquarters. Deputy Shaw was able to help all of the local agencies in the county when called upon.

As part of the FBI course, Shaw was also taught how to mold clay. Using this newfound skill, he aided in solving a cold case that had languished for seven years. The body of a murdered female had been found where it was dumped, in the Big Sur wilderness of the Los Padres National Forest. The only evidence available were her skeletal remains.

Naturally, the detectives ran through all past cases involving missing persons who could match her description. In these types of cases, communication is put out to all local, state and national agencies. All the leads were run down, but without a photograph of a face or matching physical evidence, this Jane Doe continued to be unidentified.

Deputy Shaw volunteered to sculpture a clay mold of the victim's head and facial features, onto the actual skull. The interpretation was based on anthropological research from the coroner's office and on Shaw's artist rendering. A press release was sent out to all media outlets. It was hoped that, with the new image, someone might identify her and lead us to the suspect.

A press conference was held to announce that the case was being reopened. Usually representatives of the media can be pretty loose with their arrival time, but not this one. The press release announcing the unveiling generated quite a response, everyone wanted to get a good seat with cameras up close. News agencies representing all over the Bay Area came for this unmasking. Prior to the arrival of the media, Deputy Shaw and I arranged for the sculpted head to be on display near the podium. I had a black veil draped over it well before the conference, creating an eerie scene. When Shaw unveiled his creation, those hardened members of the media let out a gasp, so vivid were the woman's features. Deputy Shaw had dazzled them with his knowledge and talent.

After the press conference, one of the local news anchors approached Deputy Shaw and remarked, "that was gruesome, man." The photo image of the "Skullpture," as it came to be known, made headlines across the region. The case was now refreshed and the image of the head was on the front page of every newspaper carrying the story. Eventually there was a break in the case and the victim was identified and the suspect prosecuted.

Officer-Involved Shootings

In police work, one can never count on a nice, quiet shift. In February 2000, for instance, the midnight crew was winding down as the sun was rising. They would be going to be off-duty in another half hour—at least, that was what they were hoping for.

There was a report of a reckless driver on Highway 1, near the mouth of the valley, and one of our units spotted him driving back and forth on the road. The erratic driver tried to evade being pulled over, despite red lights and sirens, and then doubled back. The suspect then confronted the deputy head-on, with backup units coming in. It was then that shots rang out at the pursuing deputy. His beat partners saw him collapse on the front seat and returned fire at the culprit, killing him.

None of our deputies was physically hurt, but they were all relieved of their guns and placed on administrative leave, as is protocol. This froze the crime scene on the two lane portion of Highway 1 and blocked off traffic north and south, leaving no way to get around. The incident caused traffic to back up on all roads leading to it.

I was called at home and drove straight to the crime scene to get briefed on what we knew. The media had gathered and needed the information as soon as we could put it out. As the P.I.O., I briefed the journalists and promised to have a press conference later in the day. There was much concern because our office was processing the scene and identifying and recovering all the bullets that had been fired. The suspect's car was still blocking the roadway while we worked diligently. "Push him off the side of the road!" outraged motorists yelled out. Doctors insisted that they *had* to get to Big Sur. And the county supervisor of the district was deluged with phone calls, demanding that the road be cleared.

When an officer is involved in a shooting incident like this, the D.A. investigators do their own independent investigation as well. In the days that followed, the pathologist determined the cause and manner of death, and a press release was issued. What was interesting is that the local media did its own investigating of the suspect and shared all the troubles he was encountering where he lived in San Jose. The Monterey newspaper put in print, "Suicide by Cop," a term law enforcement doesn't use, however true it may be. This person purposely sought out the attention of our deputies by taking shots at them until his final confrontation. The deputies were all impacted, but being professionals, returned to work as soon as they were clear.

Citizen's Academy

During the course of Sheriff Sonne's term, I was also the instructor for the department's citizen's academy. There was a format set by my predecessor, Sgt. Bryant, who ran a fine course. He was really dedicated to it, which was inspirational to me. I competed to get the assignment and had a lot of freedom to construct the class offerings.

One advantage the sheriff's office has on city police departments for their own citizen academy's is that we have a broader range of responsibilities. These include jail, courts, patrol procedures, the gang unit, crime prevention, and investigations. There is also our records division to maintain, and finally, the coroner's division. I arranged subject matter experts on all the topics to include judges, prosecutors, crime-scene investigations, and even a mock crime scene. The gang unit scared the hell out of our citizens; they gave inside information and even predicted the imminent murder of a soon-to-be-paroled offender. A walk through the coroner's section was an experience no other agency could match for realism.

My favorite contraption for our classroom was an electric setup and monitor of a "shoot-don't-shoot" training session. It was used for training of our deputies and was a great teaching aid for our citizen academy students. Each student had the opportunity to hold a pistol simulator while facing the giant screen. They were made aware that cops had to make a split-second decision whether or not to use deadly force. This was very stressful for most of them, but they got to experience many of the ramifications of facing a dangerous scenario.

There were about a couple of dozen different scenes recorded. As students faced the unfolding scene with plastic electric guns in their holsters, they were, naturally, apprehensive. I think the first scenario started off as almost routine until the actor suddenly pulls out a gun and shoots. No one anticipated the circumstances unraveling so soon. By the next scenario, they were ready. This time, a subject kept coming suspiciously closer and closer and whips out something from inside his coat. He was holding a business card identifying himself as hearing/speaking impaired. These untrained civilians inevitably shot the innocent man and were devastated by their decision. It was a good lesson in how cops have to evaluate and make instant decisions.

I really enjoyed my time teaching the citizen's academy. After the course's completion, I made up certificates and arranged for the sheriff (or undersheriff) to personally hand them out to the graduates. Many of them joined the ranks of the Sheriff's Advisory Committee, a non-profit organization that raises money for equipment that otherwise would go unfunded.

Monterey County Peace Officers Association President

I had been on the board of directors for the M.C.P.O.A. for five years when, in 2002, I was sworn in as president of that non-profit organization. This body was established in 1947 and was formed to recognize accomplishments of peace officers, prosecutors, and civilians. It was also a law-enforcement society that represented all cities' police departments, the county and state agencies working in Monterey County. A board meeting was held once a month to cover business and to receive recommendations for award considerations for sworn personnel or civilian actions.

There were monthly meetings of the general membership, usually at a restaurant banquet room. The respective chiefs or sheriff would read a citation acknowledging the "above and beyond the call of duty" actions of the deserving recipient. Then, to great applause from the audience, the hero would come forward to receive the certificate from the board and take part in a photo-op with their boss.

At one of those monthly meetings, I did something that had heretofore never been tried: I sent out a press release and invited the media to one of our award nights. I was especially interested in acknowledging Deputy Scott Regan who, without regard for himself, reached into a burning car to rescue a woman. A local camera crew did show up, but it became awkward fast. As the members were dining with their loved ones, the camera started panning the room. There were some undercover cops and other professionals who did not want to be seen. Needless to say, that particular experiment was never attempted again. My term expired at the end of 2002, and it coincided with a big banquet for the "Officer of the Year" honors. For this annual occasion, the board always approved a keynote speaker to lead things off. This time, we set out to acknowledge the one-year anniversary of the 9/11 catastrophe at the World Trade Center. We invited a representative of New York PD to address us, and we made it known we did not want an administrator—we wanted someone who had responded to the disaster.

A friend of a friend knew of just the person to speak to our members; he was a motorcycle cop from NYPD. He came in his uniform and motorcycle boots and told us his firsthand account of what he and his comrades went through that day. The packed room hung on his every word. It really hit home to the audience when the officer recalled, "As the people were running out of the building, we were running in." The line was repeated for emphasis, "We were running in as the people were running out."

Paul McCartney

Meanwhile, back at home, I loved being a dad. I was Doug's T-ball coach and I took him and Diana to all the "kid" movies of that era. I raised them to have an appreciation for the music of The Beatles, and I finally got a chance to see one of them perform.

In 2002, Paul McCartney came to my home town, San Jose, to perform with his new band. I was determined to go and take along Diana, who was a wide-eyed eleven-year-old at the time. There were problems at home over the dispersal of money, but I made this a priority. I announced that I was getting tickets for the April 3, 2002 concert, which immediately started an argument.

"You *can't* go," my wife said firmly. "Maybe next time he's in town . . .," which effectively meant never. I was fuming, especially when the play date came and went.

I got the surprise of my life when Paul, following his scheduled tour, announced that he was coming back for another concert, this time on the twenty-second of October. My wife couldn't say anything about it, and I secured two great seats. Diana and I went to a fancy restaurant and had the time of our lives, watching the master at work.

The day after the concert was a scheduled day off, but when I got back to work, Deputy Tim Krebs casually mentioned that he had seen Paul McCartney during his patrol duties. The former Beatle was buying a box of Girl Scout cookies at the front of Safeway at the Crossroads. I didn't know what to think at the time, but years later I learned it was true. McCartney divulged in an interview that he had always wanted to meet Doris Day, so he arranged a meeting at her house. He even mentioned that he had brought along Girl Scout cookies as a gift.

San Francisco Teens Found Dead in Greenfield

It was early in the morning on March 6, 2003, and I was just preparing for my day as P.I.O. when South County units responded to an emergency call. A hysterical female had called 9-1-1 to report that two students who had gone missing the night before had been found dead that morning. On my scanner, I heard the dispatcher update the units as the details were coming in. It was relayed that two ex-Marines were in the campground during the night and they were carrying knives. The female was certain that the Marines were responsible and that they were still in the area.

Everyone rolled on that one, including me. All the local newspaper and television stations have police scanners in their offices and they regularly hear calls coming in. The crime scene was in the unincorporated area of Monterey County, near the river gorge of the Los Padres National Forest near Greenfield. The reporting party was a student from Urban Pioneer Experiential Academy in San Francisco. She had come to the area with her classmates on a field trip and had stayed overnight. Apparently, there were three separate tents: one for the boys, one for the girls, and one for the teacher. While the teacher slept, the teenagers had a party in the girls' tent. At one point, two Marines showed up with liquor and crashed the party. This disturbed two of the male students, who set out in the darkness to reach the teacher's tent. They were slightly intoxicated and their only light source was a Bic® lighter. They were on a steep ravine trail and never came back. Their bodies were discovered in the morning light.

The two victims had fallen a great distance, and the students assumed they had been murdered because a knife was found next to them.

Naturally, the media came out in force.

Detectives and crime-scene technicians combed and secured the area. What was unusual in this case was that a local TV station crew beat the deputies to the scene and videotaped the area and especially the bodies of the two seventeen-year-old victims. I overheard that local news outlets were offering the Bay Area news teams footage, which is pretty standard. Our office assisted in securing transportation for the students after we interviewed them.

We were all there all day and, by that time, the detectives and coroner investigators had a good idea of what had transpired. The two victims were trying to walk the narrow ridge in the dark and fell. There was blunt force trauma to their heads consistent with a fall and without any other noticeable injuries. A knife they were carrying had no blood on it and laid beside their crumpled bodies. Of course, the victims would be autopsied in the days ahead for an official cause of death, but it was enough for me to realize this was an accident, not a murder.

I held a preliminary press conference at the scene and laid out a simple, overall summation of what our department was doing and gave an update on the teenagers' plight. All the media outlets were trying to interview the students and it was becoming an absolute zoo with all the "loose maniacs in the forest" theories.

I did something I had never done, before or since: I sought out a veteran news reporter from a San Francisco television station whom I recognized. It was Rigo Chacon, the same reporter who covered an attack on one of my fellow academy classmates back in 1979. I pulled him over to talk to him privately, away from the madding crowd. I said to him, "You are a veteran journalist and you can read the body language of our detectives; does it look like they're moving with adrenaline?" It was an odd question to be sure, but he understood without my having to say that this may not be the huge murder everyone is making it out to be.

Chacon let it all sink in and knew to downplay the murder scenario. This was still a sensational story, especially because the students were from San Francisco. The big question was; how did the onsite teacher and school administers agree to this arrangement? That was for someone else to answer. In my absence at the scene, our department was flooded with phone calls from reporters who wanted more information. I held a press conference with my supervisor, Sgt. Chris Pascone, back at the office, and we updated a press release, stating that we were searching for the two persons of interest.

With wide coverage and front-page newspaper headlines all across Northern California, the two adult men came to our office of their own volition to be interviewed. They had no idea of the details of the deaths. As soon as the autopsy results were available, we held yet another press conference to confirm that the victims had died as a result of an accidental fall in the darkness. Toxicology test results were pending, but it wouldn't change the boys' "accidental death" status.

By the end of the year, the charter school was discontinued and many lawsuits were pending. It was a sad situation all around. It turned out that this had been the last press conference I ever held. A promotion was waiting in the wings.

Sergeant Cassara

After twenty-two years in the department, I was promoted to sergeant by the newly elected sheriff, Mike Kanalakis. Assignments were based on seniority, so I did my turn working the midnight shift at the Salinas office. The crew was made up of both veterans and fresh rookies. There was always action in these enormous beats from North County to the valley and some of its more notorious neighborhoods.

I was now in my early fifties and had gained a vast amount of knowledge, but I was experiencing severe hearing problems. I had been exposed to close-range shooting, cumulative exposure to Code 3[97] responses, and an inordinate amount of eardrum-piercing audible alarms. I was also exposed to an accidental firing of another deputy's weapon next to me that resulted in permanent loss of hearing in one ear.

It didn't help either that I was in a Code 3 pursuit during a kidnapping in progress. I spotted the suspect, vehicle, and victim heading in a southerly direction. Even with red lights and siren blaring, I couldn't get the suspect to pull over. He continued driving south all along Highway 1 to the county line at San Luis Obispo. Reinforcements were waiting there and they took him into custody. I drove seventy-five miles with the overhead pulsating siren hitting me like angry ocean waves. As we say in the vocation, "you can't outrun Motorola" (the radio). There is an unwritten code in law enforcement that can best be described as survival of the fittest. A distinct culture of distrust takes place for anyone over fifty, especially with a perceived disability. In the profession, it is known that we will break down physically at some point—some just reach that juncture earlier than others. There is a legal mechanism in place to force peace officers from their jobs if they are a danger to others, and hearing loss can be a contributing factor.

---

97. Code Three is ten code for "Lights and sirens."

I recalled how we used to make fun of an older deputy who suffered from hearing loss; he was working his regular midnight shift and backed up another deputy for an alarm activation. Deputy Homan arrived first and waited for his fill unit. He informed the deputy who had just arrived, "There's an open door." The impaired deputy repeated, "Oh, Code-4,"[98] and then drove off. We all thought it was funny at the time, little did I know.

I continued to work swing shift at the Salinas office and later transferred back to the Monterey office to supervise many of the deputies whom I had broken in as their training officer. It was a welcome transition for me, though my hearing problems were still an issue.

Terry Melcher Dies

On November 19, 2004, Terry died at the untimely age of sixty-two, in Beverly Hills. The cause of death was announced as melanoma. It was front-page news in the *Monterey Herald* and hit the music industry right between the eyes. Terry was not recognized as an entertainer so much as a producer; he made things happen in that business.

Doris Day went into seclusion when her son died. Terry had told me that his mom offered her full support when he married Terese, there was a very tight connection there.

On December 7, 2004, Terry's son, Ryan organized a memorial service for his father at the Carmel Mission, the burial place of Father Junipero Serra, who has since been canonized. It was a beautiful short service for friends and family. Doris did not attend. The proceedings were officiated by Monsignor Declan, who gave a soothing eulogy. No one else spoke.

Of course, I went to the service and met Terry's family at their home. Ryan stood up and spoke about his dad. He became a man that day; he even got a nod of approval from his mom. There were many people there, but it was not overcrowded. There were a lot of friends of the family, but not too many from the music profession. I did notice one well-dressed gentleman with a British accent, who had traveled alone to the States to pay his respects. He was a musician and former Apple executive who had known Terry back in the day.

---

98. Code Four means "no further assistance needed."

Edgar Kennedy-Master of the Slow Burn

In 2005 I finally became the author of a book! That quest had its beginnings five years earlier when Edgar's daughter, Colleen, invited me to her residence in Sebastopol, California, and announced that I had "earned the right" to write a book about her dad. I took it on as a responsibility. She showed me a cardboard box full of old stills, which really jump-started my investigation. I read anything and everything that had been written about Edgar, which didn't amount to much. I became very skeptical of articles in movie magazines because most of these were supplied by studio publicists and bore little resemblance to the truth; it was, after all, their job to create an actor's public image. A more reliable source came in the form of old newspaper accounts. Way before the internet, I had to drive to the San Francisco library and went through microfilm of the sports pages from the *San Francisco Chronicle* to trace Edgar's amateur and professional boxing careers. I found some references in Oakland newspapers as well.

I made special arrangements to go through Radio-Keith-Orpheum (R.K.O.) scripts that were stored off campus at UCLA. The old Edgar Kennedy "Average Man" scripts had been thrown in cardboard boxes along with other two-reel comedy scripts without any organization. I pored over material at the Margaret Herrick Library in Beverly Hills and read every published review of Edgar's films in the trade journals. Among the items pertaining to Edgar was an old one sheet bio, it identified his high school as San Rafael. This was news to Colleen.

The family had an intriguing photo of Edgar in his youth posing with other actors his own age. Colleen was sure it was taken in San Francisco, but I could never figure out where. There was never a San Rafael school in San Francisco, so my investigation led me to the San Rafael city library. I asked if they might have a high school yearbook from 1905 somewhere, knowing the chances were slim. As luck had it, the librarian led me to a small area away from the other section. She pointed out old local history archives and said, "we only have a few of the older yearbooks." There were scarce yearbooks going back that far, but there was one…and it was from 1905, could there be something in there?

I opened the small cardboard backing of the yearbook and flipped to the photographs; and there it was, an exact match of the photo the family had. It also identified all the players and the date. Not only that, but the yearbook featured a winning essay by one Edgar Kennedy. I couldn't believe my luck, this sixteen-year-old student wrote about going back to his family's homestead and described his day. For an author, that is tantamount to finding gold. If that wasn't enough, I was given access to microfilm of the San Rafael newspaper and looked up the date of the play. Gold again! A reporter attended the play and described it fully, Edgar was the star with his comic performance as the lion in an adaption of William Shakespeare's, "A Midsummer's Night Dream."

In all, it took me five years to research and write the book. The last year was especially hectic after learning that Colleen had terminal cancer; she never told me this herself, but her children discreetly filled me in. It was a race against the clock. When the book finally rolled off the presses, I immediately drove to Colleen's house to give her the first copy. Fortunately, she was alert. I presented her with the first book ever written about her famous father and she clutched it to her bosom. Flipping through the pages, she remarked, "I could *never* have done this." Three days later, she died in peace.

Michelle enters my life

I met my future wife at a Sons of the Desert banquet in Los Angles. The facility was at the Culver Hotel, where many exterior scenes in Laurel & Hardy's movies had been shot. Michelle Benton and her sister, Kimm, were sitting at the wrong assigned table when I walked in. Michelle turned away from me as I sat down and didn't warm up until Mark Kennedy (Edgar's grandson) and his wife sat down. It might have been "hate at first sight," but we started talking and she was very vivacious. What impressed me most was how respectful she was to the people at the microphone; she gave them her full attention and applauded supportively. I thought she must be in the entertainment business, and she was. She worked at the Hollywood Bowl and the Pantages Theater.

She asked what I did for a living and I told her, "I'm a cop." She found that "fascinating." I asked if she wanted to go on a ride-along with me and she took me up on it—but not for a while. It finally happened during Christmas week of 2004, when I was working on the peninsula as the shift sergeant. An incident went down in Robles Del Rio (Carmel Valley) involving a domestic dispute. When the deputies and I arrived, the huge front bay window was broken out and the living room was a mess. The family had been dining when something triggered an argument, which soon turned physical. Unfortunately, there was a five-year-old child impacted by all this, and he was crying. The adults were too busy fighting to comfort the boy.

As the deputies sorted things out, I retrieved a Teddy bear from a container in my trunk (we carried such things just for this purpose). The little boy clutched the furry figure and I said some soothing words.

The primary instigator had fled the scene before the deputies arrived, and we needed to talk to him. As Deputy Irons took down the details for the report, I waited up the road in case he returned. As I blacked out the patrol car and stayed a bit hidden, I explained to Michelle that, as the sergeant, I had to look out for the deputies and, hopefully, intercept him if he came back. "But he could have a gun," Michelle said with concern.

"That's right, he could," I said. "This is our job."

It was an eye-opener for Michelle, but it was a fairly routine call. Fortunately, the suspect did not return to the scene that night.

Professional Services/Internal Affairs

There came an opening in the Professional Standards Division for a sergeant to be an internal investigator, an administration duty. I was ready for it: I was senior to most everyone and it seemed like a natural progression. The sheriff appointed me to the position after a competitive selection process.

As an I.A. sergeant, it was my job to ensure that all investigations were handled impartially and to protect the department from various liability issues. The sheriff and his staff relied on unbiased investigations.

Chapter Twenty

Wedding of the Century

SEPTEMBER 3–4, 2006. Those were the special dates when Michelle Benton and I were married in an unlikely marriage ceremony in Carmel. Our very special hostess was the legendary film actress Joan Fontaine. Joan had known of my budding relationship with Michelle and wanted to meet her. The three of us met at a restaurant, where Joan and Michelle hit it off immediately. At one point, Joan turned to me and said, "I approve." Then she surprised us by offering, "Why don't you kids get married at my place?" Michelle and I just looked at each other and quickly agreed. The thought of a wedding in front of our friends and family with a backdrop of the Pacific Ocean was almost too much of a dream.

What could go wrong?

The day of the wedding finally arrived. We all met at a designated point so no one would get lost trying to drive and park near Joan's house. Michelle and her sister (in full gown and makeup) went on ahead to prepare while the rest of us were to wait for the signal to convoy up.

Once the bride and the matron of honor made it to Joan's house, they found her in garden clothes. She walked Michelle into the back yard and announced to the gardener, "The bride thinks the wedding is today." Joan then shooed them away with instructions to "come back tomorrow, the correct date." YIKES! The girls made a graceful exit, then made a mad dash to the car, (cell phones were useless in the Carmel Highlands area). The immediate goal was to stop the guests from arriving.

The pressure came on like a tourniquet. Fortunately, the girls headed us off in the exit driveway before we could leave. Michelle gestured frantically; something was not quite right. Her sister broke the news to

Michelle, me, Joan Fontaine

me: "Joan thinks the wedding is tomorrow." We planned the wedding for the middle of the Labor Day weekend so that our out-of-town guests had time to get there and back.

Michelle and I conveyed the same goal: to get married that day while all our guests were present. I couldn't just walk up to Michelle and communicate directly; I wasn't even supposed to see her gown before the ceremony! People weren't sure if we were to be married in the parking lot, at a shopping center, or on the beach.

I made the announcement to "follow me," starting a convoy of cars reminiscent of *It's a Mad Mad Mad Mad World*, a touch of Keaton's *Seven Chances*, and various Mack Sennett car chases.

About a mile away, I knew of a very private area in Carmel Valley with a lakeside view. To access the gated community, I informed the security guard that I was the groom and that the entire wedding party was behind me. Each car then shot past the lone security guard.

We were in luck. The area was not only vacant, it was already set up for a wedding! I ran inside the adjacent barnhouse/office and yelled out for anyone to answer. I was hoping to make a quick deal/arrangement to secure the setup, but there was no one in sight.

Our guests took in the beautiful surroundings. There was a wondrous lake surrounded by woods with an overhang, complete with fresh flowers. White bridal chairs were already in rows for guests. Thousands of rose pedals lined the path. Was this divine intervention?

The groom was there, the judge, and the best man, but we had lost track of the bride. After what seemed like an eternity, Michelle and her sister arrived. I was a little nervous—not about getting married—but that the real bridal party would show up and run us out with pitchforks. I was, however, comforted by the fact that the sheriff of Monterey County was one of our guests and that a superior court judge would be presiding.

My best man was Mark Kennedy, Edgar's grandson. He was present when Michelle and I first met. We tied the knot after a brief but wonderful ceremony and retreated to the neighboring golf course restaurant (appropriately named "Edgar's") for an impromptu reception. After a few rounds of toasts, everyone took a pledge to stay an extra night so Joan wouldn't be disappointed.

The next day arrived and all was smooth, *except that the judge couldn't make it.* We were technically married, so all we needed was for someone to read our unique vows again. Mark's brother, Glenn, volunteered to do the honors. Bob Zeroun had brought along a choir robe, which Glenn wore for the ceremony. Joan was very elegant and led us to her beautiful rose garden, where we restated our vows. Joan was none the wiser. Once the ceremony was complete, Joan opened her home for a wonderful cake and champagne reception. While making a toast, I adlibbed, "On behalf of Joan Fontaine, everyone is invited to come back in fifty years to celebrate our golden anniversary." Joan had to laugh at that one.

Thankfully (or should I say *hopefully*) she never found out about our "double wedding" that weekend.

Sheriff Kanalakis Fundraiser

The time had come for local elections again and I very much wanted Sheriff Kanalakis to win. He had observed my career from the start and was the one who promoted me. I'll always be grateful to him for that.

Since I had a proven record of fundraising with film events, I suggested that we show *One-Eyed Jacks* (1961) at Monterey's Golden State Theater. The film was directed by and stars Marlin Brando, which made it unique in itself. Karl Malden was cast as the sheriff of Monterey in this Western, and his deputy was none other than Slim Pickens. The film was shot on the Monterey Peninsula and had some prominent scenes in Pebble Beach, making it perhaps the only Western with the Pacific Ocean as its backdrop.

Prior to the event I managed to obtain Mr. Malden's phone number via actor Anthony Caruso's widow, they were family friends for years. I arranged for Malden and Kanalakis to talk to each other by phone. Malden was very obliging and the two talked "sheriff to sheriff." I got a big kick out of that. Naturally, the sheriff extended a welcome to Malden; he even offered to sponsor his transportation. The ninety-two-year-old actor begged off, citing a previous golf commitment.

Slim Pickens

Whenever I went to the Sheriff's Posse clubhouse, I would look at a plaque on the wall recognizing Slim Pickens as an "Honorary Monterey Sheriff's Posse." It was awarded to him in 1961 while Slim was in the area making *One-Eyed Jacks*. He had begun his career in show business as a rodeo clown. He was absolutely loved by the hard-drinking, hard-swearing members of the Sheriff's Posse, a non-profit organization. Slim had appeared in more than 170 films and TV shows. His most famous role was as a crazy cowboy who rides a launched nuclear bomb in Stanley Kubrick's *Dr. Strangelove, or How I Learned to Stop Worrying and Love the Bomb* (1964).

Aimee Semple McPherson

The noted faith-healing evangelist made her way into folklore by claiming she had been a victim of a kidnapping in 1926. There is a Salinas and Carmel connection to this story, and I'm thankful that Henry Brandon filled me in on it back in 1988.

Aimee Semple McPherson built a temple in Glendale, California, and claimed to have great powers of healing. The people who couldn't flock to her place of worship benefited by the power of the relatively new medium of radio. Her sermons were broadcast by her in-house radio hookup. She was a superstar during her lifetime and probably as well known as the president of the United States, Babe Ruth, and Jack Dempsey.

McPherson went missing in May of 1926, much to the concern of her followers, who feared she had been washed out to sea at Venice Beach. The newspapers followed the story for weeks. Eventually, she reappeared in Mexico, telling a tall tale of being kidnapped, held for ransom, and finally managing to escape her captors. The story was a sensation and held the nation's interest during the five weeks she had been missing. One of her followers actually drowned while searching for her in the Pacific Ocean. During McPherson's disappearance, she was spotted in Carmel with her radio man. They hunkered down in a bungalow overseeing the ocean.

The Los Angeles County district attorney charged McPherson with numerous counts. A preliminary trial was held at great expense to the city and to international attention. She maintained that she had been kidnapped, but the evidence never matched up. The prosecutor questioned her on the stand and asked if she "would like to change any of your testimony?" McPherson famously answered, "That's my story and I'm sticking to it."

I became interested in this case because of what Henry Brandon said to me, "They got caught shacking up in Carmel." It always struck me as very strange that during McPherson's disappearance, her mother gave up hope immediately that she would ever return. In law enforcement we learned behavioral patterns of mothers with missing offspring, they *never* give up hope, even years after.

I was retired by now and got Michelle interested in the case. Together we sought out old issues of the *Carmel Pine Cone* of the period. We started at the Carmel library and were redirected to an archive in a separate facility. This small town newspaper covered the story worthy of a Pulitzer Prize for journalism. The locals had recognized McPherson and her guest and reported them to the authorities. The bungalow where they stayed was still intact by 2005.

Michelle and I in Nottingham, England

Chapter Twenty-one

Death Denied and the Rest of My Life As an Author

ALL CALIFORNIA PEACE OFFICERS know there are physical standards we must maintain, but there is no denying the aging process. I was lucky: some officers get injured on the job and can no longer work in the profession. It was my inability to hear high-frequency sounds that did me in. I also could not hear whispers or children's voices. There is a statute on the books in California that allows the agency to impose retirement to those whose hearing is not up to set legal standards. It is based on a case in which a traffic sergeant had a hard time discerning when people were talking to him. No one wants a hearing-impaired cop working in life and death situations wherein comprehending language is all-important.

Peace officers who have lost their hearing have a hard time testifying in court. I personally had a couple of instances when I thought the opposing attorney was deliberately trying to wear me down by asking question while his back was to me. There were only so many times when I could ask the attorney to repeat or rephrase the question before becoming the subject of negative attention and/or lack of credibility. The year was 2007 and it was time for me to go back on patrol. I wanted to get out of office work and work swing shift back in Monterey, something for which I had the seniority to do. Prior to obtaining approval, I had to have my hearing tested. I was sent to a specialist in San Francisco, where I spent half a day going through sundry hearing challenges. What really got me was an audio with background noise that I was supposed to decipher. I'm not sure *anyone* could pass that test. So that was it, the department was going to impose retirement on me, but I had my pride. I elected to have a service retirement instead. I went out the way I wanted. For the next three years, I became a sheriff's civil processor on a part-time basis.

Dorothy DeBorba

Dorothy DeBorba had been a dear friend of the Sons of the Desert through the years. Best known as "Little Echo," she had been one of the members of Hal Roach's Our Gang. She lived in Livermore on the East Bay and made a point of attending our banquets on a yearly basis. On those occasions, she often stayed at my house. The last time I saw Dorothy was when our Midnight Patrol tent was celebrating its twenty-fifth anniversary. The venue for the event was the Edison Theater in Niles (Fremont District), California. It was now 2009 and Dorothy was confined to a wheelchair and dependent on an oxygen bag, but she was not going to miss this event! The last image I have of her is Dorothy sitting in her wheelchair, laughing at the antics on the screen. She was not conscious of it, but directly behind her was a large cardboard cutout of the Keystone Cops in their automobile during a chase scene. The camera captured the seemingly merged images; it looks like Dorothy's wheelchair was the rear tire and along on the pursuit, a perfect symbolic exit. This was Dorothy's last public appearance, she died shortly afterwards.

Vernon Dent: Stooge Heavy

\Back in 1986, I bought a book entitled, *The Columbia Comedy Shorts*, by Ted Okuda and Ed Watz. That book was a revelation to me. I had always been interested in the Three Stooges, but I found myself wondering more and more about the supporting players in their two-reel comedies. This book provided the most thorough information about everyone associated with the studio. What floored me most of all was a short bio on actor Vernon Dent. The authors had interviewed Vernon's widow and identified his place of birth as San Jose, California! I never heard that before.

Vernon Dent (1895–1963) was a singer, songwriter, and comedian who more or less followed Roscoe "Fatty" Arbuckle's career path. Roscoe had also made his singing debut in San Jose and became a popular film comedian who worked for Mack Sennett. Vernon broke into movies in 1919 and was active in the industry until 1954.

I set out to find more information on Vernon and his family and eventually hit pay dirt with the census of 1900. I found out his saloon keeper father was murdered in 1909, a crime well covered in newspapers of the time. Trips to the main library were also fruitful: I was able to confirm where Vernon's family originated, going back to his grandfather's fruit orchard estate. It turns out that this particular residence is within walking distance of the neighborhood in which I grew up. Equating research with investigating a case, I tried to visit every residence at which Vernon once lived. Using old-fashioned gumshoe techniques, I was able to discover many interesting facts about my subject's life and career.

My mentor, Ed Watz,[99] was a source of great encouragement on the Vernon Dent book. Since he was partially responsible for interviewing Vernon's widow back in the 1980s, I was anxious to learn many more details that didn't make it into his (and Ted Okuda's) book, *The Columbia Comedy Shorts*. These table scraps were like gold to me; I used them to pursue fresh leads. Ed contributed many photographs to the book, as well as the foreword. He did a terrific job.

As word spread about the book I was writing, illustrator and humorist Drew Friedman approached me with an offer to help. Drew is the author of many books and a first-class caricaturist. He gave me the most fantastic drawing of Vernon bumping Moe, Larry, and Shemp's heads together. It graces the book's back cover.

After *Vernon Dent: Stooge Heavy* was published, I got the biggest surprise: my aunt informed me that my grandmother, who had also been born in 1895, attended the Horace Mann school in San Jose. My grandmother and Vernon not only went to the same school, *they were in the same class*! My aunt didn't know a thing about Vernon until she read my book, and my grandmother (who died in 1967) certainly never mentioned anything about Vernon to anyone. The right question might have prompted her memory, but who would have done that?

Giants Win World Series

During 2010, I began to feel ill, light-headed, and faint. I couldn't imagine what was wrong with me and I didn't have enough sense to make an appointment with a doctor. My mind was more occupied by the Giants,

---

99. Ed Watz also authored the book, *Wheeler and Woolsey: The Vaudeville Comic Duo and Their Films, 1929–1937* (Jefferson, NC: McFarland & Company, 1994).

who were on fire that year. They not only made the playoffs, they plowed through each playoff rung to qualify for the World Series!

I was also preoccupied by the process of finishing up the Vernon Dent book, so I was busy. When it was published in October of that year, I decided to take a nice, long train ride to Oregon to visit my friend, fellow author Lon Davis. The trip was something of a pilgrimage for me. Lon and his wife, Debra, lived in Eugene, not far from the town of Cottage Grove, where Buster Keaton had shot *The General* in 1926. Lon, a silent film historian, and one of the world's nicest people, took me on a tour of the little town and even showed me the diamond where Buster and his crew played baseball between takes. I always embraced the fact that Buster used to play baseball when he was stuck on the next scene during filming, and I can relate to how that all works.

The Giants were on the cusp of winning, but sleep eluded me and I was still feeling quite ill. While having dinner at my hosts' home, my cell phone rang. It was a call from my son, which was quickly followed by one from my wife. They were both calling to celebrate the Giants' victory in the World Series. It was a moment I had waiting for my entire life! On the long journey home, the train went through the Bay Area on the very day of the World Series victory parade. All travel venues were blocked by hordes of Giants' fans traveling to San Francisco by way of Oakland.

Illness Strikes Me Down

My health continued to deteriorate. I felt weak and dizzy all through Christmas and into the New Year. Once I retired from the sheriff's office, there were no health benefits, so I just hoped to ride out the symptoms. Things finally caught up to me on April 15, 2011. That was the day I almost died.

My wife had made an especially delicious dinner that night, but I was distracted by a sharp pain in my solar plexus. Prior to this, I might have attributed the discomfort to a previous lower back injury. Hoping my symptoms amounted to everyday heartburn, I took some antacids. Later that evening, I voided black blood. With my coroner's experience, I should have recognized this as an emergency, but I did not. I was, however, concerned that I was not experiencing any relief, so I decided to lie down and sleep for a while. As I did so, I felt as though I was hit by a lightning bolt. I jumped up and—blackness descended. I collapsed on the hardwood floor, unconscious. I was hemorrhaging blood; it was pumping out of me. Michelle tried to rouse me but could not. She also attempted to move me as I was blocking the doorway. Her first thought was to jump out the bedroom window to a phone, but the seconds were ticking away and I was still bleeding. Michelle's adrenaline and good sense gave her superhuman strength; she grabbed my arm, slid me across the floor and sat me up against the wall. It was then that I started to come around. I could hear her scream, "Bill! Bill!" She slapped my cheek, causing me to open my eyes. That was the positive sign she needed; she then scrambled up to kitchen's phone.

As I slowly regained consciousness and strength, I could hear Michelle talking with a 9-1-1 emergency dispatcher. "My husband . . . my husband!" then I could hear her retching. She was calmed down by the dispatcher enough to get the basic details; an ambulance was dispatched to a victim of a "G.I. [gastro-intestinal] bleed." Michelle was told to wait outside to wave in the ambulance crew.

I was conscious enough to survey the large amount of blood on the floor and clinically knew I might only have a few moments left before shock set in. Then the strangest thing happened. I stood up, walked into the bathroom, and started to *wash my feet*! I was, remarkably, free of pain.

When the ambulance crew arrived, I could tell from their reactions that they were seeing a dramatically large amount of blood. With an upright and empty gurney facing me at the door of the bathroom, I took one slow step after another to reach them. By this time I was experiencing an endorphin rush and even hallucinated that I was entering the gates of Heaven. In the ensuing medical reports, it was documented that I lost 40 percent of my blood; had it been 41 percent, I would have died. In fact, it was a miracle that I survived. A John Lennon song, "She Said, She Said," includes the lyric, "I know what it's like to be dead." I shudder at the recollection.

I was fully alert when they took me Code 3 to the hospital, with intravenous drips in place. I knew that if I bled again it would be all over, but once I made it to the hospital they began immediate transfusions. Two doctors were attending to me; they were also trying to figure out the cause of my bleeding. I heard one said to the other, "We may have to do exploratory surgery." I almost popped up to object. I lay there, seemingly for hours, wondering how my dear wife was coping.

Michelle told me later that once I was enroute to the hospital she got on the phone to tell her sister in the Los Angeles area to come on up, but what amazed me was she had the determination to soak up the blood with towels—every last towel in the house. She then bolted to the hospital to see me. I could tell she was more traumatized than I. She stayed there and helped wipe my legs and feet. I warned her that the blood might be contaminated, but she continued.

They finally wheeled me into the critical care unit and, amazingly, my Michelle was there to greet me with a reassuring smile. It was that million-dollar brightness about her that inspired me. The medical personnel fitted me with three IV's on each arm and, as I was set down in my bed, I thought I must be pretty important as I had my own room. Michelle sat next to me but— fearing that she needed sleep even more than I did—I sent her home. I was almost afraid to go to sleep, believing I might never wake up again. There was so much more for me to accomplish in my life, and I wanted to see my children grow up.

I spent six days in the hospital undergoing every test imaginable. I was told that it was a good thing that I had bled out like I did; otherwise, I most likely would have died from peritonitis. The cause of my illness was ulcers that had triggered bleeding into my abdomen. As a result, I was woefully anemic for the next couple of years.

Joan Fontaine's Death

By 2013, Michelle and I moved back to San Jose to further my recovery. It was a most welcome homecoming for me; I had been gone since 1979. It was wonderful to rediscover the old haunts in the neighborhood where I grew up.

Joan and I had kept up communication through the years and we always exchanged Christmas cards. One summer day in 2013, Joan called me. It was evident that she was feeling a little down; I could even hear a few sniffles. I offered to come see her, but she told me that she would call me when she wanted me to come to her home. That was our last communication. Joan Fontaine died peacefully at the age of ninety-six on December 15, 2013. Joan tried very hard to outlive Olivia, but it was not to be. I learned of Joan's death via social media. I wasn't sure what to do, so I immediately phoned Joan's house, not knowing if anyone would pick up. Someone named Susan answered the phone; I was thankful she knew who I was; Joan had kept a framed photo of Michelle's and my wedding picture with Joan posing with us on her vanity desk. I asked if

I was needed to come over to the house as per Joan's wishes, but Susan reassured me that "everything was under control." That was good enough for me. The attorney took charge of her estate.

Joan's personal effects were auctioned off by Christie's in New York, Her Academy Award statuette (for her role in Alfred Hitchcock's 1941 drama *Suspicion*) was reportedly worth $300,000. There were 104 lots of fine art, silver, furniture, and jewelry, as well as a 1935 painting by Marc Chagall, "Vase of Flowers in the Window," valued at $600,000. Her elegant home was also auctioned off as real property. Her total assets amounted to $40 million, bequeathed mostly to the Salvation Army. She had also earmarked $1 million to the S.P.C.A. of Monterey. Joan had always loved dogs, particular golden retrievers.

Ted Healy: Nobody's Stooge (2015)

While I was recovering from my illness, I was very interested in learning about Ted Healy, that oft-maligned creative genius who discovered Samuel Horwitz, Moses, Horwitz, Jerome Horwitz, and Louis Feinberg. They became better known in their own Columbia Pictures short subject film series as Shemp Howard, Moe Howard, Curly Howard, and Larry Fine—The Three Stooges.[100]

I was pretty well informed about the comedy team, having read every book written by and about them. Most of them begrudgingly gave Healy credit for their discovery, then quickly moved on. I had always wanted to know how the act got started.

I was able to dedicate a lot of time searching through old newspapers that were available online. I queried the name Ted Healy and got piles of hits from all over the county. The first accounting of his professional act surfaced in, of all places, San Jose, and even more coincidentally, it was on August 18 [1918], the same month and day as my birthday! These were good signs to me to dive into his life to see if he was book worthy.

I compiled all the data I could find about the successful vaudevillian who had been born Charles Earnest Lee Nash in Texas on October 1, 1896. Facts were sporadic because, during his lifetime, no one had ever interviewed him in depth. Ted Healy and his wife starred in the 1925 Earl Carrol *Vanities* on Broadway, their first stooge was a dog. I followed

---

100. As Vernon Dent's widow, Eunice, told Ed Watz, "The Three Stooges were weird—all four of them."

a story from the *New York Times*, describing how Healy and his crew were lost at sea and could not show up for his starring performance. During the days he and his crew were missing, it was big news. The harbor police were worried that he was lost at sea. When his yacht was recovered offshore from New Jersey, it made headlines across the region. If Healy wasn't a big name before, he certainly had name recognition now.

Yes, Ted Healy was book worthy. By following his career in the newspaper accounts, I was able to cobble together pre-Three Stooges history and detailed the evolution of the act.

Meeting Moe Howard's Daughter

I have always had great respect for Moe Howard, who died on May 4, 1975. I read his autobiography when it was posthumously published in 1977 and latched onto every word. He spoke so respectfully about his mentor, Ted Healy, and how he had learned the art of comic timing from him. I took a chance and handwrote a letter to his only daughter, Joan Howard Maurer, requesting an interview for the book. She contacted me via email and invited me to visit her at her home in Los Angeles.

Michelle and I were greeted warmly by Joan; she was intrigued that I was researching Healy's life. Joan brought out a special file of photographs marked "Ted Healy." They were precious original photos of Ted and Moe dating back to 1929–1933, when the Stooges were firmly part of Healy's act. Moe had saved them all those years.

Before she brought out the pictures, Joan impressed on me that "Ted Healy was *very* generous to our family." She was speaking from personal experience. One of her first memories was Christmas of 1929. Healy sent for the family to spend the holidays at his palatial home in Connecticut. Joan still vividly remembered the huge ornaments on the giant Christmas tree, as well as petting one of Healy's horses.

She also had some snapshots taken by her mother, Helen, during that weeklong visit. The images of Ted and Moe were casual and friendly. It was, in fact, a turning point in Moe's career: he had been out of show business since 1925.

Moe's older brother Shemp returned to support Healy in 1926 and, two years later, he and Healy discovered violinist Larry Fine working as the emcee at Chicago's Rainbo Gardens nightclub.

Joan generously offered some of her Ted Healy photos for the book. I picked a few images and also some clippings, one from a column titled "The Daily Stooge." It offered an account of the creation of the stooges and was written by Healy.

Just prior to wrapping up the visit, Michelle asked Joan if we could see her wedding photos. Only a few minutes later, she returned with her wedding album in hand. The professionally photographed pictures from the 1947 ceremony, joining Joan Howard and Norman Maurer in holy matrimony, were lovingly preserved in a bound white book. Outside of the immediate family, not many people have had the honor to view these priceless photos. Her dad, Moe, was one proud papa. It was so refreshing to see him posing out of character.

In 2015, *Ted Healy—Nobody's Stooge* was published by BearManor Media and had a wonderful foreword by Drew Friedman, and that was not his only contribution. He also drew an original image of Ted Healy for the back cover. What a talent! This new book, containing revelations about the real history of the Three Stooges act, caused a sensation. I was invited to speak at the Three Stooges convention held in Springhouse, Pennsylvania, in April 2016. I gave power-point presentations on both Vernon Dent and Ted Healy. Afterward, Stooge fans stood in line to buy my books. I was happy to give back and thankful for all the laughter the Stooges have given me.

Another appearance I made was at the Cinecon, the annual convention celebrating classic films. Cinecon has a long history, and in recent years it has been held at the Egyptian Theater on Hollywood Boulevard. Stan Taffel, Cinecon's president, has personally invited me to be a guest author over the years. In 2015, I introduced the film *Myrt and Marge* (co-starring Ted Healy and His Stooges) and, in 2018, my co-author Rick Greene and I introduced one of Henry Brandon's films, *The Golden Horde*. The latter event was a promotional effort for *Henry Brandon: King of the Bogeymen*, a book about my late actor friend.

With the encouragement of Native American, Lisa Ballantyne,[101] Rick Greene and I were determined to commemorate Henry Brandon and his varied film career.[102] Our goal was to research, accumulate, write, and have it published by the time of the next Sons of the Desert convention in Cincinnati. With a big push by our publisher, Ben Ohmart of BearManor

---

101. Lisa Ballantyne is the administrator of the Facebook site; "For the Love of Henry" in celebration of the life and career of Henry Brandon

102. Henry Brandon died suddenly at age seventy-eight in 1990

Media, the book came out ten days before the convention. We put the whole volume together in a year's time—breakneck speed. It was topped off by a brilliant foreword by our pal Stan Taffel, who also knew Henry. In 2017 I turned sixty-six years old and had long-since retired from law enforcement. I signed up to work security for the Sacramento Rivercats, the San Francisco Giants' top minor league affiliate. The Giants came to play an exhibition game towards the end of spring training and there I was, sharing the cherished field with my favorite team.

The ballpark was sold out and the fans were in a festive mood. As part of the pregame festivities, there was a table display on the field with the three World Series championship trophies from 2010, 2012 and 2014. The Giants had a special employee whose sole job was to keep watch on these treasures. Just before the start of the game, it was time to get the trophies off the field. I assisted by lifting each one and handing it on to the designated handler, who carefully packaged and transferred them onto a small truck. I suddenly recalled how each trophy, in its respective champion post-season, had been circulated throughout cities in Northern California and how, in 2010, the trophy came to Salinas. I was too sick then to even go out of the house, much less stand in line for hours to see them. Those thoughts passed quickly when I briefly held each one. There were no photographers, no spotlight, and no music. It was a thrill just to hold them for a moment.

The ballplayers were introduced in ceremonial fashion on each of the baselines while I hurried across the field to the dugout position. Just then, the national anthem started and the players removed their caps. I had to stop and found myself just behind home plate, I too participated by taking off my ball cap. Right in front of me was Giants manager Bruce Bochy. I had come full circle, paying homage to the summers of my youth, with memories of Willie Mays and his Giants.

Final thoughts:

I would like to think I had a positive impact on people's lives during my career, judging on the many letters, community awards and in-house memos. A real highlight was being recognized by the California Assembly (1988) for being "One of the top five cops in California." In the years after "retirement," I have been contributing, researching and writing whenever I can for other authors. Foremost I still consider myself a historian, a documenter of facts.

As I write this final passage, I am now 68 years old. The exact age as Ralph Rambo, when he wrote "Almost Forgotten" in 1963. That author was so inspiring to me about the history for where I grew up, it proved as a framework of recording my own life's work. The past is our greatest teacher. Let us hope that "The talking rings" (computers?) do not relegate the books to dust as they do in Jules Verne's novel, "The Time Machine."

Photo by Jack Taylor, 2020

Index

Made in the USA
Coppell, TX
04 December 2020

42788684R00164